CONSTRAINT THEORY

An Approach to
Policy-Level Modelling

Laurence D. Richards

Department of Administrative Science
Colby College

SCHOOL OF

CALIFORNIA

PROFESSIONAL

PSYCHOLOGY

LOS ANGELES

UNIVERSITY
PRESS OF
AMERICA

LANHAM • NEW YORK • LONDON

Copyright © 1983 by

University Press of America,™ Inc.

4720 Boston Way
Lanham, MD 20706

3 Henrietta Street
London WC2E 8LU England

Printed in the United States of America

ISBN (Perfect): 0-8191-3513-5
ISBN   (Cloth): 0-8191-3512-7

TO SHIV, KLAUS, and JANE

You may look at the world any way you please, through
any window you choose. Nor does it always have to be
the same window. Naturally how the world appears, what
you see and what you miss, and the angle on what you
see, depends on which window you are using, but how can
a window be right or wrong? A window is a window.
(George Spencer Brown [James Keys], Only Two Can Play
This Game, with a Preface by R. D. Laing. New York:
Julian Press, 1972, p. 98.)

ACKNOWLEDGEMENTS

The research reported here would not have been possible without the continuing guidance, constructive criticism, and encouragement of a number of individuals. The bulk of the work was performed while I was a doctoral student at the University of Pennsylvania. Shiv Gupta, Chairman of the Operations Research Program at The Wharton School, was invaluable in keeping the research, to as great an extent as possible, oriented to real-world management problems. Klaus Krippendorff, a cybernetician at the Annenberg School of Communications, provided an essential interdisciplinary focus to the research and helped me articulate concepts which are relatively new to management science. Eric Trist and Jim Emshoff, who were directors of research centers at The Wharton School and who initially encouraged me to pursue this research, also provided valuable insights.

A special acknowledgement is due Murray Geisler, the project leader for the research performed for the Department of Defense. For his open-mindedness and the sharing of his logistics expertise, I am deeply appreciative. Other members of that project, for whose cooperation and ideas I am grateful, were Mary Hutzler and Bob Kaiser.

The corporate research project was made possible through contacts generated by Bob Graham. For reasons of confidentiality, the corporation concerned has chosen to remain anonymous. We refer to it as the MFS Finance Corporation. However, this research could not have been completed without the full support of the Chairman of the Board and President of that company.

I would like to thank the Logistics Management Institute, and in particular its past and current presidents, Hugh McCullough and Perkins Pedrick, for its financial support throughout the duration of the research. Dorothy Dean did an excellent job in preparing the initial document.

My wife, Jane, put in many hours preparing the final manuscript. This book would have been impossible without her encouragement and understanding, as well as the support of our two children, Doug and Greg.

TABLE OF CONTENTS

APPENDICES

LIST OF TABLES

LIST OF ILLUSTRATIONS

PREFACE

Management science is currently searching for methodological approaches to what has come to be called the "ill-structured" problem. Top-level managers in large corporations and administrators in government agencies are particularly aware of this class of problem. It is inevitably encountered in the process of formulating broad, organization-wide policy. When this type of problem is characterized by conflict in the values and perceptions of the participants in the policy formulation process, we refer to it as an "issue." This book examines the characteristics required of quantitative models that address policy issues, and the role of modelling in the policy formulation process in general.

The book is divided into three parts. Part I is a synthesis of the literature relevant to policy-level modelling. This includes a review of the schools of thought on the nature of policy formulation and a survey of management science approaches used to deal with "ill-structured" problems. We argue that certain characteristics of the policy formulation process suggest a need for model structures based on philosophical foundations different from those of most management science models. These foundations do not replace, but rather complement, the "rational" foundations of current modelling practice.

Part II presents a theoretical framework built on the philosophical foundations previously introduced. We contend that the language and mathematical assumptions of management science models represent barriers to the structuring of policy issues and hence to the use of those models in policy formulation. The theoretical framework proposed, then, includes a modelling language for describing policy issues and a modelling mathematics that is consistent with that language. We label the framework "constraint theory."

Part III presents an integrated approach to policy-level modelling. This approach evolved from two major research projects, one sponsored by the Office of the Secretary of Defense in the Department of Defense, the other by the President and Chairman of the Board of a consumer finance company. The approach requires the use of the modelling language and mathematics developed in Part II, but it also uses other management science and operations research methods. The results of the research projects should not be viewed as tests of the validity of the total approach, but rather as demonstrations of the specific methods used.

A number of themes recur throughout the book. "Complexity" is a word often used to characterize the ill-structured nature of policy issues. "Negative reasoning" is a term we use to distinguish the logic of constraint theory from that of the rational decisionmaking framework. The role of subjectivity and of "mental models" is central to the modelling approach. The contribution of the approach is in the facilitation of participation and communications and in the stimulation of creative thinking in the policy formulation process, the end result being "value-rich" or "robust" policy. These themes serve to integrate ideas from the more qualitative, behaviorial sciences with those from the more quantitative, systems sciences.

The novel and interdisciplinary nature of the research should make the results of interest to individuals with a wide diversity of backgrounds and training. As such, we attempt to introduce logical and mathematical concepts in the context of human behavior, and behavioral concepts in the context of logic and mathematics.

CHAPTER 1

INTRODUCTION

This book reports on research into the structure of policy-level models and the role of modelling in the policy formulation process. Chronologically, the research began with a study directed at developing a policy-level management support system (i.e., a policy support system[1]) for the Assistant Secretary of Defense for Installations and Logistics. Two overwhelming methodological issues emerged during the course of that study. First, available modelling techniques by themselves were not able to capture the full complexity of the Department of Defense logistics systems which represent the policy responsibility of the Assistant Secretary. We traced part of the problem to structural assumptions that underlie both normative and descriptive operations research models. Second, the role typically assigned to management models, that of an input-output device that can be operated independently of the policy formulation process, was not well suited to the behavioral and political aspects of policymaking.

The product of the Defense study was a conceptual design for a policy support system, accompanied by a theoretical framework providing some foundations for policy-level modelling in general. For want of a better title, we coin that theoretical framework "constraint theory"[2] for its focus on a generic concept of constraint. In this book, constraint theory consists of a modelling language and a set of mathematical concepts which contrast with, but also complement, the language and concepts supporting the "rational" decisionmaking framework for management oriented modelling.[3] The development of constraint theory requires the integration of both qualitative and quantitative insights from a number of different disciplines. Furthermore, the proposed framework builds on a logic and philosophical heritage relatively new to management science and operations research.

The role of modelling in the policy formulation process that emerged from the Defense study was one of

1

facilitating communications and stimulating creative thinking. The desired result is "value-rich" policy. In this context, the subjective content of the model becomes the critical focus.

The second piece of field work, then, was directed at demonstrating the tractability of a constraint theoretic structure for collecting and analyzing subjective information. With the approval and support of the President and Chairman of the Board of the MFS Finance Corporation, a sequence of interviews and questionnaires were administered to employees at various levels of the organization. The choice of the questionnaire as the instrument for demonstrating the proposed structure was made for reasons of expediency. As a communications mechanism, questionnaires present some methodological problems. If the primary intent of the study had been to augment the MFS policy formulation process, gaming, computerized conferencing, etc., would have been better choices and the research approach would have been different.

A primary conclusion of the MFS study is that subjective information filtered through a constraint theoretic model structure can provide rich insights into value relationships among the actors in a policy issue. As a result, the involvement of a larger number of participants in the policy formulation process is facilitated and the acceptability of alternative policies is clarified. The study did not explicitly consider the dynamics of the political and group processes inherent in policy formulation. A policy support system designed to augment these processes would probably involve some form of structured group process. The computational effort required to filter information through the model structures and feed it back in a timely manner suggest that computer assisted methods may be useful in such a system.

From the two projects, an approach to using quantitative modelling techniques in the policy formulation process evolved. While this book emphasizes the structure and role of mathematical models in policy formulation, we believe the implications of the approach as a paradigm for any systematic examination of complex policy issues is even more significant.

This chapter motivates the sequence of topics considered in the three parts of the book by

2

illustrating and briefly summarizing the research need. The specific research issues confronted in the two organizational studies are described first. Next, the characteristics of these issues which render them methodologically difficult are discussed in the context of assumptions underlying most management science models. Finally, the central premises of the constraint theoretic approach to policy-level modelling are summarized.

1.1 POLICY-LEVEL RESEARCH ISSUES ILLUSTRATED

The Department of Defense (DoD) and the MFS Finance Corporation provide examples of two very different organizations -- one government, the other corporate; one huge, the other medium-sized. Yet both confront complex situations which require the formulation of organization-wide policy and strategy.[4]

1.1.1 A Government Agency

The Assistant Secretary of Defense (Installations and Logistics), at the time the study reported here was initiated, had policy responsibility for DoD logistics and installations management. The boundaries on the DoD logistics system, however, are not well defined; there are overlaps with other defense functions and organizations. It was generally agreed that at least 1.5 million civilian and military employees performed logistics related tasks and 40% of the annual defense budget (i.e., $40-$50 billion dollars in 1977) was being channelled to logistics activities. The function of the logistics system is to supply and maintain defense assets with an original acquisition cost in excess of $240 billion. These assets include over 500 major military installations, 20,000 aircraft, and large numbers of ships and other military weapon systems. In addition, the logistics system is responsible for procurement and transportation of spare parts and consumable operating supplies, as well as official and wartime transportation of personnel. Personnel policies have recently been added to the responsibilities of the Assistant Secretary under his new title, Assistant Secretary of Defense (Manpower, Reserve Affairs, and Logistics).

The Department of Defense is divided into three Military Departments (Army, Navy, and Air Force), each

3

with its own logistics organization. The top-level administrators, including the Assistant Secretary, his Principal Deputy, and the Deputy Assistant Secretaries within the Office of the Secretary of Defense (OSD) and the Military Departments, are appointed to their positions by the President. Many of the Deputy Assistant Secretaries, however, are considered career civil servants and will retain their positions with the changeover of administrations; but the turnover rate for these top-level positions in general is relatively high. The result is little continuity in the management practices and processes which involve the Assistant Secretary in policy formulation. The Planning, Programming, and Budgeting System (PPBS) was an attempt to provide continuity, and, in DoD, is still the single most valuable mechanism for that purpose. However, its structure does not easily accommodate the political process which is an essential and intrinsic aspect of policymaking.[5] Management By Objectives (MBO) has also been implemented, but has been of limited, if any, value as a policy tool.[6]

The generally recognized objective of Defense policy is embodied in the word "readiness." That is, the formulation of logistics policy should be directed at maintaining or improving the state of military readiness. However, there are many definitions of readiness and attempts to develop readiness measures have not adequately captured the concept in its totality. The ambiguity associated with the word "readiness," then, is a result of the complexity of Defense operations and organizations, as well as of the value tradeoffs and conflicts inherent in the concept.

The Assistant Secretary of Defense, realizing the dilemma he faced in fulfilling his policy role without an adequate understanding of the macrostructure of logistics and its relation to readiness, commissioned the Logistics Management Institute to undertake developmental work on a policy support system.[7] That system was initially envisioned to be simply a set of management indicators and a few basic modelling techniques to assist in interpreting historical trends. The data employed were to be extracted from historical data files. As we discuss in Part III, methodological difficulties led to a conceptual design for a policy support system of a very different character.

4

1.1.2 A Corporation

The MFS Finance Corporation is a consumer finance company which currently operates in ten states. The company has experienced very rapid growth over the last few years, nearly twice the industry average. Its long-term strategy is to continue to grow at better than the industry average (although not at as rapid a rate as in recent years) through the acquisition of other companies and expansion nationwide. However, top management expresses real concern about certain aspects and possible consequences of this strategy. Uncertainty about the future of the national economy and the possibility of socioeconomic shifts means that the strategy is not without substantial risk. There is also concern about internal stability and capability. The turnover rate among new managerial employees is very high, for example. While the industry average is also high, if MFS is to develop the level of skill it needs to exploit the markets it plans to enter, the retention rate may become a very significant factor. Another concern of top management is that the level of creative marketing and management ideas being generated by middle and top management is not adequate. Opinions about these strategic issues vary significantly among employees of the corporation.

To help ensure the success of their long-term strategy, MFS has initiated a program that is intended to change the prevailing management "style" of the corporation. The program is called "management by planning" and is designed to increase the involvement and participation of MFS personnel in setting operational goals and developing plans to attain them. If this program is to achieve the results intended, certain changes will have to occur in the allocation of managerial time and in the amount and nature of communications between managerial levels. The degree of change will depend on the extent to which the planning activity is given priority over other managerial activities. Likewise, the success of the program in reducing personnel turnover, developing managerial skills, and stimulating creative thinking will depend on these priorities.

The research issue this situation poses for the management scientist is one of identifying the best way to use his expertise to make a contribution to the formulation of policy supportive of the new management style. Traditional model structures, particularly those requiring the specification of an objective function, do not capture the complex value conflicts inherent in the consequences of potential policies. Attempts to explicitly identify individual objectives leads to a long list of divergent items, with many individuals having difficulty in articulating objectives at all. Furthermore, the modeller cannot divorce his own values from the model development process.

1.2 METHODOLOGICAL COMPLEXITY

The one word consistently used to characterize the difficulty with modelling policy issues is "complexity." However, to refer to the task of policy formulation as one of managing complexity may be a contradiction in terms, for complexity implies a situation that is perceived by a particular individual to be unmanageable. For a complex situation to become manageable, it must be simplified (i.e., decomplexified).

Simplification involves the filtering of information is such a way that meaning and purpose are attributed to the situation. Filtering information is the role of human mental processes and models. The manager or administrator who has an apparently superior ability to deal with situations that others perceive as complex is one who has developed a mental model which gives more meaning to those particular types of situation than do other mental models. The individual, however, is generally not aware of the structure of his/her mental models and cannot, therefore, articulate the thought process utilized. To the outcome of this mental activity, then, we typically assign the ubiquitous terms "judgment" and "intuition."

Nevertheless, managers and administrators are expressing the concern that the context of strategy and policy formulation is becoming increasingly "complex." Throughout the remainder of this book, the conditions contributing to this perceived complexity are assumed to be the following:

1. The large number of interacting subsystems and variables within the organization and through-out its environment.

2. The highly interdependent and circular nature

6

of these interactions.

3. The significant degree of conflict between the value systems and perceptions of the actors involved in the strategy/policy formulation process.

Steinbruner also identifies three conditions that characterize the complex decision problem: uncertainty, value conflicts, and multiple decisionmakers.[8] We have chosen to divide uncertainty into two aspects (items 1 and 2) in order to better distinguish the structural concept of uncertainty that we develop later from the probabilistic concept of uncertainty. Likewise, we have combined value conflicts and multiple decisionmakers into a single aspect (item 3) in order to highlight the relationship between value conflicts and the distribution of power among the various policy actors.

1.2.1 Variables and Relationships

Practicing policymakers and strategic planners recognize these different aspects of complexity. For example, consider the following:

Econometric models have gone to pot because of the inability to quantify variables going into a model. If you are forecasting the replacement tire market, you have to go back and decide how many miles will be driven, driving patterns, etc. My problem is that relationships never stay the same.[9]

You can't just extend the graphs on these things ["social factors" such as predicted modes of transportation and consumer preferences], you've got to really understand them. They're not governed by economics.[10]

[with respect to future consumer behavior]... the computers can't possibly handle things that have this many uncertainties.[11]

The emphasis in these comments is on the illusiveness of multiple variables, the dynamic nature of environmental relationships, and the uncertainty that results. Growth in the number of interdependent subsystems and variables in the social environment of

7

organizations has been attributed to a number of factors. Emery and Trist list four.[12]

1. Growth in population and organizations.

2. Interdependence between the economic and other facets of society.

3. Reliance on scientific research and development.

4. Radical increase in speed, scope, and capacity of intraspecies communication.

Environments exhibiting such interdependent characteristics have been given the label "turbulent."

The type of system which the scientist studies in these environments is one exhibiting "organized complexity," as opposed to "organized simplicity" or "unorganized complexity." As characterized by Weinberg[13] "organized simplicity" is exhibited by machines and simple physical systems. The subsystems may be interrelated but there are only a few of them. Deterministic analytical techniques can be used to study these systems. "Unorganized complexity" is exhibited by relatively homogeneous populations. These systems contain a large number of subsystems, but the subsystems are not highly interrelated. They exhibit sufficient randomness to be adequately treated with statistical techniques. "Organized complexity" characterizes systems with a large number of highly interrelated subsystems. These systems are heterogeneous, i.e., the subsystems are diverse and the relationships between them are mutually causative as opposed to lineally causative.[14] The analytical and statistical techniques which constitute management science contain structural assumptions that preclude a rich treatment of organized complexity.

1.2.2 Value Conflicts

Even more difficult from a methodological point of view is consideration of the value tradeoffs, dilemmas, and conflicts inherent in the political process of policy formulation. Consider the following observations, the first by a director of program evaluation for the United States Commission on Civil Rights and the second by two prominent public policy analysts:

8

We have been encouraged to believe that
quantification is impersonal and objective
and, therefore, more reliable than qualitative methodology which takes into consideration such relatively intangible factors as
values...The canard that "objective" is good
and "subjective" is bad denies the fundamental worthiness of human endeavor--of
creativity, imagination, ingenuity, and
spontaneity.[15]

Science seeks to establish patterns of
experience that all may share...Politics is
quite different from science: The intent is
to find one purpose, or course of action,
acceptable to individuals espousing diverse
purposes, values, and courses of action.
Politics is value-expressive; facts are
subordinate to and sustaining of values, and
only contribute to the delineation of an
issue.[16]

The emphasis here is on the subjective content of
scientific methodology and the process of reconciling
the personal agendas of the individual policy actors
versus the "objective" and detached position typically
assumed in conducting quantitative analysis. The pros
and cons of qualitative methodology of the type
proposed by Siedman will be discussed in Chapter 4.

In management science and operations research
modelling practice, situations involving a group
decisionmaking process are often simplified by assuming
that the group as a whole can be treated as a single,
rational decisionmaker. If one can identify objectives
which can be attributed to the group and specify a set
of alternative courses of action, the rational
decisionmaking framework provides a structure for
optimizing the group decision. Since conflicting
values are treated simply as multiple objectives, one
of a variety of schemes can be used to weight or order
each objective with respect to its relative importance
to the decisionmaker.[17]

Many students of political and managerial
processes, however, have observed that policy-oriented
group behavior is often not comparable to individual
behavior, and that neither group nor individual
behavior can always be explained with the rational

9

decisionmaking paradigm.

Steinbruner, in attempting to analyze the politics of nuclear sharing policy during the period 1956-1964, and in particular, the concept of the multilateral force (MLF), concluded that "the analytic [rational] paradigm, which currently provides the base decision theory for most political analysis, is not adequate to account for all of the forces which affect the conduct of public affairs. The analytic paradigm encounters serious anomalies in the events of the MLF."[18] Mintzberg, et al., found a similar divergence in corporate strategy formulation.[19]

Despite the inconsistency between actual and predicted behavior based on the rational paradigm, the rational decisionmaking approach to modelling is still defended by many for its normative value. Some of the resistance to implementation of decision technology, however, might be explained by the incompatibility of its model structures with the structure of human mental processes, including managerial judgment and intuition. Argyris and Schön describe the situation in a case study:

> ...when the models were presented, even though they met the client's requirements, they were resisted for reasons that had little to do with the technique involved. The response seemed irrational to the professional. What sense does it make for executives to resist the very models they have requested?[20]

But the strongest criticism of the mathematical structure of decision models has been in the context of group decisionmaking, and particularly in light of Arrow's Impossibility Theorem. Scientists who have been staunch proponents of "rational" method, have been forced to conclude that "assumptions which we found hard to reject as rational for a single decision-maker become not only dubious or unrealistic, but logically impossible when applied to groups."[21] In the closing chapter of his book, Making Decisions, Lindley similarly concedes:

> It is a major deficiency of the method of decisionmaking described in this book (or of any other method known to me) that it does not offer a precise solution to either the

10

committee or the conflict situation...The
provision of such a method is one of the
greatest needs of our time.[22]

1.2.3 Self-Reference

An additional complication in the conduct of
research on the policy formulation process is that the
researcher cannot intervene without having an impact on
the process. Neither can he remain objective; the
values of the researcher cannot be divorced from the
research itself.[23] Hence, the researcher himself
becomes an actor with a set of values and perceptions
which may conflict with those of the other actors.
This classic research dilemma in the social sciences
has been labeled a problem in "self-reference."[24]
The influence of the observer on the social system
being observed requires a logical framework which
incorporates consideration of the values and
perceptions of the observer along with those he is
observing.

Self-reference has also been a concern in logic
and mathematics in the form of paradox and
contradiction. In particular, Bertrand Russell's
paradox involving classes which contain themselves as a
member has resulted in a reconsideration of the
foundations of mathematics.[25] The point is that
traditional mathematical structures based on two-valued
logic, functional relationships, and infinitely
extended spaces present methodological difficulties
with respect to self-reference. The theoretical
framework proposed in Part II deals with self-reference
indirectly by specifying a process-oriented role for
policy-level models.

1.3 CENTRAL PREMISES OF CONSTRAINT THEORY

In this book, a constraint theoretic framework is
being proposed as a complement to the rational
decisionmaking framework. The central premises that
motivate a constraint theoretic approach to
policy-level modelling include the following:

1. In complex policy issues, the goals and objectives
of an individual decisionmaker are illusive, and the
specification of a realistic objective function (or
social welfare function) for an organization is
virtually impossible.[26]

11

2. Policy criteria and values, both individual and social, can be treated as a dynamic system of constraints; such a treatment can accomodate the political process inherent in policymaking.

3. The structure of interaction among policy variables is best characterized as mutually causative rather than lineally causative. The specification of these relationships can be accomplished by the identification of constraint in the system of variables.

4. Uncertainty in policy formulation tends to be structural and fuzzy in nature, and manifest in disagreement among the policy actors.

5. To operationalize these concepts of policy criteria, relationship, and uncertainty requires the development of new modelling mathematics and a new modelling language.

6. Since the political process which characterizes policy formulation involves, in some way, the reconciliation of the mental models of the participating actors, the logical structure for deriving this mathematics and language should be representative of the structure of human mental processes.

7. Recent developments in logic, Spencer Brown's laws of form, fuzzy set theory, and second order cybernetics, provide foundations for generating new model structures.

8. Consideration of self-reference requires the specification of a process-oriented role for policy-level models, and a participant-observer approach for the modeller.

Perhaps the most distinguishing characteristic of constraint theory is its emphasis on "negative reasoning,"[27] i.e., on the states of a system which are excluded from consideration, whether through natural or technological constraints or through perceptual and value constraints, rather than on most probable states.

The next three chapters support these premises by reviewing and synthesizing some of the relevant literature on concepts of policy formulation and on

12

methodological approaches to policy issues. A discussion of selected philosophical perspectives provides a linkage between these concepts and approaches.

NOTES

1. A policy support system, as we use the term, is similar to a decision support system in that it provides structured information useful to the actors in the policy formulation process. However, a policy support system addresses the ill-structured problems that decision support systems explicitly avoid. See Peter G. W. Keen and Michael S. Scott Morton, Decision Support Systems: An Organizational Perspective (Reading, Mass.: Addison-Wesley, 1978).

2. The word "theory" used here refers to a systematic statement of axioms and principles, not to the more narrow usage referring to a formulation of apparent relationships in observed phenomena. These axioms and principles, while consistent with observed relationships, are not sufficiently specific to be subjected to direct test. They do, however, provide the basis for deriving more specific hypotheses and theories with respect to policy issues and the policy formulation process.

3. The rational decisionmaking framework will be described and dissected fully in later chapters.

4. The words "strategy" and "policy" are used almost synonymously throughout this book. In the organizational literature, these words are sometimes differentiated, but the distinction is blurred. "Strategy" connotes a shared mental model of the direction an organization is and ought to be moving, while "policy" connotes the manifestation of that mental model in the form of various organizational artifacts and patterns of communication. It makes little sense, however, to speak of mental models that are never manifest or of manifestations divorced from the mental and group processes that produced them. The word "plan," however, does connote something different. Strategic planning is a very specific form of strategy formulation, and a plan is but one of its many possible policy manifestations.

5. For an excellent discussion of the shortcomings

13

of PPBS, see Allen Schick, "A Death in the Bureaucracy: The Demise of Federal PPB," Public Administration Review, March/April 1973, pp. 146-156. For example: "One line of reasoning, first developed by Lindblom and Wildavsky, but now widely held by political scientists, is that PPB failed because it ran roughshod over some important American political values. The argument is that the bargaining-incremental mode of budgeting gives expression and representation to diverse political interests which might be neglected if budget choice were centralized in the hands of analysts."(p.149)

6. Havens argues that the decision to institute MBO is based on the same mentality as was the decision to institute PPBS, and has the following to say about both:
"It seems to me that the recent history of efforts to improve techniques for strengthening management in the public sector is characterized by:
-A simplistic view of the process of decision making in the public sector;
-A simplistic view of the nature of public policy decisions;
-An implicit assumption that all important public goals are quantifiable;
-An implicit assumption that the appearance of neatness can create the fact of rationality."
(Harry S. Havens, "MBO and Program Evaluation, or Whatever Happened to PPBS?", Public Administration Review, January/February 1976, p. 40.)

7. The precise wording of the task order agreed upon by the Assistant Secretary includes the following: "An examination of this DoD logistics complex from a macro point of view would be a useful aid in understanding OSD's role with respect to DoD logistics, and in providing appropriate tools for the exercise of that role." (Department of Defense Task Order SD-321-47, 16 June 1976)

8. John D. Steinbruner, The Cybernetic Theory of Decision (Princeton, N.J.: Princeton University Press, 1974), p. 16.

9. A. J. Ashe, Vice President for Planning and Development, B. F. Goodrich Company, quoted in "Piercing Future Fog in the Executive Suite," Business Week, April 28, 1975, p. 50.

10. Robert E. Wycoff, Director of Corporate

Planning, Atlantic Richfield Company, quoted in "Future Fog," p. 50.

11. George R. White, Vice President for Product Planning, Xerox Corporation, quoted in "Future Fog," p. 50.

12. F. E. Emery and E. L. Trist, Towards a Social Ecology (London: Plenum Press, 1972), pp. 52-53.

13. Gerald M. Weinberg, An Introduction to General Systems Thinking (New York: Wiley-Interscience, 1975), pp. 18-19.

14. See Gregory Bateson, "Effects of Conscious Purpose on Human Adaptation," in Steps to an Ecology of Mind (New York: Ballantine Books, 1972), pp. 444-445; and Magoroh Maruyama, "Hetergenistics: An Epistemological Restructuring of Biological and Social Sciences," Cybernetica 20(1977):69-86.

15. Eileen Siedman, "Why Not Qualitative Analysis?," Public Administration Review, July/August 1977, p. 415.

16. Martin Rein and Sheldon H. White, "Can Policy Research Help Policy?," The Public Interest, Fall 1977, p. 135.

17. For an excellent discussion of these issues in the context of utility theory, see Ralph L. Keeney and Howard Raiffa, Decisions with Multiple Objectives: Preferences and Value Tradeoffs (New York: John Wiley & Sons, 1976).

18. Steinbruner, p. 327.

19. H. Mintzberg, D. Raisinghani, and A. Théorêt, "The Structure of 'Unstructured' Decision Processes," Administrative Science Quarterly 21(June 1976): 246-275.

20. Chris Argyris and Donald A. Schön, Theory in Practice: Increasing Professional Effectiveness (San Francisco: Jossey-Bass, 1974), p. 165.

21. Karl Henrik Borch, The Economics of Uncertainty (Princeton, N.J.: Princeton University Press, 1968), p. 224.

15

22. D. V. Lindley, _Making_ _Decisions_ (London: Wiley-Interscience, 1971), p. 165.

23. As noted by Myrdal, the mystique of "objectivity" in the scientific community results in a barrier to dialogue on this issue. "In our profession there is a lack of awareness even today that, in searching for truth, the student, like all human beings whatever they try to accomplish, is influenced by tradition, by his environment, and by his personality. Further, there is an irrational taboo against discussing this lack of awareness." [Gunnar Myrdal, _Objectivity_ _in_ _Social_ _Research_ (New York: Pantheon Books, 1969), p. 4.] Kaplan puts it more succinctly: "the problem for methodology is not _whether_ values are involved in inquiry, but _which_, and above all, how they are to be empirically grounded." Abraham Kaplan, _The_ _Conduct_ _of_ _Inquiry_: _Methodology_ _for_ _Behavioral_ _Science_ (New York: Chandler Publishing Company, 1964), p. 387.

24. As Umpleby points out: "The social scientist constructing a theory of the society of which he is a part must explain that an element of a society [e.g., himself] can construct a theory of the operation of the society and that those theories may influence the behavior of society. [A] successful theoretical treatment...would appear to require a logical system and a scientific method that permits self-reference." (Stuart A. Umpleby, "Second Order Cybernetics and the Design of Large Scale Social Experiments," _The_ _Proceedings_ _of_ _the_ _XXth_ _Annual_ _North_ _American_ _Meeting_ _of_ _the_ _Society_ _for_ _General_ _Systems_ _Research_, 1976, p. 71.)

25. For a discussion of this and other paradoxes and their impact on mathematics, see W. V. Quine, "Paradox," _Scientific_ _American_, April 1962, pp. 84-95. See also, Douglas Hofstadter, _Gödel_, _Escher_, _Bach_: _An_ _Eternal_ _Golden_ _Braid_ (New York: Vintage Books, 1979) for a popularized discussion of the self-referential paradox.

26. A past president of The Institute of Management Sciences states: "Management scientists working in both the private and the public sectors are facing problems that do not lend themselves to relatively straight forward criteria, such as profit maximization or simple measures of cost; they must

deal with problems in which objectives are most difficult to identify and to specify in terms that make possible the applications of traditional analytical methods to help the decision maker." [Donald B. Rice, "New Challenges--and Some Old Ones," OR/MS Today 3 (November/December 1976):18.]

27. See Gregory Bateson, "Cybernetic Explanation," in Steps to an Ecology of Mind (New York: Ballantine Books, 1972), pp. 399-410; and Klaus Krippendorff, "Information Theory," in Communication and Behavior, ed. Gerhard J. Hanneman and William J. McEwen (Reading, Mass.: Addison-Wesley, 1975), pp. 486-487.

PART I

IN SEARCH OF THEORY AND METHOD

CHAPTER 2

POLICY FORMULATION CONCEPTS

Models intended for use in policy formulation make implicit assumptions about the policymaking process. However, the process of policy and strategy formulation in organizations has been studied from a number of different perspectives; psychologists, sociologists, anthropologists, political scientists, and management scientists have all produced slightly different descriptions of the process. The descriptions presented in this chapter are based on four overlapping sets of concepts: structural concepts, functional concepts, decisionmaking (or organization process) concepts, and political concepts. While each set of concepts views organizational strategy from a different perspective, they are not independent; they are related through their evolutionary development and their complementarity.

Structural concepts explain policy formulation in the context of formal organizational structures, particularly the managerial roles at different levels in bureaucratic and other hierarchical organizations. Functional concepts explain policy formulation from the point of view of its relation to management processes -- planning, organizing, and controlling. Decisionmaking concepts are those that view policy formulation as an organizational process. With origins in the rationalism of scientific management and the classical study of bureaucracy, these concepts represent a synthesis of the structural and functional descriptions, but have tended to be limited in scope to formal decisions. Stressing the importance of the informal organization, the human relations or social psychological school of thought has questioned the validity of these decisionmaking descriptions. Political concepts build on both the decisionmaking concepts and the behaviorist criticism of them. Policymaking is viewed as a group process involved in resolving differences of opinion and value conflicts. Bargaining, compromise, gamesmanship, and use of influence are an inherent behavioral aspect of this process.

21

For the purpose of synthesizing the various concepts of policy formulation, it proves useful to distinguish well-structured "problems" from ill-structured "issues." This synthesis is made possible by introducing a generalized concept of organizational communications and control.

2.1 CONCEPT I: ORGANIZATIONAL STRUCTURE

The organization charts of corporations and government agencies have provided management theorists with an easily accessible way of identifying organizational roles. Most organization charts depict a hierarchical structure; even most matrix organizations have a hierarchical authority structure superimposed on the matrix responsibility chart, implicitly if not explicitly.

2.1.1 Levels of Management

The literature on organizational structure has typically specified three levels of the hierarchy. Anthony labels the functions performed by these levels strategic planning, management control, and operational control respectively.[1] Thompson prefers the adjectives first suggested by Parsons -- institutional, managerial, and technical -- to describe the roles of the three levels.[2] Although these levels are generally associated with a hierarchically structured organization, they represent functions or aspects of management which must be performed in any large organization, irrespective of its structure. In a hierarchical organization the technical/operational control functions are associated with those individuals at the bottom of the organization chart, while the institutional/strategic planning functions are associated with the individuals at the top. In more pluralistic organizations, the functions are performed by individuals throughout the organization, possibly on a rotating basis.[3] "Levels," then, should more appropriately refer to the level of complexity involved in performing the functions, rather than to a specific hierarchical level on an organization chart. Despite the connotations of the terms, we will refer to the levels as the strategic or policy level, the intermediate level, and the technical or operational level.

The responsibilities of lower-level management lie primarily in the control of relatively routine, technical tasks. Decisions must be made on production schedules, inventories, manpower assignments, and working conditions. Performance standards and incentives are commonly used as the primary means of managerial control. The concern of management at the technical level is to produce the best product or provide the best service for the least cost. In the economic marketplace, "best" translates into that which provides the largest profit or profit margin, market share, etc. Organizational policies, plans, rules, procedures, goals, and standards constrain the behavior or lower-level management by limiting the alternative actions available and the criteria used in selecting an appropriate action.

The responsibilities of top management include broad policymaking, long-range planning, and resource guidance. Decisions must be made on centralized vs. decentralized operations, diversification vs. market penetration, labor intensive vs. capital intensive production, vertical vs. horizontal growth, and long-term vs. short-term payoffs. In effect, top management identifies a strategy of survival for the organization and implements it through policy. The word "policy" represents a broad spectrum of modes of control, and the implementation of policy comes in many forms. At one extreme are artifacts as simple as organizational slogans and logos symbolizing certain strategic inclinations of management. At the other extreme are rigid plans, goals, and rules. Between the two extremes are procedural guidelines which are recommended but not mandatory. Irrespective of their form, policies serve the primary purpose of constraining organizational behavior.

The responsibilities of intermediate-level management include a wide range of activities which fall somewhere between the two extremes just described. These activities tend to be tactical in nature rather than strategic. The utilization and management of scarce resources is a primary responsibility, but in addition this level performs the delicate task of interpreting and implementing top-level policies. In this capacity, intermediate-level management must serve as a buffer between the strategic and technical levels and between the technical levels and the organizational environment.

In discussing the basic function of policy-level management, Thompson introduces the idea of a "paradox of administration."[4] The role of strategy formulation is one of "co-alignment in time and space not simply of human individuals but of streams of institutionalized action."[5] Because this target of coalignment is continually moving, adaptive policy must be oriented to a search for flexibility. But the orientation at the technical levels is toward uncertainty reduction and efficiency. There is then a dialectical tension between the strategic concerns and the technological/economic concerns of an organization. The rational decisionmaking framework successfully operationalizes the concept of efficiency for use in technical problem solving. A limited notion of flexibility is embodied in the concept of slack as developed by Simon to support his "bounded rationality" view of organizational decisionmaking.[6] But, as will be argued later, to fully operationalize the concept of flexibility requires a framework supportive of "negative reasoning."

2.1.2 Contingency Theories

While this efficiency/flexibility dialectic is a useful way of highlighting one distinction between policymaking and technical problem solving, the organizational structure perspective on policy formulation is otherwise misleading. It does not account for the interdependence of strategy, structure, environment, and technology. Chandler advanced the proposition that structure follows strategy.[7] In fact, the formal organization chart can be viewed as one form of artifact of the policy/strategy formulation process. But the organization chart does not, of course, include consideration for the diversity of individual styles and personalities and the informal channels of communication they propagate and maintain.

To better explain the relationship between strategy and structure, contingency theories of organizations have emerged which map strategy-structure relations onto technology/environment types. The result is a spectrum of organizational designs from mechanistic (hierarchical) to organismic (network)[8] and centralized to decentralized[9]; specifications for information systems[10] and multidimensional matrix structures[11]; and propositions on technology dependencies.[12] While contingency theory is regarded as the dominant school of thought in

24

organizational behavior,[13] it is severely limited by its emphasis on formal structure. The observed dynamics of organizations are usually difficult to explain in isolation of the interpersonal conflicts and coalitions that exist.

2.2 CONCEPT II: MANAGEMENT FUNCTIONS

While the classical view of management as consisting of several functions[14] is often discredited as a useful framework for theory development and empirical research, it still holds an influential place in modern management thought and deserves brief mention. The three management functions which are consistently cited in the literature are planning, organizing, and controlling.[15] All managers perform these functions in one form or another. Adam and Ebert have organized their book on operations management around these three functions.[16] They assign most operations research techniques to the planning function -- capacity planning, plant location, product planning, transportation planning, forecasting, scheduling, assignment, and project planning. A few techniques contribute to the function of controlling technical operations -- inventory control and quality control. Only industrial engineering techniques assist in the organizing function. They argue that behavioral factors dominate here, hence the limited contribution of formal models. While these three functions can often be separately identified at the technical level of management, policy formulation inherently involves the integration of all three. The concern at the policy level is with sociotechnical systems, and one of the themes of the framework proposed in Part II is the inclusion of both the social/behavioral and technical aspects of a policy issue. The controlling function is seen as the key to integration, but a much broader concept of control is needed than that associated with technological control.

2.3 CONCEPT III: DECISIONMAKING

2.3.1 Scientific Management

Rationality in decisionmaking has been a central theme in organization and political theory. It has origins in scientific management[17] and the classical study of bureaucracy.[18] In scientific management, rationality involves the identification of economic incentives to match worker production goals. Since the assumption is that the organizational objective function is to minimize costs and maximize revenues, i.e., maximize efficiency, models which support scientific management are optimization models. These models require very precise measurement techniques to provide data. The time and methods techniques developed for scientific management and industrial engineering measure physiological variables, ignoring social psychological variables. March and Simon criticize this approach: "it is a matter of record that time- and methods-study efforts have been far from successful in persuading workers that their long-run interests lie in maximizing their incentive pay."[19] In fact, the rapid rise in popularity of the "human relations" approach and the contingency theories previously mentioned can be seen as a "reaction to the excessive rationalism and formalism of Taylor's philosophy."[20]

2.3.2 Bureaucracy

Max Weber, considered the father of the study of bureaucracy, tried to show how bureaucratic organizations, through centralization and delegation of authority, specialization and departmentalization, and rules and procedures, represent an efficient structure for rational decisionmaking. The information processing limitations on individual decisionmakers could be overcome by exercising the above prerogatives. However, Merton, Selznick, and Gouldner focus attention on the unanticipated and dysfunctional consequences of bureaucratic organizations and purposive social action. Merton is concerned with the standardization of rules and procedures and the rigidity of behavior that results.[21] Selznick emphasizes specialization of tasks and, like Merton, the dysfunctions resulting from conflict in highly interrelated systems of interpersonal relations.[22] Gouldner similarly shows that rational control techniques, designed to decrease interpersonal conflict in a subsystem through equality norms, can disturb the equilibrium of the larger system of which it is a part, with feedback to the subsystem in unanticipated form.[23]

These latter theories of bureaucracy share a view that rationality (focus on efficiency) engenders a loss of flexibility to adapt. Hence, adaptation generally takes the form of growth in specialization and role differentiation, rules and procedures, and hierarchical control, often manifest by appending of additional departments, divisions, etc., to the organization to deal with the unanticipated dysfunctions that occur.[24] Crozier provides a very negative definition of the bureaucratic organization as one "where the feedback process, error-information-correction, does not function well and where consequently there cannot be any quick readjustment of the programs of action in view of errors committed."[25] Furthermore, he argues that a bureaucratic organization is blindly perpetuated through a self-reinforcing "vicious circle," despite the rational intentions of the top-level administrators. If one is to propose alternatives to circumvent this phenomenon, the role of policymaking from other than a rational point of view needs to be advanced. Also, the theory of the organization as a homeostatic system (i.e., deviation counteracting) needs to be complemented with a theory of the organization as a morphogenetic system (i.e., deviation amplifying[26]), the latter being in part the result of complex interpersonal relationships within the organization. Optimization models assume that all variables, except those to be consciously acted upon by the decisionmaker, will remain within certain limits and that probabilities can be assigned to the values of these variables (a homeostatic assumption).

2.3.3 Organization Process

Partially in response to the difficulties of rationality as a basis for explaining organizational behavior, Simon developed the notions of "bounded rationality" and "satisficing" behavior.[27] Limitations on human cognitive processes in decisionmaking result in actions which are suboptimal; hence, there is "slack" in the system and perfect efficiency is sacrificed in order to absorb uncertainty. There is a cost associated with the search for acceptable alternatives, so the decisionmaker generally stops looking when an alternative is found which is satisfactory to current levels of aspiration. As an alternative to the bureaucratic model of organization, March and Simon stress the interrelationship between levels of aspiration, satisfaction realized, the rate of search for alternatives, and the expected value of reward.[28] Changes in the levels of aspiration themselves may be an outcome of search, a possibility not permitted in optimizing behavior.

Cyert and March attempt to extend Simon's framework to better formulate a theory of collective choice.[29] They hypothesize a dominant coalition in an organization, consisting of individuals whose personal goals may be in conflict. "Quasi-resolution" of this conflict involves some form of conjunction of these individual goals, which the coalition imposes on the organization as a series of aspiration level constraints.[30] Policy can be viewed as embodying these constraints. Uncertainty avoidance, problemistic search, and organizational learning are also part of the framework. Although the "human relations" school has criticized the framework for its apparent emphasis on formal decisions and deemphasis on interpersonal relations[31] (other than those among a hypothetical dominant coalition), the Cyert/March theory remains the definitive formulation of organization process as decisionmaking and problem solving. Perhaps the weakest link in the theory is the assumption of a dominant coalition. In actuality there are multiple coalitions, with some disappearing and others being formed continually, and different coalitions exhibiting different degrees of dominance in the resolution of different issues. The interaction among coalitions and issues creates an atmosphere conducive to an organizational dynamics of significantly greater severity and discontinuity than that implied by organizational learning.

Satisficing has been incorporated into a number of decision models, including goal programming, compromise programming, dominance methods, and other sequential elimination techniques. These modelling techniques, however, are all derivatives of the "positive" reasoning of rationality. Slack is seen as a necessary evil, and it is assumed that levels of aspiration will and should be increased once current levels are realized.

This order of decisionmaking [joining available means to ends] we call routine, distinguishing it from the realm of critical decision. The latter, because it involves choices that affect the basic character of the enterprise, is the true province of leadership...Such choices are of course often made unconsciously, without awareness of their larger significance, but then the enterprise evolves more or less blindly.[32]

28

The role of policy is to provide guidance and hence reduce some of the blindness. The distinction between the process of routine decisionmaking (based on a "positive" form of reasoning) and critical decisionmaking (based on a "negative" form of reasoning) corresponds to the distinction made by Alexander between selfconscious and unselfconscious modes of design[33] and Steinbruner's distinction between the analytic and cybernetic paradigms.[34]

2.4 CONCEPT IV: POLITICS

Only the political concept of policy formulation approaches the "negative" reasoning paradigm. Lindblom[35] and Braybrooke and Lindblom[36] have developed in considerable detail the concept of "disjointed incrementalism" or what Lindblom first referred to as "muddling through." The concept accepts the limitations on information processing, the complexity of policy issues, and the social conflict inherent in policymaking as was implicit in the Cyert-March-Simon framework. But the conclusion is different; ends and means are viewed as inseparable and, hence, means-ends analysis is usually inappropriate. Incrementalism limits analysis only to alternatives in the immediate neighborhood of existing policy. The emphasis is on the policy actors, their relative power and influence, and the rules of the policy game.

While disjointed incrementalism represents a type of negative reasoning, it does so without realizing it. By denying that theory can serve any useful role in policy formulation, a theory of negative reasoning is also denied. Although admittedly descriptive of much that is observed in policymaking, the result of the incremental concept is one of cynicism, with little allowance for hope that the policy process might be improved and little faith in human ingenuity.[37] Lindblom himself admits that "the method is unquestionably one of less than universal usefulness."[38] Our approach assumes that there is a role for theory and models in policy formulation and that policymaking need not be relegated the fate imposed by Lindblom. But for this to be realized, not only must the character of negative reasoning be recognized, a theory of negative reasoning (constraint theory) must also be incorporated into the policymaking process. An interactive, process oriented model provides one mechanism for this purpose.

Lindblom's identification of the key factors in policy formulation is an important contribution, and Allison has successfully used the political model to analyze the events surrounding the Cuban missile crisis.[39] The importance of the policy actors, their interpersonal relationships, and the implicit rules and dynamics of coalition formation have also been recognized by others.[40] Modern evolutionary theories of organization also place greater emphasis on conflict resolution and less on means-ends rationality. Weick, in fact states:

> Rationality makes sense of what has been, not what will be. It is a process of justifica-tion in which past deeds are made to appear sensible to the actor himself and to those other persons to whom he feels account-able.[41]

Hence, the public image portrayed by an administrator is usually one of rationality, as that is the socially accepted behavior of a person in such a position.

2.5 SYNTHESIS

If policymaking as politics is to provide the behavioral basis for constraint theory, a more rigorous development of the elements and their interrelationships in the policy formulation process is necessary. This will be done in detail in the form of a language for policy-level modelling (Chapter 6). For now, let it suffice to make a distinction between the "technical problems" addressed by optimization and predictive models and the "issues" addressed by policy-level models.

2.5.1 Technical Problems vs. Policy Issues

Optimization and predictive models are developed to assist in operational decisionmaking (i.e., problem solving). The classic definition of a problem is depicted in Figure 2.1. A problem exists when, in the mind of the decisionmaker, the desired situation is sufficiently separate from the perceived situation that it is called to his/her attention. In an optimization model, the desired situation is specified in the form

30

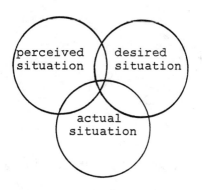

Figure 2.1 A Problem[42]

of goals and objectives; in a predictive model, the
desired situation is not explicitly incorporated in the
model but is implicit in the selection of model
variables. The perceived situation, in an optimization
model, can take the form of a functional relationship,
as in an inventory model, or of a well-defined set of
constraints, as in mathematical programming. In a
predictive model, the perceived situation is inevitably
structured as a set of cause and effect relationships,
as in a regression model or a queuing model. If a
technical-level problem fits one of these structures,
an optimization or predictive model is appropriate.

A policy issue represents a whole system of
problems, what Ackoff has referred to as a "mess."

> The "solution" to a mess--whatever it may
> be--is not the simple sum of the solutions to
> the problems which are or can be extracted
> from it. No mess can be solved by solving
> each of its component problems independently
> of the others, because no mess can be decom-
> posed into independent problems...We need a
> theory and methodology for coping with
> systems of problems as systems, as wholes,
> as indivisible sets of interdependent
> elements.[43]

Compared to a "problem," a policy "issue" is better
represented by Figure 2.2. The perceptive, cognitive,
and affective differences between the actors in a

31

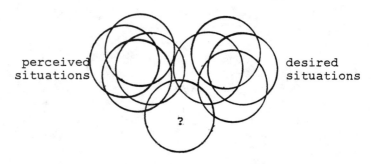

perceived
situations

desired
situations

Figure 2.2 A Policy Issue

policy issue result in conflicting perceptions and values.

In Department of Defense logistics, a policy-level "issue" with significant ramifications for strategic posture concerns the centralization of logistics management. During the early phases of our Defense study, interviews with over fifty top-level logistics managers surfaced a very divergent set of perceptions and opinions about this issue. The issue has important organizational implications and, therefore, implications for the policy formulation process itself. In the MFS Finance Corporation, an "issue" which is related to the company's strategic posture was evidenced by a high turnover among loan office personnel. What an acceptable turnover rate is, or whether it can (or should) even be reduced, produced different responses from questioned individuals.

Conflicting perceptions occur, in part, because a policy issue involves a large number of interdependent variables and relationships. One of the difficulties in political processes is that the participants have selected different sets of variables and hence are looking at the situation from entirely different perspectives (i.e., they have different mental models). Furthermore, perceptions cannot be divorced from values, and conflicting values complicate a policy issue even more. Because the dimensionality of an issue varies from actor to actor, ambiguity, inconsistency, intransitivity, and contradiction are inherent characteristics of an issue; and bargaining, compromising, negotiating, and other political maneuvering characterize the dynamics of the resolution process. Tradeoffs across dimensions, rather than simply across outcomes, is typical. In this context, incrementalism appears inevitable.

However, the diversity of perspectives and values need not be viewed as an obstacle to policy formulation; they can serve to generate creative alternatives and insights. If the actors are inclined to take a cooperative rather than an adversarial posture, learning can occur with respect to both the system being observed and the individual values being imposed on it. "Value-rich" policy becomes a real possibility, one that policy-level models can help facilitate.

Steinbruner has developed a theory of political decision which goes beyond that of Lindblom and Allison.[44] He develops a paradigm which explicitly incorporates individual perception and cognition, and successfully uses it to analyze the events surrounding United States/NATO nuclear sharing policies between 1956 and 1964. The constraint theoretic framework we propose in Part II also emphasizes perception and cognition, i.e., mental models.

2.5.2 Organizational Communications and Control

The transfer of information on individual values and perceptions through both the formal and informal channels of communication in an organization results in a complementary relationship between technical problems and policy issues.

Figure 2.3 depicts this complementary relationship between technical problem solving and policymaking in terms of levels of management in an organization. A technical problem arises in the context of an explicit set of goals and objectives for the efficient functioning of a technological system.[45] If goals and objectives are not being adequately achieved, alternatives for improving the situation are considered and the best one selected. Not only will the solution selected have an impact on the technological system, but also the problem solving process itself will have an impact on the larger sociotechnical system. The sociotechnical system is the subject of policymaking. The set of alternatives considered, the problem criteria used, and the decision rules employed in the problem solving process are constrained by organization-wide policy.

33

There are usually, of course, many levels of management between the two extremes depicted in the

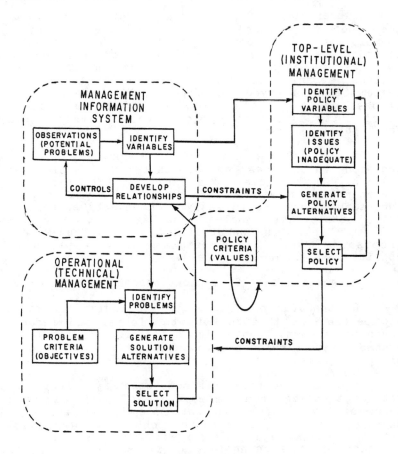

Figure 2.3   Relationships between Technical
Problem Solving and Policymaking

diagram, the intermediate levels performing a hybrid of the two extremes. To depict the policymaking process as a sequence of steps, as in the diagram, is misleading; we do it only to make a comparison with the technical problem solving process. The steps cannot in reality be so separated. A policy issue often surfaces through intuition or as the result of conflicting or ambiguous opinions or information. The resolution of

34

an issue involves a process of exploring the policy space, evaluating current policy, and, if necessary, creating alternative policies. The selection of a policy represents the resolution of the conflict. Policy "criteria" are seldom explicit and are embedded in the entire process.

The role of what is labelled the Management Information System is critical. "Management Information System" does not refer simply to a computerized MIS, but rather to all organizational communications. It therefore includes much more than data storage and retrieval. In fact, it is the informal communications and the "institutional knowledge" of individuals with exposure to the sociotechnical system being managed which are particularly relevant to policy-level management.

For purposes of modelling, two categories of information, not mutually exclusive, are identified: information on the state of system variables and information on relationships among those variables. The state of technological variables are usually measureable and the relationships relatively easy to develop. That is, the relationships in technical problems tend to be adequately formulated as linear, or at least curvilinear functions. At the policy level, system variables are aggregations of a large number of interrelated variables. The relationships in policy issues, then, tend to be fuzzy and often characterized by discontinuity. The human factors which can often be ignored at the technical level become very significant at the intermediate and top levels of management. Some relationships can be directly measured, but many must be exposed through interpersonal communications and modelling. The relationships define the set of viable policy alternatives. Limited knowledge of relationships, then, constrains the capability of policy-level management to generate and evaluate policy alternatives.

The concept of control implicit in the two processes -- problem solving and policymaking -- is also very different. The concept of control derived from rationality and appropriate for technical-level management is one of error detection and correction. If a standard or goal is not being met, the manager takes action (often in the form of sanctions). Furthermore, if the manager can predict a discrepancy before it occurs, corrective action can be taken in

35

advance. At the policy levels, the key to control is flexibility, i.e., keeping as many options open as possible. This is accomplished at the expense of efficiency and stability. Identifying a balance between the two modes of control is the role of policy management. By specifying the class of behavior which should be excluded from occurring, policy formulation employs the negative form of reasoning. A generalized concept of control, then, emphasizes relationships between people, not the imposition of authority.[46] Relationships are realized through the channels and nature of interpersonal communication.

This chapter has emphasized a dichotomy between the positive reasoning of rationality and negative reasoning. The next chapter explores the philosophical heritage of this dichotomy.

NOTES

1. Robert N. Anthony, Planning and Control Systems: A Framework for Analysis (Boston: Division of Research, Graduate School of Business, Harvard University, 1965).

2. James D. Thompson, Organizations in Action: Social Science Bases of Administrative Theory (New York: McGraw-Hill, 1967), p. 10; Talcott Parsons, Structure and Process in Modern Societies (New York: The Free Press of Glencoe, 1960).

3. Experiments with more pluralistic structures are reported in David Jenkins, Job Power (Baltimore, Md.: Penguin Books, 1974); Ph. G. Herbst, Alternatives to Hierarchies (Leiden, The Netherlands: Martinus Nijhoff Social Sciences Division, 1976); and Russell L. Ackoff, Creating the Corporate Future (New York: John Wiley & Sons, 1981).

4. Thompson, pp. 148-150.

5. Ibid., p. 147.

6. Herbert A. Simon, Administrative Behavior (New York: The Free Press, 1957).

7. Alfred D. Chandler, Jr., Strategy and Structure: Chapters in the History of the American Industrial Enterprise (Cambridge, Mass.: The M.I.T.

Press, 1962).

8. Thomas Burns and G. M. Stalker, The Management of Innovation (London: Tavistock Publications, 1961).

9. Paul Lawrence and Jay Lorsch, Organization and Environment (Homewood, Ill.: Richard D. Irwin, 1969).

10. Jay Galbraith, Designing Complex Organizations (Reading, Mass.: Addison-Wesley, 1973).

11. Stanley M. Davis and Paul R. Lawrence, Matrix (Reading, Mass.: Addison-Wesley, 1977).

12. Thompson, pp. 51-65; Joan Woodward, Industrial Organization: Theory and Practice (London: Oxford University Press, 1965).

13. Jay R. Galbraith and Daniel A. Nathanson, Strategy Implementation: The Role of Structure and Process (St. Paul, Minn.: West Publishing Company, 1978), p. 55.

14. Henri Fayol, Industrial and General Administration, trans. J. A. Coubrough (Geneva: International Management Institute, 1929).

15. Richard M. Hodgetts, Management: Theory, Process, and Practice (Philadelphia: W. B. Saunders Company, 1979), p. 64.

16. Everett E. Adam, Jr. and Roanld J. Ebert, Production and Operations Management (Englewood Cliffs, N.J.: Prentice-Hall, 1978).

17. F. W. Taylor, Scientific Management (New York: Harper & Brothers, 1911).

18. Max Weber, The Theory of Social and Economic Organizations, trans. A. M. Henderson, ed. Talcott Parsons (New York: The Free Press of Glencoe, 1947).

19. James G. March and Herbert A. Simon, Organizations (New York: John Wiley & Sons, 1958), p. 19.

20. Graham T. Allison, Essence of Decision (Boston: Little, Brown, and Company, 1971), p. 299.

21. Robert K. Merton, "The Unanticipated

Consequences of Purposive Social Action," American Sociological Review 1(1936): 894-904.

22. Philip Selznick, TVA and the Grass Roots (Berkeley, Calif.: University of California Press, 1949); Leadership in Administration (New York: Harper & Row, 1957).

23. Alvin W. Gouldner, Patterns of Industrial Bureaucracy (New York: The Free Press of Glencoe, 1954).

24. See Elliott Jacques, "Growth in Bureaucratic Systems," in A General Theory of Bureaucracy (London: Heinemann Educational Books, 1976), pp. 305-308.

25. Michel Crozier, The Bureaucratic Phenomenon (Chicago: The University of Chicago Press, 1964), p. 187.

26. Magoroh Maruyama, "The Second Cybernetics: Deviation-Amplifying Mutual Causal Processes," American Scientist 51(1963): 164-179.

27. Herbert A. Simon, "A Behavioral Model of Rational Choice," in Models of Man (New York: John Wiley and Sons, 1957), pp. 241-260.

28. March and Simon, pp. 47-52.

29. Richard M. Cyert and James March, A Behavioral Theory of the Firm (Englewood Cliffs, N.J.: Prentice-Hall, 1963).

30. For an expanded discussion, see Herbert A. Simon, "On the Concept of Organizational Goal," Administrative Science Quarterly 9(1964): 1-22; Allison, pp. 75-78; Joseph L. Bower, "Descriptive Decision Theory from the 'Administrative' Viewpoint," in The Study of Policy Formation, ed. Raymond A. Bauer and Kenneth J. Gergen (New York: The Free Press, 1968), pp. 103-148.

31. Barnard was perhaps the first organization theorist to fully emphasize the informal organization, but he failed to adequately develop the process of conflict resolution. Selznick's theory of leadership, on the other hand, advances a normative model of conflict resolution. Drawing on the self-actualizing model of man developed by Maslow, Hertzberg, McGregor,

and Likert, Argyris levels perhaps the strongest criticism against the Cyert-March-Simon framework, complaining that the creative and emotive aspects of the individual are not adequately considered. Chester Barnard, The Functions of the Executive (Cambridge, Mass.: Harvard University Press, 1938); Selznick, Leadership; Abraham Maslow, Motivation and Personality, 2nd ed. (New York: Harper & Row, 1954); Frederick Hertzberg, Bernard Mausner, and Barbara Bloch Snyderman, The Motivation to Work, 2nd ed. (New York: John Wiley & Sons, 1959); Douglas McGregor, The Human Side of Enterprise (New York: McGraw-Hill, 1960); Rensis Likert, New Patterns of Management (New York: McGraw-Hill, 1961); Chris Argyris, The Applicability of Organizational Sociology (London: Cambridge University Press, 1972) and "Some Limits of Rational Man Organization Theory," Public Administration Review, May/June 1973, pp. 253-267.

32. Selznick, Leadership, p. 135.

33. Christopher Alexander, Notes on the Synthesis of Form (Cambridge, Mass.: Harvard University Press, 1964).

34. John D. Steinbruner, The Cybernetic Theory of Decision (Princeton, N.J.: Princeton University Press, 1974).

35. Charles E. Lindblom, "The Science of 'Muddling Through'," Public Administration Review XIX (Spring 1959): 79-88.

36. David Brayrooke and Charles E. Lindblom, A Strategy of Decision (New York: The Free Press, 1970).

37. Yehezkel Dror, "Muddling-Through--'Science' or Inertia?," Public Administration Review XXIV (September 1964): 153-157.

38. Charles E. Lindblom, "Contexts for Change and Strategy: A Reply," in Readings on Modern Organizations, ed. Amitai Etzioni (Englewood Cliffs, N.J.: Prentice-Hall, 1969), p. 171.

39. Allison, Essence of Decision.

40. For example, Ian C. MacMillan, Strategy Formulation: Political Concepts (St. Paul, Minn.: West Publishing Company, 1978).

41. Karl E. Weick, The Social Psychology of Organizing (Reading, Mass.: Addison-Wesley, 1969), p. 38.

42. Adapted from Edwin M. Bartee, "A Holistic View of Problem Solving," Management Science 20(December, Part I, 1973): 440.

43. Russell L. Ackoff, "Beyond Problem Solving," General Systems XIX (1974): 238.

44. Steinbruner, The Cybernetic Theory of Decision.

45. There is nothing to preclude a technological system from consisting of human operators, as long as those human operators have well-defined and rigid tasks to perform (e.g., an assembly line).

46. See Weick, p. 37.

CHAPTER 3

PHILOSOPHICAL PERSPECTIVES

Any research or modelling approach is based on certain philosophical assumptions. These assumptions are often not well articulated, nor are the scientists using these assumptions always aware of them. They are, however, implicit in the theories which emerge from a particular science and in the language and mathematics used to describe those theories. It became apparent as the theoretical framework and field work unfolded that the foundations for policy-level modelling being proposed are based not only on different assumptions about organizations and the policy formulation process, but also on a philosophical heritage different from that of most modelling practice.

This chapter briefly discusses some of these assumptions and their adequacy as the foundations for policy-level modelling. Raymond Hainer has provided a classification scheme which we use to subdivide the discussion of alternative philosophical assumptions into three categories: rationalism, pragmatism, and existentialism.[1] In addition, developments in phenomenology are particularly relevant to modern existentialism. While the framework proposed in Part II is compatible with the assumptions of the latter category, these assumptions are not sufficiently formalized to accomodate the development of new mathematical structures and a new modelling language. Hence, the final section of the chapter discusses some recent developments in cybernetics[2] which do provide the needed formalism.

3.1 PERSPECTIVE I: RATIONALISM

Two forms of rationalism can be identified: idealism and positivism. Plato's idealism takes as its basic assumption that concepts, logic, and mathematical principles are independent of the world of phenomena; they are simply waiting to be discovered.[3] Once a concept or principle is "discovered," it enters the body of institutionalized knowledge and need not be questioned again. If observation does not confirm the rational view, the observations may be ignored or explained away as errors in human perception. Hence, idealism has a built-in safeguard which assures its perpetuation. It is in this context that Aristotle's laws of logic[4] still remain the foundations of modern rationality. Euclidean mathematics, Newtonian mechanics, and the bureaucratic form of organization can be traced to this two-valued logic. Much of modern technology has been made possible by the structure of mathematics and physical science that has resulted. The same logical structure is reflected in the formal design of social institutions to manage this technology. Furthermore, it could be argued that modern technology and the bureaucratic form of organization mutually reinforce each other.

Positivism assumes that concepts, logic, and mathematical principles exist, but are not independent of the world of phenomena. In fact, the method for discovering these concepts and principles is through empirical investigation. Since these principles are verifiable in the objective, external world and independent of the subjective world, an observation that violates a previously "proven" relationship may be explained as imperfection in the method of measurement or experiment. When this is not a satisfactory explanation, the phenomenon may be described as stochastic. The probability of occurrence of stochastic events can also be verified through empirical test.

Descartes provided the formalism needed for a methodology of rationalism later developed by the English empiricists Locke, Berkeley, and Hume.[5] If contradiction or inconsistency arises, it is treated either as not founded in reality or by appending new concepts or principles to the existing body of knowledge which resolve the inconsistency.[6] In this way, a hierarchy of laws and principles develops and continues to grow, analogous to the hierarchical growth of bureaucratic organizations discussed in the previous chapter. Herbst, in fact, calls this form of logic "totalitarian" and credits it with a narrowminded focus on "the quest for certainty."[7]

Most management science models, while pragmatically implemented, are rationalistic in structure. The mathematics of functional relationships, differential calculus, graph theory, and

42

probability distributions has foundations in two-valued logic. By forcing this dichotomous structure on the system being modelled, ends are separated from means, causes from effects, the objective from the subjective, and the modeller from the model. Given a sufficiently developed system of logic and mathematics, events can be predicted either with certainty or with knowable probabilities. The mode of management control which derives from rationalism is authoritative, for with sufficient knowledge of cause and effect, events can be forced to exhibit a consciously planned pattern. A modern critic of rationalism, Bateson responds to this "positive" form of reasoning:

> "D is desirable; B leads to C; C leads to D; so D can be achieved by way of B and C." But if the total mind and the outer world do not, in general, have this lineal structure, then by forcing this structure upon them, we become blind to the cybernetic circularities of the self and the external world. Our conscious sampling of data will not disclose whole circuits but only arcs of circuits, cut off from their matrix by our selective attention.[8]

As the basis for policy-level modelling, rationalism by itself is not adequate, for it cannot deal with:

--the ambiguity, inconsistencies, and intransitivities inherent in policy issues;

--the interrelationship of values and perceptions;

--the social and political patterns of communication and control in the policy formulation process; and

--the interrelationship between the modeller and the model.

3.2 PERSPECTIVE II: PRAGMATISM

It is not clear, historically, where the bridge between rationalism and pragmatism occurred.[9] Certainly the development of inductive logic by John Stuart Mill had a significant impact. While the primary justification for induction is that it works, Mill, in trying to explain why it works, postulated the existence of structure in the external world. Of course, it is only by induction that Mill could know that.[10]   But, the development of statistical inference as an inductive tool has served a key role in pragmatic thinking.

Pragmatism assumes concepts, logic, and mathematical principles only tentatively. "The method of pragmatism is that of recurrent formulation, deduction, test in reality, detection of difference between expectation and findings, and feeding back of the error into the formulation until the difference between the new expectation and the latest look at reality becomes arbitrarily small."[11]   The appropriateness of concepts and principles is relative to a specific task, and if they prove useful in a test, they are retained until others prove more useful. In modelling practice, pragmatism involves continual revision of the model.

Two difficulties arise with pragmatism as a basis for policy-level modelling. First, an intellectual formulation is prerequisite to any experimentation. While this may not be formally and rigorously accomplished, it is implicit in the mental processes that produce assumptions and hypotheses. Hence, the method of pragmatism is not divorced from a system of logic, which historically has been the logic of rationalism. The mental models of the participants in policy formulation (including the modeller), each of which presupposes structure in a policy issue, are, at least in part, socially and culturally conditioned. Pragmatism has problems dealing with social process, first because of the large amount of information required to support a rationalistic model of such a process, and second because pragmatic inquiry is in effect a social process itself.

The second difficulty with pragmatism as a basis for policy-level modelling, lies in the concept of "usefulness," a concept which is also socially and culturally dependent. If usefulness itself is to be the subject of a model, pragmatism has no way to deal with it -- How can the concept of usefulness be evaluated if the criterion of evaluation is usefulness?

As mentioned in the previous section on rationalism, most modelling practice is pragmatic with respect to implementation. If a model does not work, i.e., is not acceptable to the client, it is revised until it does. The danger of this approach is that the management consultant tends to assume a "hard sell" advocacy role. There is little "science" involved; the success of the professional lies in his intuition, judgment, and persuasive skills. Without some set of underlying axioms or theoretical framework, criticism and advancement of the science of policy-level modelling cannot be realized, for there is no basis for communication between scientists nor any structure on which to build additional theory. Much of the process-oriented, organizational development technologies are based in pragmatism.

3.3 PERSPECTIVE III: PHENOMENOLOGY AND EXISTENTIALISM

Science as a social process with origins in cultural presuppositions is the perspective of modern phenomenology. Although relying heavily on rational reasoning, Kant developed a theory of phenomena which was to prove a turning point in modern philosophy. Kantian theory assumes that concepts of logic, time, and space are mental constructs and do not exist and cannot be verified in the external world.[12] The rationalist content of the theory is evident in the dichotomy between internal and external, subjective and objective, self and environment. But by shifting attention to subjectivity and social/political processes, Kant initiated a transcendental or "meta" system of thinking which incorporated frames of reference into philosophical inquiry. Hegel, by postulating that the act of defining any phenomenon automatically creates its opposite, initiated the development of a system of dialectical logic. Focusing on dialectical relationships as the essence of mental constructs, he went a step beyond the rationalist, self/environment dichotomy of Kant. However, Hegelian theory assumes an ultimate truth which can be approached through the thesis-antithesis-synthesis process. In so doing, it follows the tradition of rational idealism.

Existentialism assumes that "concepts arise out of the uniquely human process of perceiving, of pattern (Gestalt) forming, of symbolizing, of comparing, and of conceptualizing, which are not explicitly conscious."[13] The definitions, assumptions, and relationships in a theory are inevitably incomplete, and characterized by ambiguity and inconsistency.

...anyone predicting the future with certainty is engaged in misrepresentation...
Causality, implying temporal connection or
correlative association, is a concept which
is not justified unless or until the aggregate of existence-phenomena-experience indicates its presence without ambiguity. Probability, as a frequency within a presumed
finite set of events, does not have a priori
meaning; information content is not known to
be finite, and reproducibility is not
assumed.[14]

It is little wonder that the early existentialists,
e.g., Kierkegaard, Nietzsche, Heidegger, Jaspers,
Satre, and Camus, reflect a philosophy of despair and
loneliness, not unlike the feelings aroused by
disjointed incrementalism.

Modern existentialism, however, takes as its point
of departure the notion of metaconcepts, metalogic,
metalanguage, and metamathematics.[15] "Meta" here
implies the inclusion of frames of reference in the
system of knowledge, i.e., knowledge is context
dependent. In so doing, metaconcepts highlight the
ambiguity, inconsistency, and incompleteness of
assumptions, theory, and information content in
experience. Metalogic, rather than stating what can
follow from theoretical propositions, focuses on what
can be excluded from consideration. Hence, the meta
form of reasoning is "negative" reasoning.
Furthermore,

Existentialism is unceasingly preoccupied
with the human condition: with the constraints to which man is subject...Existen-
tialism emphasizes not only constraints but
also possibilities. There must be alternative possibilities of action, or choice
would be meaningless; and there must be
alternative possibilities of existence, or
it would be predetermined by essence. This
manifold of possibility gives rise to a final
basic existentialist category: ambiguity...
choice is continuous as we go through life,
and with each choice some possibilities
vanish forever while new ones emerge for the
next choice.[16]

Phenomenology, as the science of existentialism,

attempts to take advantage of the tremendous number of conceptual possibilities available to generate radically new insights into phenomena, as Einstein did in using alternatives to Euclidean mathematics to develop the theory of relativity.

Metamathematics is the mathematics of mathematics and, as a discipline, has been preoccupied with inconsistency and paradox in mathematical proof and symbolic logic. Russell and Whitehead's Theory of Logical Types, for example, was an attempt to transcend a system of mathematics and logic which had produced irreconcilable paradoxes. The theory, however, requires certain limitations on the classes of things being considered.[17] Gödel's Incompleteness Theorem proves that any formal system of logic or mathematics is necessarily incomplete, and that consistency can only be proved by recourse to methods of proof which the system itself cannot generate.[18] Watzlawick, et al., argue that Wittgenstein, a student and colleague of Russell, had formulated the Gödel paradox in philosophical terms ten years prior.[19] But the greatest contribution to modern logic and mathematics may prove to come from another of Russell's students, George Spencer Brown, who in his Laws of Form transcends the Theory of Logical Types.[20]

As a brief diversion, it may be useful to note that existentialism has many similarities with Eastern, particularly Buddhist, philosophies. "In Buddhist thought, the contradictions generated by any set of logical axioms are used to destroy specific axioms and ultimately the logic itself and thus to transcend it."[21] Contradictions are the focal point of the metalogic, and the act of negation produces a smaller, more flexible system of logic, in contradistinction to the certainty sought in rationalism.

As the basis for policy-level modelling, existentialism emphasizes ambiguity, inconsistency, possibilities, and constraint. Furthermore, the role of the model is to generate insight and creative alternatives through a communications experience. The structure of the communication channel should accommodate different frames of reference and, specifically, different perceptions and values.

47

3.4 SYNTHESIS: SECOND ORDER CYBERNETICS

While existentialism provides philosophical foundations with the attributes necessary for policy-level modelling, it is no accident that it is not sufficiently formalized for that purpose. As the "science of communications and control in the animal and the machine,"[22] cybernetics does provide a formalism consistent with the concepts of constraint, circularity, and possibility. Its mathematical development has been rigorous,[23] as has its application to social/political science,[24] psychotherapy,[25] and management science.[26] However, it is the development of "second order" cybernetics[27] as an extension of the original formulation which is particularly relevant for policy-level modelling.

By emphasizing the relationship between observer and observed, modeller and model, knower and known, the new formulation directly addresses self-referential paradox, metaknowledge, and the role of observation and modelling in scientific inquiry. The logical empiricism of the pragmatists, which currently dominates method in the social sciences, and which assumes that knowledge can be logically derived from empirical experience and science advanced through continual improvements in method, gives way to a concept of knowledge as a state of consciousness. But consciousness is multi-level, self-referential, and self-reflective, and a conscious representation of phenomena cannot be complete and unambiguous. Burton, citing Feyerabend, argues for a dialectical science, one involving continual structuring, tearing down, and restructuring of theories and research programs.[28] This is consistent with Kuhn's theory of scientific revolutions.[29] In this context, the role of science becomes one of raising questions which force the reframing of knowledge, rather than one of building an ever increasing system of laws and theories.

Another important aspect of second order cybernetics is its preoccupation, not with "change," but with the "change of change," i.e., higher order change. While this was also included in the initial formulation of cybernetics,[30] it was explicitly excluded by Aristotle.[31] Policy issues represent situations,

48

...in which first-order change...is incapable
of effecting the desired change, because
there the system's structure itself has to
undergo change, and this can be effected only
from the second-order change level...The
attempt to effect first-order change under
these circumstances either greatly contri-
butes to the problem which it is supposed to
solve, or actually is the problem.[32]

It is in this context that Spencer Brown's logic of
distinctions, and its extension to a calculus of
self-reference,[33] is particularly relevant.
Furthermore, developments in set theory provide an
initial, although admittedly limited, mathematical
structure for operationalizing the logic for use in
policy-level modelling.[34]

Finally, second order cybernetics as a basis for
modelling has implications for the rationalist
distinction between art and science. Burton motivates
the argument:

ᵣeyerabend wants to develop a conception of
science that takes fuller account of the
artistic and creative impulses of human
beings, that enables the criticism and transformation of conceptual and social worlds
rather than just the representation of
them...it argues for "irrational" and
"subjective" influences in scientific work.
It is contrary to the mainstream philosophy
of science because it argues for the centrality of human values and concerns in the
motivation for, as well as the conduct of,
science.[35]

But subjectivity and human values are characterized by
high degrees of ambiguity and overwhelming numbers of
possibilities.

This is why existentialism turns so charac-
teristically to literature to express its
philosophy. For poetry and myth--indeed, art
in general--is ambiguous in just this way.
The existentialist believes that only the
riches of the artistic consciousness can be
adequate to the rich ambiguity of life
itself.[36]

49

One of the conclusions of the field work reported in Part III is the need to incorporate more artistic content into the modelling process. To facilitate communications, information needs to be displayed in other than numerical and simple graphical forms, forms that do not capture the richness of the information content in a policy issue.

The methodological approaches discussed in the next chapter have a basis in different philosophical traditions. The proposed synthesis of those methods has a basis in second order cybernetics.

NOTES

1. Raymond M. Hainer, "Rationalism, Pragmatism, and Existentialism: Perceived but Undiscovered Multicultural Problems," in The Research Society, ed. Evelyn Glatt and Maynard W. Shelly (New York: Gordon and Breach Inc., 1968), pp. 7-50.

2. These recent developments in cybernetics have been coined "second order cybernetics." The distinction is that first order cybernetics can be referred to as the science of observed systems, second order cybernetics as the science of observing systems. See Stuart A. Umpleby, "Second Order Cybernetics and the Design of Large Scale Social Experiments," The Proceedings of the XXth Annual North American Meeting of the Society for General Systems Research, 1976, p. 72.

3. Ph. G. Herbst, Alternatives to Hierarchies (Leiden, The Netherlands: Martinus Nijhoff Social Sciences Division, 1976), p. 85.

4. The cornerstones of Aristotelian logic are the law of identity ($A=A$ and $A \cap A = A$), the law of the excluded middle ($A \cup \bar{A}=U$), and the law of noncontradiction ($A \neq \bar{A}$ and $A \cap \bar{A} = \emptyset$).

5. Hainer, pp. 33-34.

6. See, for example, the discussion of the concept of infinity and infinitesimal in W. V. Quine, "The Foundations of Mathematics," Scientific American, September 1964, pp. 113-127.

7. Herbst, pp. 69-83.

8. Gregory Bateson, "Effects of Conscious Purpose on Human Adaptation," in Steps to An Ecology of Mind (New York: Ballantine Books, 1972), p. 445; Bateson expands these ideas in Mind and Nature: A Necessary Unity (New York: E. P. Dutton, 1979).

9. The principal proponents of pragmatism have been William James, Charles Pierce, and John Dewey.

10. Martin Gardner, "On the Fabric of Inductive Logic, and Some Probability Paradoxes," in Mathematics: An Introduction to its Spirit and Use, Readings from Scientific American, with introductions by Morris Kline (San Francisco: W. H. Freeman and Company, 1979), pp. 161-164.

11. Hainer, p. 21.

12. Herbst, p. 85.

13. Hainer, p. 24.

14. Ibid., p. 25.

15. Ibid., p. 29.

16. Abraham Kaplan, The New World of Philosophy (New York: Vintage Books, 1961) pp. 116-117.

17. For a discussion of the Russell paradox and the theory of logical types, see Paul Watzlawick, John Weakland, and Richard Fisch, Change: Principles of Problem Formation and Problem Resolution (New York: W. W. Norton & Company, 1974), pp. 6-10; and W. V. Quine, "Paradox," Scientific American, April 1962, pp. 84-95.

18. For a discussion of Gödel's incompleteness theorem, see Quine, "Paradox;" Michael A. Arbib, Brains, Machines, and Mathematics (New York: McGraw-Hill, 1964), pp. 119-140; and Ernest Nagel and James R. Newman, Gödel's Proof (New York: New York University Press, 1958).

19. Paul Watzlawick, Janet Helmick Beavin, and Don D. Jackson, Pragmatics of Human Communication (New York: W. W. Norton & Company, 1967), p. 270.

20. G. Spencer Brown, Laws of Form (New York: The Julian Press, 1972).

21. Herbst, p. 80.

22. Norbert Wiener, Cybernetics, 2nd ed., (Cambridge, Mass.: The M.I.T. Press, 1961).

23. W. Ross Ashby, An Introduction to Cybernetics (London: Chapman & Hall, 1956) and Design for a Brain (London: Chapman & Hall, 1960).

24. Karl W. Deutsch, The Nerves of Government (New York: The Free Press, 1966); and Walter Buckley, Sociology and Modern Systems Theory (Englewood Cliffs, N.J.: Prentice-Hall, 1967).

25. Watzlawick, et al., Human Communication.

26. Stafford Beer, Decision and Control (London: John Wiley & Sons, 1966); Designing Freedom (London: John Wiley & Sons, 1974); Platform for Change (London: John Wiley & Sons, 1975); The Heart of Enterprise (Chichester: John Wiley & Sons, 1979); and Brain of the Firm, Rev. ed. (Chichester: John Wiley & Sons, 1981).

27. Heinz Von Foerster, Cybernetics of Cybernetics (Urbana, Ill.: Biological Computer Laboratory, University of Illinois at Urbana-Champaign, 1974).

28. Dudley J. Burton, "Methodology and Epistemology for Second-Order Cybernetics," The Proceedings of the XXIst Annual North American Meeting of the Society for General Systems Research, 1977, pp. 324-333; Paul Feyerabend, Against Method (London: Verso Editions, 1975).

29. Thomas S. Kuhn, The Structure of Scientific Revolutions, 2nd ed. (Chicago: University of Chicago Press, 1970).

30. As Ashby states:"...the word 'change'...can refer to two very different things. There is the change from state to state...which is the machine's behavior, and which occurs under its own internal drive, and there is the change from transformation to transformation...which is a change of its way of behaving." (Ashby, Cybernetics, p. 43)

31. Watzlawick, et al., Change, p. 10.

32. Ibid., p. 38.

33. Francisco J. Varela, "A Calculus for Self-Reference," International Journal of General Systems 2(1975): 5-24.

34. W. Ross Ashby, "The Set theory of Mechanism and Homeostasis," General Systems IX (1964): 83-97; and "Constraint Analysis of Many-Dimensional Relations," General Systems IX (1964): 99-105; L. A. Zadeh, "Fuzzy Sets," Information and Control 8(1965): 338-353.

35. Burton, p. 328.

36. Kaplan, p. 117.

CHAPTER 4

METHODOLOGICAL APPROACHES

Research methods designed to aid in the formulation of policy can generally be classified into one of two categories. Diesing labels the two extreme categories "formalist methods" and "participant-observer methods."[1] Formalist methods tend to be quantitative and to rely on a mathematical model to guide the collection and analysis of data. The responsibility of the scientist is to maintain as detached and objective a position of observation as possible. The purpose of formalist empirical research is to verify the model; if the data do not verify the model, the model is changed to reflect the discrepancy. These methods have a basis in rationalism and logical empiricism.

Participant-observer methods, on the other hand, assume that it is impossible for a researcher to avoid the influence of his own subjectivity on the organization being researched. The collection of data takes the case study form and the results are used to try to develop qualitative theories which describe the phenomena observed. In management science these methods have had a basis in pragmatism, although some methods in anthropology and psychoanalysis are existential in character. The result of participant-observer research can be a thick, detailed documentation of observations to which little meaning or insight can be imputed. The value of such research is questionable. Successful case studies tend to be those for which the scientist has some preconceived model prior to or during the course of the study, although he may not be able to articulate the substance and structure of the model. When these models are made explicit, they are typically presented in verbal form, and may use schematic block diagrams, multidimensional matrices, etc., to represent the model structure.

Both the formalist and participant-observer approaches to research present certain methodological difficulties when applied to policy issues. Furthermore, attempts to merge the two approaches have not been as successful as one might anticipate.[2] One reason is that the two methods are based on two separate and conflicting philosophies. Formalist methods are used primarily to develop predictive or normative models and are outcome-oriented, while participant-observer methods are process-oriented. Bridging the gap between the two extremes requires a modelling approach with a basis in modern existentialism. The language and mathematics of this approach must reflect the structure of mental modelling processes and social/political processes, and the role of the model should reflect the self-referential nature of the model/modeller relationship.

This chapter critically discusses some of the modelling approaches, both quantitative and qualitative, which have been used to treat ill-structured problems and hence could be applicable to policy formulation. It would be impossible to review all the relevant literature, so most of the approaches discussed have been reported in Management Science. A synthesis is proposed which takes as its point of departure a cybernetic view of the structure of mental models. The problem of self-reference is subsumed in the logic that emerges.

4.1 APPROACH I: FORMAL MODELS

The hallmark of formalism is the mathematical model. Two classification schemes are used here to evaluate various models for their potential contribution in policy formulation. The first scheme is simply descriptive (behavioral) versus normative (decision). The second is based on alternative model structures and quantification methods, the two methodological requirements of all empirically-based mathematical models.

Model structures can be deterministic, probabilistic, or generalized. A deterministic structure is one where, for a given set of inputs, the outputs are always identical. A probabilistic structure is one where, for a given set of inputs, the outputs are always distributed over the identical probability density function. A generalized structure is one where, for a given set of inputs, the outputs fall within some range of values but are not necessarily identically distributed. Furthermore, the range may change over time, indicating change in the structure itself (second-order change). Quantification

56

of the structure, i.e., parameter estimation, can be performed with data from historical or experimental measurements or with data from subjective judgments. A classification scheme based on model structure and parameter estimation is shown in Figure 4.1. The assignment of models to the various categories is not clearcut, and a given model may be developed differently in different circumstances; but for the purpose of critical discussion, most models exhibit more characteristics of one category than another.

Model Structure

Parameter Estimation	Deterministic	Probabilistic	Generalized
Data from Measurements	D_1	P_1	G_1
Data from Judgements	D_2	P_2	G_2

<u>Figure 4.1</u> Model Classification

Parameter estimation through observation and physical measurement of behaviour is very difficult in the generalized case. A generalized structure focuses on variable state combinations that are possible. In sociotechnical systems, the number of possibilities is very large and historical experience or controlled experimentation seldom produces even close to all the possibilities. Furthermore, the set of possibilities is continually changing. With a generalized structure and highly subjective parameter estimation (category G_2), then, validation becomes a process of demonstration and user acceptance (i.e., implementation). This category of model is inherently process-oriented, and there are virtually none that we discuss in this section. The more structured, outcome-oriented models require validation <u>prior</u> to implementation. In order to attain broader structural scope, policy-level management must be willing to sacrifice precision and objectivity in parameter estimation and, hence, in model validation.

57

Four areas of modelling research will be briefly discussed in the context of these classification schemes. First are normative group decisionmaking techniques. The focus here is on combining individual preferences into a group preference or social welfare function, and on resolving the intransitivity that results. Second are multiple criteria decisionmaking techniques, where the concern is with combining multiple and conflicting criteria. These are also normative, but assume that if a group is involved, it can be treated as a single decisionmaker. Third are simulation techniques, which represent the state of the art in response to the deficiencies of descriptive statistical techniques (e.g., multiple regression, factor analysis, canonical-correlation analysis, and discriminant analysis) in modelling large-scale systems with high degrees of interdependence among the variables. Statistical techniques are, of course, extremely useful in developing hypotheses about such systems. Last are the various techniques associated with the Delphi method. These may be either descriptive or normative, but they all involve the use and combination of subjective judgment.

4.1.1 Group Decisionmaking Models

The problem which has received the most research in normative group decisionmaking concerns specifying rules for combining individual preferences. Of particular interest is the simple majority rule. As early as the 18th century, however, it was recognized that majority rule can lead to intransitivity in group preferences, and that the selection of alternatives based on these preferences is not independent of the order in which the alternatives are compared. This phenomenon is known as the paradox of voting,[3] and led to Arrow's formulation of the Impossibility Theorem.[4] Because the axioms upon which the Impossibility Theorem is developed are so important in understanding the problem of the rational approach to individual and group preference, they are reproduced here:[5]

Axiom 1: (Positive Association of Social and Individual Values) If the group ordering indicates alternative A is preferred to alternative B for a certain set of individual rankings, and if (1) the individual's paired comparison between alternatives other than A are not changed, and (2) each individual's paired comparison between A and any other alternative

58

either remains unchanged or is modified in A's favor, then the group ordering must imply A is still preferred to B.

Axiom 2: (Independence of Irrelevant Alternatives) If an alternative is eliminated from consideration and the preference relations for the remaining alternatives remain invariant for all the group members, then the new group ordering for the remaining alternatives should be identical to the original group ordering for these same alternatives.

Axiom 3: (Individual's Sovereignty) For each pair of alternatives A and B, there is some set of individual orderings such that the group prefers A to B.

Axiom 4: (Nondictatorship) There is no individual with the property that whenever he prefers alternative A to B, the group will also prefer A to B regardless of the other individuals' preferences.

Impossibility Theorem: If there are at least two individual members in a group, at least three alternatives, and a set of all possible individual members' orderings, there is no social welfare function defined on the set of individual orderings and satisfying Axioms 1 through 4.

"Arrow's Theorem is considered by many people to say some very negative things about the possibility of truly democratic decisionmaking."[6] The position taken in this book is first that most policy formulation is not simply a matter of voting. Even when voting is the formal mechanism for approving a policy recommendation, as in legislative bodies, the outcome is generally decided before the vote takes place through "behind the scenes" maneuvering and negotiating. However, Riker has suggested that the paradox may actually have occurred in the United States Congress.[7] This is not necessarily an aberration; it may be that acceptance of intransitivity is the most expedient method of resolving a conflict. Also, preferences change over time, a consideration not included in most group decisionmaking models, but one which could give the appearance of intransitivity. The real aberration would be if alternatives are excluded from consideration simply because they would produce intransitivity and give the appearance of violating the axioms of rational thought.

59

Social welfare models have dealt with the
Impossibility Theorem by either challenging the axioms
or revising them by establishing conditions on the
individual and/or group orderings. Arrow[8] and
Black,[9] for example, showed that by requiring
individual preferences to be "single-peaked,"
transitivity in the group ordering was assured.
Sen[10] and Davis, et al.,[11] have identified other
sufficient conditions, and Inada[12] and Sen and
Pattanaik[13] have proposed the necessary and
sufficient conditions for a transitive group preference
function. Bowman and Colantoni formulate the problem
of finding such a function as an integer programming
problem,[14] Blin and Whinston as a quadratic
assignment problem[15] and later as a discriminant
pattern classification problem,[16] and Merchant and
Rao as a set covering problem.[17]

Another approach has been to specify a distance
measure between pairs of individual rankings and to
minimize the sum of the distances. Kemeny and Snell
develop the axioms that a distance function should
satisfy, and propose that either a median or mean
ranking are acceptable forms of consensus.[18]
Implicit in the concept of a distance measure is a
measure of disagreement between individual rankings.
Bogart revises the axioms for the case where partial
orders only are given for each individual, and shows
that a unique distance function also exists under these
conditions.[19] Cook and Seiford use the distance
function on ordinal preferences expressed as priority
vectors.[20] The distance axioms are consistent with
all of Arrow's axioms except Axiom 2, the independence
of irrelevant alternatives. This axiom is the one
which has been relaxed more than any other, and, in
fact, the position of this book is that the
"irrelevant" alternatives, i.e., those excluded from
consideration, are the most relevant to group and
social processes involving the resolution of value
conflicts. We use a variation of a distance measure to
analyze the first questionnaire distributed to the MFS
Finance Corporation (Chapter 10).

Based on the argument that the difficulty with
Axiom 2 can be traced to the inability of an ordinal
ranking to account for strength of preference, utility
functions have been suggested as an alternative method
for representing individual preferences. Sen has shown
that a social welfare function which incorporates as
arguments the preferences of all individuals requires

60

the interpersonal comparison of utilities.[21] Fishburn postulates conditions where a group ordinal preference function can be written as the sum of individual ordinal utility functions.[22] Keeney and Kirkwood develop other forms of group utility function under more generalized conditions.[23] Keeney then shows that rules of aggregation consistent with Arrow's axioms imply that the group utility function must be a linear combination of the individual utilities.[24] The interpersonal comparisons that must be made to specifiy this linear combination can be performed by a "supra Decision Maker" (benevolent-dictator) who wishes to incorporate in some way the preferences of all individuals in the group preference function, or by the group as a whole, indicating the relative power/influence of each individual.

The difficulty with all these formulations of group preferences is the misplaced preoccupation with identifying a unique and complete preference ordering or utility function. For such an ordering or function to be meaningful, certain conditions must be placed on individual behavior: each individual has only one preference ordering, possibly a partial ordering; each individual ordering is transitive; and individual preferences are relatively stable. In reality, individuals devote attention selectively to sets of alternatives and may have contradictory preferences over those sets. Bargaining and compromising between individuals, then, can occur not only across alternatives but also across sets of alternatives. These sets may represent different aspects of an issue or different issues. Hence, independence of issues cannot be assumed in group preference functions, even if an individual is totally indifferent on the issue. Further complicating the situation is that bargaining and compromising occur not only between individuals but between groups of individuals, and that these groups can carry greater power/influence than the sum of that of the individuals who constitute the group. All these factors lead to a dynamic view of group values, rendering the concept of a group preference function of questionable relevance. Of greater relevance is the set of alternatives excluded from consideration, for these define the domains within which negotiating takes place, and the boundaries where adjustment will be required if reasonable resolution is not possible within present domains.

Normative group decisionmaking models fall into category D_2. Consideration of uncertainty with individual subjective probabilities (category P_2) presents problems of aggregation. As a result, expected utilities are usually employed in the formulation.[25]

4.1.2 Multiple Criteria Decisionmaking Models

Closely related to group decisionmaking models are multiple criteria decisionmaking (MCDM) models. MacCrimmon has provided two classification schemes for MCDM models. The first scheme groups the models on the basis of whether the criteria or attributes are reduced to a single dimension or treated in intermediate or full dimensionality.[26] In the single dimensionality category are maximax, maximin, lexicographic, additive weighting, effectiveness index, and utility theory approaches. These approaches assume that alternatives are comparable on a common scale and that a complete accounting of feasible alternatives is available. In the intermediate dimensionality category are tradeoff analysis and non-metric scaling. In the full dimensionality category are dominance and conjunctive procedures.

The other classification scheme groups the models on the basis of their distinguishing structural characteristic: weighting, sequential elimination, mathematical programming, and spatial proximity methods.[27] It is interesting to note that the modelling techniques which treat a problem in its full dimensionality, dominance and conjunctive procedures, are both sequential elimination methods. In addition to these two modelling techniques, interactive goal programming and compromise programming are particularly relevant to the policy formulation process. Weighting techniques, most prominently multiattribute utility theory, have already been discussed in the group context. Starr and Zeleny[28] and Zeleny[29] discuss the difficulties and shortcomings of this approach in greater depth. Spatial proximity methods are more specialized than the others, and include indifference maps, multidimensional scaling, and graphical overlays. Multidimensional scaling with ideal points has similarities with compromise programming, but will be discussed in a slightly different context as a Delphi technique.

Dominance methods involve identifying those alternatives which are superior to others on all criteria and attributes. The dominated alternatives can then be eliminated from further consideration. The nondominated alternatives are referred to as the "efficient frontier" or "Pareto optimal set." In the group decisionmaking context, Pareto optimality refers to an alternative for which it would not be possible to improve the satisfaction of some without diminishing the satisfaction of others.[30] The difficulty with dominance methods is that in complex policy issues they are not likely to succeed in eliminating many alternatives. But dominance does provide the foundations for an alternative to multiattribute utility theory, namely compromise programming.

Conjunctive procedures and goal programming represent two attempts to incorporate consideration for Simon's insights into satisficing behavior. In a conjunctive decision model, a set of standards, including aspiration levels, must be satisfied for an alternative to be acceptable. The first alternative to meet the standards is selected and the search procedure terminates. The procedure is heuristic, and is based on research into information processing in human problem solving activities. It has been highly successful in predicting the decisions of managers in investment portfolio selection,[31] personnel selection,[32] and pricing,[33] and has been applied to consumer behavior.[34] If the constraint-theoretic framework proposed in Part II were developed for technical-level problem solving, it would take on many of the characteristics of the conjunctive model. The difficulty at the policy level is that there may be no alternatives which satisfy all the standards of all the policy actors. Furthermore, each actor may not be considering the same set of alternatives. In fact, it is precisely this complexity that makes policy "domains" a useful concept distinct from the single alternatives considered in a decision. Furthermore, one role of policymaking is to identify creative alternatives and sets of alternatives (i.e., policy domains).

Goal programming, originally proposed by Charnes and Cooper[35] and popularized by Lee,[36] treats goals, i.e., levels of aspiration, as constraints. Goal programming is, however, an optimization model, requiring that weights or priorities be assigned to the deviations from each goal that are to be minimized.

While the conjunctive decision model could be adapted to a generalized structure (categories G_1 and G_2) by permitting continual changes in the heuristic and in the order that alternatives are considered, goal programming is a category D_1 or D_2 model. Some interesting work has been done with an interactive version of goal programming which allows a decisionmaker to adjust goals to a specific situation.[37] That such a model could be used in a policy formualtion context, however, is questionable; for as Keen points out:

> ...objectives must be predefined and the choice rule expressed. It relieves the decision maker of the computational burdens of defining cost and utility but the speci- fication of priorities and weights remains complex and risky...It does not seem behaviorally-grounded...Goal programming accepts the rational axioms of the need for prior objectives and of optimality as a characteristic of the solution.[38]

The user of the model is merely the provider of inputs, inputs which are not necessarily consistent with his mental model.

A recent, but as yet relatively unvalidated, attempt to circumvent the difficulties of MCDM models is the development of compromise programming by Zeleny.[39] This approach assumes explicitly that ends (objectives, preferences, goals, etc.) are not independent of means (alternatives), and in so doing that the excluded set of alternatives do influence individual preferences. An ideal point is hypothesized which is invariably outside the feasible set. A compromise set of alternatives is then identified by taking the minimum of all L_p distance metrics from the ideal point to the set of nondominated alternatives. Hence, the compromise set is a subset of the Pareto optimal set. Zeleny defines the ideal point as the intersection of the extensions of the extreme value of each attribute of potential alternatives in the direction of increasing preference (see Figure 4.2). That is, the ideal represents the maximum that one could acquire of each attribute if the attributes were unrelated or if one attribute were pursued at the expense of all others. The ideal point is not stationary, and in fact shifts simply by eliminating alternatives from consideration; as a result,

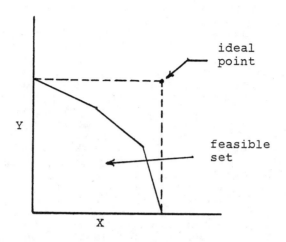

Figure 4.2   Ideal Point

preferences are dependent on the "irrelevant"
alternatives. Zeleny has developed the model for use
in assessing consumer preferences toward alternative
product designs.[40]

Compromise programming has many appealing
characteristics. It does not assume comparability of
alternatives on a single scale; it is oriented to
aiding the decision process, not making a decision; and
it is dynamic. It is a G_1 model to the extent that as
the ideal point shifts, the structure of preferences
changes and, used in an interactive mode, approaches
the G_2 category model. Two difficulties with
compromise programming arise in the context of
policy-level modelling. First, it is explicitly
oriented to a single decisionmaker.[41] Yu, however,
has used the concepts of domination structures,
"utopia" point, and compromise solution to model a
class of group decision problems. The resolution of
conflict is accomplished by minimizing group regret,
which is assumed to vary with the L_p class of distance
functions.[42] But again, the problem is simply to
select one of a set of mutually exclusive alternatives.
In policymaking, the concern is to identify the
excluded set of alternatives or outcomes, i.e., to
establish the rules within which decisionmaking is to

65

take place.

The second difficulty with compromise programming is in the apparent arbitrariness of the ideal point. Implicit are some assumptions about the nature of human values, not only that they are dependent on perceptions of available alternatives (probably a reasonable assumption), but also that they are unidimensional and conditionally independent. These assumptions may be reasonable in situations where the attributes are clearly identified and their interrelationships well structured, but in policy issues these conditions do not often obtain. Even though Yu uses utility functions to find his "utopia" point, these utility functions must be accurate and complete for the compromise solutions to be meaningful. Yu further states that, "threat, collusion, and bargaining then need to be considered. We shall not stop to do so."[43] The point is that while compromise programming represents a substantial contribution to modelling technology, there is further research needed to verify the ideal point assumptions, and to extend the framework to the policy formulation context.

4.1.3 Simulation Models

Simulations are perhaps the most widely used type of model as aids to policy formulation. Policymakers and corporate planners are apparently more comfortable with models that attempt an "objective" and detached description of the system under consideration. Three simulation models, in particular, are widely used: forecasting(D_1), Monte Carlo methods (P_1), and system dynamics (D_1 or D_2). Naylor and Schauland found that "the number of firms using or developing corporate simulation models has increased from less than 100 in 1969 to over 2000 in 1975."[44] Furthermore, "the vast majority (94%) of these models are what management scientists call deterministic models...Most (76%) of the corporate planning models are what if models, i.e., models which simulate the effects of alternative managerial policies and assumptions about the firm's external environment."[45] The average number of equations in the models was 545, with a range from twenty to several thousand. In addition to the implicit philosophical assumptions of the simulation approach, there are also practical difficulties. A large simulation is expensive and very time consuming to build. A large quantity of data is generally required, and model validation is not an inconsequential task.[46] The simulation models used by policy-level management are designed to be predictive, and therefore require as accurate and complete a quantitative representation of the relevant variables and their relationships as possible. Even in a totally technological system, however, the overwhelming number of variables and their interrelationships can make this a difficult task. In more than a few instances, the important variables and relationships have changed by the time the model is eventually operational.

System dynamics (SD), as developed by Forrester, is one of the fastest growing and most popular simulation techniques.[47] The first SD models were limited to a few variables, although efforts are currently underway to build an SD model of the National economy which incorporates thousands of variables. The mathematical structure of SD takes the form of sets of differential or difference equations. The modelling approach can be criticized not only for the same practicality reasons given above, but also for the limits on its structure:

> Attempts at complete quantification run into some special problems in the area of behavioral interactions..."soft facts" may be equally influential: the pressures on him [the manager] from the production manager on the one side and the sales manager on the other, his perception of the kind of performance (conservative or aggressive) desired by his immediate superior, the amount of personal exposure to criticism which will result from a particular decision. It is not clear that converting these facts into quantitative single independent variable table functions will enhance understanding of the complex power and social variables which influence decision making, nor that this will lead to desirable recommendations for systems redesign.[48]

The amount of feedback, and feedback of feedback, etc., is so intense in social systems that it is almost inconceivable that it can be captured in a simple control system model like SD.

The construction and validation of an SD model (or for that matter any simulation model) generally relies on historical performance data. In policy issues, the situation is generally unique, i.e., it has never occurred in precisely the same form before, rendering historical experience of less usefulness than it would be in a replication of past successes and failures. In the policy support system presented in Chapter 9, we use a flow graph structure similar to the SD graphical representation. The emphasis, however, is on the subjective assessment of asset and flow capacity constraints in the system, not on rates of flow and stocks at a hypothetical point in time. Hanssmann[49] has made a strong argument against dynamic simulation models in strategy formulation, arguing for a more static approach similar to that of Gupta and Rosenhead.[50]

4.1.4 Delphi Techniques

The Delphi method[51] was for a long time very popular in R&D planning and forecasting, and is still used in modified form in technology impact assessment studies. Designed to combine the opinions of "experts" and hopefully to converge toward a consensus through feedback of results and iteration of the procedure, Delphi has been criticized by many. While not unlike the problem of group decisionmaking, Delphi has been concerned with reaching a consensus on cause and effect relationships and probabilities of events, rather than just preferences. Some systematic procedure is employed to obtain the group output. Some of the more common Delphi procedures include cross impact analysis,[52] digraph analysis,[53] hierarchical analysis,[54] Bayesian procedures,[55] and various scaling techniques, of which multidimensional scaling[56] is one of the more sophisticated. An impact type of approach has been used in selecting R&D projects.[57] Sackman has been the chief critic of Delphi techniques, arguing that the future is too important to be left to "fortune tellers."[58] The counterargument is that the Delphi technique is not intended to produce "facts," but rather to search for judgment and wisdom.

Linstone has listed some qualitative pitfalls to avoid in implementing a Delphi;[59] but the greatest criticisms in the constraint-theoretic context are first, the preoccupation with cause and effect and predicting the "future," and second, the almost universal use of pairwise comparisons to make assessments. Current Delphi techniques, as

68

unstructured as they are, are still D_2 and P_2 category models. The statistical forms of analysis generally performed on the solicited data consider primarily binary relationships. We argue that in complex policy issues it is the higher order relationships which are often of particular significance and that new methods of mathematical analysis are needed to adequately treat these.

Turoff has proposed the "policy Delphi" with a role quite different from that of the predictive Delphi.

> The Policy Delphi...seeks to generate the strongest possible opposing views on the potential resolutions of a major policy issue...a policy issue is one for which there are no experts, only informed advocates and referees...The Policy Delphi rests on the premise that the decisionmaker is not interested in having a group generate his decision; but rather, have an informed group present all the options and supporting evidence for his consideration. The Policy Delphi is therefore a tool for the analysis of policy issues and not a mechanism for making a decision. Generating a consensus is not the prime objective, and the structure of the communication process as well as the choice of the respondent group may be such as to make consensus on a particular resolution very unlikely.[60]

Turoff still suggests linguistic scales as the mechanism for soliciting responses, however. The policy support system proposed in Part III, is based on the same logic expounded by Turoff, but the method of solicitation and analysis of responses is new. A variation of the digraph format is also incorporated, namely the bipartite graph. But the focus is not on how decisions will impact on system stocks and flows, but rather how resource and policy constraints will effect the capacity (potentiality) of the system. A modified form of hierarchical analysis is also incorporated, but again treating values and perceptions as systems of constraint, rather than as weights or utilities arrived at by pairwise comparisons.

4.2 APPROACH II: CASE STUDIES

The title of this section may be misnamed, for there is very little policy research reported in the management science literature which is truly in the spirit of the participant-observer approach, and its principal method, the case study.[61] The discussion here will be limited to approaches directed at altering or augmenting policy formulation through process-oriented methodology. The models utilized in these approaches lean very heavily on qualitative description, as opposed to the quantitative focus of formalism. However, some formal models are discussed in the context of topics not included in the previous section. Relevant research includes studies in model and management information system (MIS) implementation, organization design, strategic planning systems, and organizational development (OD) and gaming.

4.2.1 Implementation Studies

The implementation literature has dealt with the interpersonal relationship between modeller and user,[62] cognitive style differences and how to adjust to them,[63] and the role of intuition and the subconscious in managerial problem solving.[64] Since the implementation of a management-oriented model in an organization is itself a policy issue with social ramifications, it is to be expected that the themes of this literature would be individual style and interpersonal relationships.

The literature on the design and implementation of management information systems (MIS), once thought to be the answer to the manager's policymaking problems, follows similar lines. An initial critique of the MIS approach came from Ackoff, who particularly emphasized the problem of information overload,[65] and from Argyris, who claimed that a new MIS can result in a reduction of space of free movement, psychological failure and double bind, decreasing feelings of essentiality, and reduction of intra- and inter-group politics.[66] Charnes, et al.,[67] and Johnson and Ward[68] proposed some MIS guidelines to assist in urban policymaking and facilitate participation in the policy process; and Mason and Mitroff established a framework for research on MIS which suggested a variety of MIS formats to meet the needs of different psychological types, problem types, methods of generating evidence, and modes of presentation.[69]

Since then, many articles have appeared that either advocate or delineate certain aspects of information systems which claim to lead to success or failure in implementation.[70] Dickson, et al., in a series of experiments identify what appear to be key factors in an MIS, two of which are its availability as an interactive tool and the display of output information.[71] The policy support system presented in Part III diverges from the traditional MIS format to the extent that it is the communications system which is important, and that any computer-based portion of such a system must be highly flexible with respect to both hardware and software.

4.2.2 Organization Design Studies

The design of an MIS has unmistakeable implications for organizational design. Most of the management science literature on organization design has centered on the centralization/decentralization issue. Beged-Dov talks of the tradeoff between cost of coordination and "control" (low in centralized organizations) and the cost of information (low in decentralized organizations).[72] Decentralization is one area where mathematical models have been used for descriptive purposes. Building on Whinston's internal pricing framework,[73] Ruefli uses a goal programming formulation, which requires no global organization objective function, as a tool for control in decentralized organizations.[74] Sweeney, et al., develop an alternative model.[75] Kochen and Deutsch model the decentralization of facilities for a system supplying services to customers.[76] The centralization issue, while somewhat peripheral to the subject of this dissertation, is a crucial one. The policy support system proposed in Part III does not involve any change in the formal organization structure, but a change in patterns of communication will inevitably alter the informal organization, in the spirit of Swinth, away from authoritarian and incrementalist approaches.[77] It is not clear whether the centralization/decentralization dichotomy is meaningful; perhaps decentralization in one aspect of an organization, for example, is inevitably accompanied by centralization elsewhere. What is clear, however, is that the balance between the two can take on many configurations. Those configurations can have an impact on the balance of power in an organization,[78] and cannot be divorced from the values of the individuals involved.[79] Furthermore, computerized

71

MIS's which at one time implied greater centralization of information, are now being introduced to more flexible, dispersed, and distributed technologies.[80]

4.2.3 Strategic Planning Studies

The one form of policy that receives more attention than any other is the strategic plan. The literature on strategic planning has been both descriptive and normative and is much too diverse to give it fair coverage here. In 1966, Starr identified three types of planning model: the fully-constrained (e.g., PERT), the partially-constrained (e.g., simulation, heuristics), and the threshold-constrained (no adequate models exist to deal with the high levels of discontinuity and vulnerability to ruin that this category represents).[81] It has been the inadequacy of forecasting models that has stimulated interest in other forms of planning models. While Starr's definition of policy is different than the one we use, his discussion of the need for planning models is otherwise relevant. Since then, a diverse literature has evolved on planning systems, summarized to some extent in Ansoff[82] with an extensive bibliography appearing in Steiner and Minor.[83]

Most of this literature deals with the process of matching organizational strengths and weaknesses with environmental threats and opportunities. The models underlying the various approaches, both descriptive and normative, are invariably expressed in terms of block diagrams or matrices, often accompanied by a list of steps (i.e., a process) to follow in formulating a "good" plan. The one characteristic that most of these planning systems have in common is the centrality of goals and/or objectives, and their assumed independence from means (courses of action) and environmental constraints.[84] It is our opinion that this literature is jargon-laden, and hence very difficult to generalize; different writers tend to use the same words with different meanings.[85]

Because they capture the essence of policymaking better than the majority of mainstream planning systems, two management science approaches deserve special mention: dialectical planning and situational normativism. Mason introduced the concept of dialectical planning as an alternative to the "expert approach," represented by the planning models in the above paragraphs and econometric forecasting models,

72

and the "devil's advocate approach," represented by the Harold Geneen (ITT) attitude that a "good" plan will survive the toughest of criticism. The latter approach reflects the Harvard Business School program, and Mason points out the high turnover rate among the upper echelons of management in ITT.[86] The dialectical approach pits a proposed plan against an equally plausible counterplan through a structured debate aimed at illuminating the underlying assumptions (frames of reference) of each alternative. Mitroff mathematically formalizes the dialectical planning system,[87] and Mitroff and Betz present it as a "meta-theory" of decisionmaking.[88] More recently, Mitroff, et al., have proposed a radically different form of information system to accommodate the dialectical approach, the Management Myth-Information System. In such a system, a set of data is not information unless it is associated with a particular "story" which has meaning to an individual. The story represents the individual's set of assumptions and perspectives, and hence frame of reference.[89] This is definitely in line with the information needs of policy-level management.

Situational normativism is a term which has been applied by Shakun to the combination of both analytic and heuristic reasoning in complex problem solving.[90] The proposed model structure is very simple, and has many similarities with the constraint theory structure:

$$g_i(x_1, x_2, \ldots, x_n) \geq b_i \text{ for } i=1,2,\ldots,m \qquad (4-1)$$

where x_1, x_2, ..., x_n are the strategy variables; g_1, g_2, ..., g_m are the set of constraint relations; and b_1, b_2, ..., b_m are the constraint levels. The constraints may be aspiration levels, technological and resource constraints, or cognitive style and political constraints. With respect to policymaking, values and norms play a central role, and influence the design of the g_i.

> Hence, at the policy level we must design the system's "culture" or capability with respect to its goals (and underlying values), structure, technology, information processing, and the perceptions, attitudes, and skills of its people. Thus, policies are largely concerned with what we ought to do and with design; strategies with what we can do and with analysis; tactics with what will happen if we

73

do it and with operation.[91]

The analytic power of this simple formulation of policymaking, however, has not yet been realized either in the language or mathematics of modelling.

Evaluating the effectiveness of various planning systems has been attempted, but such studies invariably encounter problems in identifying appropriate performance measures. Nutt compared the systems approach (i.e., using a professional planning group tasked with identifying a global hierarchy of objectives), the behavioral approach (i.e., using a mixed group focusing primarily on client needs), and the heuristic approach (i.e., using an informal group in an unstructured, interactive planning mode). The results showed that each approach had its deficiencies and merits.[92] Cosier, et al., evaluated the dialectical planning process and produced inconclusive results.[93] As mentioned in the previous section of this chapter, it is doubtful that any validation or verification of such planning systems, or of the category G_2 model in general, is possible in any rigorous sense.

4.2.4 Organizational Development and Gaming

The final topic of this section is organizational development (OD) and the role of the policy-level model in the OD process. Most of the OD literature is in the form of guidelines which often involve intensive training sessions, e.g., T-groups and sensitivity training.[94] Of particular relevance is the work by Nadler,[95] for this was essentially the approach taken with the MFS Finance Company. Constraint theory provides a different structure for collecting and processing the data. As previously mentioned, however, the potential of the proposed modelling approach lies in structured group processes, not in questionnaires. Gaming provides one such format, although most business games are directed at financial and marketing policies in relatively stable environments.[96] Gaming structures of the G_2 category need to be developed for sociotechnical policy issues in general.

Because gaming techniques deal directly with conflict and have explicitly incorporated coalition formation topics, they can provide valuable insights.[97] The current structure of mathematical game theory, however, makes it impractical for other

74

than pedagogic or controlled experiment purposes. Emshoff reports research using a generalized game theoretic framework, metagame theory, in a controlled experiment format. The results provided rich insights into the role of individual perception and policy formation in conflict situations. The use of a rational theory of behavior, however, led to problems in explaining the <u>dynamics</u> of conflict, forcing a reformulation of the theory in terms of aspiration levels.[98] We believe that a constraint-theoretic formulation of game theory could provide a basis for gaming exercises in government and corporate policy formulation.[99] These would be examples of G_2 models.

4.3 SYNTHESIS

4.3.1 Summary of Deficiencies and Future Directions

It is evident that the literature relevant to the topic of policy-level modelling is voluminous. The following is an attempt to summarize:

1. Formal Models

1.1 The mathematical models of the formalist approach exhibit one of the following limitations:

--based on the rational decisionmaking framework (group decisionmaking and multi-attribute utility theory);

--oriented to a single decisionmaker (multi-criteria decisionmaking);

--assumes lineal cause-effect mathematical structure (simulation); and/or

--treats binary relations only (scaling methods used in Delphi techniques).

1.2 The heuristic, conjunctive modelling approach represents the constraint-theoretic approach when applied by a single individual to a technical problem.

1.3 The compromise programming approach represents a necessary shift <u>away</u> from the mean-ends dichotomy and from the assumption of independence of irrelevant alternatives.

1.4 The policy Delphi represents the proper role of the policy-level model, but the modelling mathematics and language need to be developed.

2. Process-Oriented Models

2.1 The qualitative models of the process-oriented (quasi-participant-observer) method represent a response to the deficiencies of the formal, mathematical modelling approach; but the implicit (or explicit) models underlying most of these methods are invariably based on the rational decisionmaking framework. Most planning systems are, by definition, models of rational choice, and the centralization/decentralization dichotomy is similarly rooted.

2.2 Qualitative model descriptions use words which are often ambiguous and confusing, and while they may serve the immediate needs of an OD or planning consultant, they offer little in the way of scientific generalization.

2.3 Two themes which emerge in the research on model implementation are cognitive constraints (mental models) and interpersonal relationships, both key concepts for policy-level modelling.

2.4 Dialectical planning, in stressing frames of reference and multiple perspectives, is a significant contribution. But the formalization of the approach has had a basis in the rational choice model.

2.5 Situational normativism captures, qualitatively, the vitality of the constraint-theoretic modelling approach, but the analytical power of the approach has yet to be developed.

2.6 Gaming or pseudo-gaming represents one means for implementing structured interaction between policy actors, but new modelling structures need to be demonstrated before such a technology can become viable.

Despite the polemics with respect to the rational decisionmaking paradigm, it remains the dominant force in modelling thought in management science. Perhaps the aura of intellectuality that surrounds the concept

76

of optimality is partially responsible; but optimization is only meaningful when explicitly stated goals or objectives are available. As Bauer points out:

> ...there is every evidence that in complex policy situations, so called decision makers do not strive to optimize some value nor is the notion of optimization a useful way of ordering and analyzing their behavior regardless of their intentions.[100]

Murray supports this empirically with research on a major electric utility: "...conventional concepts which portray corporate strategy formulation as a rational, comprehensive decisionmaking activity are not descriptively accurate and perhaps not even as prescriptively useful as they might be."[101]

Keen responds by proposing a hybrid methodology that shifts the focus of the model from choice to intelligence and the design of alternatives. The role of the modeller similarly shifts to one of providing a supportive and interactive methodology.[102] In their definitive work on decision support systems, however, Keen and Scott Morton back off from the "unstructured" decision task, leaving it to the realm of "human intuition."[103] Policy issues are never completely unstructured, however, for if so they would be unrecognizable. It is exactly this "unstructured" region that this book addresses. That human intuition can be supported with some form of modelling was shown by Botkin, but the success of such a modelling technology depends significantly on the personalities and cognitive styles of its users.[104]

4.3.2 Mental Models and Self-Reference

We argue that the link between the formalist and process-oriented approaches lies in formalizing and integrating the mental models of policy actors. Emshoff has called this an "Experience-Generalized orientation," and details the need for new techniques which can test the assumptions and relationships inherent in "mental models." The policymakers themselves will formulate the models; the role of the modeller will be to formalize them for ease in communication and constructive interaction.[105] Linstone and Turoff further point out that this methodological shift must eventually be accompanied by

77

a sociological or cultural shift.[106] This shift has perhaps best been described by Maruyama.[107] It involves a reconceptualization of perceptive, cognitive, and affective processes, of social relationships, and hence of logic and knowledge itself.

That mental models must exist has been shown by Conant and Ashby:

> ...Model-making has hitherto largely been suggested (for regulating complex dynamic systems) as a possibility: the theorem shows that, in a very wide class (specified in the proof of the theorem), success in regulation implies that a sufficiently similar model must have been built, whether it was done explicitly, or simply developed as the regulator improved...There can no longer be question about whether the brain models its environment: it must.[108]

To formalize the structure of the mental model does not imply that a complete, detailed, and precise representation is necessary.

Our view of cognition is that it is a process of representing the possible states that a perceived system can adopt. The variables specifying these states form a "cognitive domain." This view is consistent with those of Simon, who interrelates cognition with motivation and emotion,[109] and of Garner, whose emphasis is on the recognition of structure and uncertainty.[110]

As Steinbruner does, Maturana extends the concept of cognitive domain to social systems:

> Cultural differences do not represent
> different modes of treating the same objec-
> tive reality, but legitimately different cog-
> nitive domains. Culturally different men
> live in different cognitive realities that
> are recursively specified through their
> living in them.[111]

This statement has implications not only for the nature of mental models, but for the role of the modeller, who has his own mental model of the situation. In arguing for a participant-observer approach to policy analysis, Archibald proposes ignoring the complexity of the world itself, concentrating on problems of perception, values, and skills within the policy agency. In this way, the cognitive boundaries on the client-system are identified, and if need be, expanded.[112] The self-reflective, self-referencing role of the modeller is essential.

The development of concepts of time in mental models, and hence of anticipatory action, are not explicitly included in the framework of Part II. The proposed logic and mathematics accommodates dynamic concepts, we argue, but substantial research is yet needed. The affective aspects of mental processes assume a prominent role in the dynamics of behavior. Simon, for example, argues that emotions serve as interrupters to sequences of cognitive or motor operations.[113] Miller, Gallanter, and Pribram, building on Simon's work in heuristic problem solving, hypothesize a metaprocess for controlling sequences of operations.[114] At the present state of knowledge of mental concepts of time, the existentialist response is to project perceptions of past and future behavior to the present; to attempt to understand the projected relationships and the nature of change; and to formulate policy that allows sufficient flexibility in behavior to respond to unanticipated change.

Two relevant topics in the management science literature have been intentionally omitted from the discussion of this chapter: fuzzy set theory and robustness. Fuzzy set theory has an enormous literature outside management science/operations research, but the literature within the field has not generally been empirically-based. It has made recent and significant contributions, however, to group decisionmaking and multiple criteria decisionmaking, and Delphi advocates anticipate its use there. Simulation models using subjective judgments for parameter estimation (category G_2) may, in the future, also utilize fuzzy set concepts. Robustness provides an alternative to optimality in policymaking, but as yet has been applied only to decision problems where the alternatives are easily enumerable. Fuzzy sets and robustness are central concepts in the theoretical framework of Part II, and are generalized to accomodate the more complex aspects of mental models, and the overwhelming number of interrelated sets of alternative possibilities in a typical issue.

1. Diesing also discusses other methods, e.g., experimentation and statistical surveys, many of which are overlapping. The distinction between formal methods and participant-observer methods provides a sharp dichotomy useful for discussing extremes in management research. Paul Diesing, Patterns of Discovery in the Social Sciences (Chicago: Aldine-Atherton, 1971).

2. Two notable exceptions deserve mention here. Friend and Jessop explicitly consider organizational and political processes, as well as individual perceptions and values, in developing a management technology (both quantitative and qualitative) for a city government in England. J. K. Friend and W. N. Jessop, Local Government and Strategic Choice, 2nd ed. (Oxford: Pergamon Press, 1977). Keen and Scott Morton build a framework based on the work of Herbert Simon and Robert Anthony, and also consider organizational and political processes and human problem solving processes in their development of a computer-based technology for policy-level management. Peter G. W. Keen and Michael S. Scott Morton, Decision Support Systems: An Organizational Perspective (Reading, Mass.: Addison-Wesley, 1978).

3. That the paradox of voting is not trivial has been shown by a number of authors. Furthermore, as the size of the group and the number of alternatives increases, the probability of intransitivities increases. Richard G. Niemi and Herbert F. Weisberg, "A Mathematical Solution for the Probability of the Paradox of Voting." Behavioral Science 13(1968): 317-323.

4. Kenneth J. Arrow, Social Choice and Individual Values, 2nd ed. (New York: John Wiley & Sons, 1963).

5. Quoted from Ralph L. Keeney and Howard Raiffa, Decisions with Multiple Objectives (New York: John Wiley & Sons, 1976), pp. 523-524.

6. Fred S. Roberts, Discrete Mathematical Models (Englewood Cliffs, N.J.: Prentice-Hall, 1976), p. 437.

7. W. H. Riker, "Arrow's Theorem and Some Examples of the Paradox of Voting," Arnold Foundation Monograph (Dallas, Texas: Southern Methodist University Press,

1965).

8. Arrow, Social Choice.

9. Duncan Black, The Theory of Committees and Elections (London: Cambridge University Press, 1958).

10. A. K. Sen, "A Possibility Theorem on Majority Decisions," Econometrica 34(1966): 491-499.

11. O. A. Davis, M. H. Degroot, and M. J. Hinich, "Social Preference Orderings and Majority Rule," Econometrica 40(1972): 147-157.

12. K. Inada, "On the Simple Majority Decision Rule," Econometrica 37(1969): 490-506.

13. Amartya Sen and Prasanta K. Pattanaik, "Necessary and Sufficient Conditions for Rational Choice Under Majority Decision," Journal of Economic Theory 1(1969): 178-202.

14. V. J. Bowman and C. S. Colantoni, "Majority Rule Under Transitivity Constraints," Management Science 19(May 1973): 1029-1041.

15. J. M. Blin and A. B. Whinston, "A Note on Majority Rule Under Transitivity Constraints," Management Science 20(July 1974): 1439-1440.

16. J. M. Blin and Andrew B. Whinston, "Discriminant Functions and Majority Voting," Management Science 21(January 1975): 557-566.

17. Deepak K. Merchant and M. R. Rao, "Majority Decisions and Transitivity: Some Special Cases," Management Science 23(October 1976): 125-130.

18. J. G. Kemeny and J. L. Snell, Mathematical Models in the Social Sciences (New York: Blaisdell Publishing Co., 1962), pp. 9-23.

19. Kenneth P. Bogart, "Preference Structures I: Distances Between Transitive Preference Relations," Journal of Mathematical Sociology 3(1973): 49-67; and "Preference Structures II: Distances Between Asymmetric Relations," SIAM Journal of Applied Mathematics 29(1975): 254-262.

20. Wade D. Cook and Lawrence M. Seiford,

"Priority Ranking and Consensus Formation," Management Science 24(December 1978): 1721-1732.

21. Amartya Sen, Collective Choice and Social Welfare (San Francisco: Holden-Day, 1970).

22. Peter C. Fishburn, "Preferences, Summation, and Social Welfare Functions," Management Science 16(1969): 179-186.

23. Ralph L. Keeney and Craig W. Kirkwood, "Group Decision Making Using Cardinal Social Welfare Functions," Management Science 22(December 1975): 430-437.

24. Ralph L. Keeny, "A Group Preference Axiomatization with Cardinal Utility," Management Science 23(October 1976): 140-145.

25. Ibid.

26. K. R. MacCrimmon, Decisionmaking Among Multiple-Attribute Alternatives: A Survey and Consolidated Approach RM-4823-ARPA (Santa Monica, Calif.: The RAND Corporation, 1968).

27. Kenneth R. MacCrimmon, "An Overview of Multiple Objective Decision Making," in Multiple Criteria Decision Making, ed. J. L. Cochrane and M. Zeleny (Columbia, S.C.: University of South Carolina Press, 1973), pp. 18-44.

28. Martin K. Starr and Milan Zeleny, "MCDM--State and Future of the Arts," in Multiple Criteria Decision Making, ed. Starr and Zeleny (Amsterdam: North-Holland Publishing Company, 1977), pp. 20-21.

29. Milan Zeleny, "The Attribute-Dynamic Attitude Model (ADAM)," Management Science 23(September 1976): 13-16.

30. Keeney and Raiffa, Decisions, p. 534.

31. Geoffrey P. E. Clarkson, Portfolio Selection -- A Simulation of Trust Investment (Englewood Cliffs, N.J.: Prentice-Hall, 1962).

32. Robert D. Smith and Paul S. Greenlaw, "Simulation of a Psychological Decision Process in Personnel Selection," Management Science 13(April

1967): 409-419.

33. John A. Howard and William M. Morgenroth, "Information Processing Model of Executive Decision," Management Science 14(March 1968): 416-428.

34. James R. Bettman, "A Graph Theory Approach to Comparing Consumer Information Processing Models," Management Science 18(December 1971, Part II): 114-128.

35. A. W. Charnes and W. W. Cooper, Management Models and Industrial Applications of Linear Programming (New York: John Wiley & Sons, 1961).

36. Sang M. Lee, Goal Programming for Decision Analysis (Philadelphia: Auerbach Publishers, 1972).

37. J. S. Dyer, "Interactive Goal Programming," Management Science 19(September 1972): 62-70.

38. Peter G. W. Keen, "The Evolving Concept of Optimality," in Starr and Zeleny, p. 48.

39. Milan Zeleny, "Compromise Programming," in Cochrane and Zeleny, pp. 262-301. See also, Milan Zeleny, Multiple Criteria Decision Making (New York: McGraw-Hill, 1982).

40. Milan Zeleny, "(ADAM)."

41. As Zeleny puts its, "it is always individuals who make decisions." Milan Zeleny, "Adaptive Displacement of Preferences in Decision Making," in Starr and Zeleny, p. 148.

42. P. L. Yu, "A Class of Solutions for Group Decision Problems," Management Science 19(April 1973): 936-946.

43. Ibid., p. 939.

44. Thomas H. Naylor and Horst Schauland, "A Survey of Users of Corporate Planning Models," Management Science 22(May 1976): 936.

45. Ibid., p. 932.

46. For comments on the validation and verification of simulation models see Richard L. Van

Horn, "Validation of Simulation Results," Management Science 17(January 1971): 247-258; and Thomas H. Naylor and J. M. Finger, "Verification of Computer Simulation Models," Management Science 14(October 1967): B92-B101.

47. Jay W. Forrester, Industrial Dynamics (Cambridge, Mass.: The M.I.T. Press, 1961).

48. H. Igor Ansoff and Dennis P. Slevin, "An Appreciation of Industrial Dynamics," Management Science 14(March 1968): 391.

49. Fred Hanssmann, "The Case for Static Models in Strategic Planning," in Studies in Operations Management, ed. Arnoldo C. Hax (Amsterdam: North-Holland Publishing Company, 1978), pp. 117-136.

50. Shiv K. Gupta and Jonathan Rosenhead, "Robustness in Sequential Investment Decisions," Management Science 15(October 1978): B18-B29.

51. N. Dalkey and O. Helmer, "An Experimental Application of the Delphi Method to the Use of Experts," Management Science 9(February 1964): 458-466.

52. Norman C. Dalkey, "An Elementary Cross-Impact Model," in The Delphi Method: Techniques and Applications, ed. Harold A. Linstone and Murray Turoff, with a Foreword by Olaf Helmer (Reading, Mass.: Addison-Wesley, 1975), pp. 327-337.

53. Fred S. Roberts, Signed Digraphs and the Growing Demand for Energy, R-756-NSF (Santa Monica, Calif.: The RAND Corporation, May 1971).

54. Thomas L. Saaty, "A Scaling Method for Priorities in Hierarchical Structures," Journal of Mathematical Psychology 15(1977): 234-281.

55. Norman C. Dalkey, "Toward a Theory of Group Estimation," in Linstone and Turoff, pp. 236-261; and Michael Bacharach, "Group Decisions in the Face of Differences of Opinion," Management Science 22(October 1975): 182-191.

56. J. Douglas Carroll and Myron Wish, "Multidimensional Scaling: Models, Methods, and Relations to Delphi," in Linstone and Turoff, pp.

402-431; and Paul E. Green and Frank J. Carmone, Multidimensional Scaling and Related Techniques in Marketing Analysis (Boston: Allyn & Bacon, 1970).

57. William E. Souder, "Achieving Organizational Consensus with Respect to R&D Project Selection Criteria," Management Science 21(February 1975): 669-681.

58. H. Sackman, Delphi Assessment: Expert Opinion, Forecasting, and Group Process, R-1283-PR (Santa Monica, Calif.: The RAND Corporation, April 1974).

59. Harold A. Linstone, "Eight Basic Pitfalls: A Checklist," in Linstone and Turoff, pp. 573-586.

60. Murray Turoff, "The Policy Delphi," in Linstone and Turoff, p. 84.

61. Some exceptions include James R. Emshoff, "Planning the Process of Improving the Planning Process: A Case Study in Meta-Planning," Management Science 24(July 1978): 1095-1108; Ian I. Mitroff, Vincent P. Barabba, and Ralph H. Kilmann, "The Application of Behavioral and Philosophical Technologies to Strategic Planning: A Case Study of a Large Federal Agency," Management Science 24(September 1977): 44-58; and Ian I. Mitroff, "Fundamental Issues in the Simulation of Human Behavior: A Case in the Strategy of Behavioral Science," Management Science 15(August 1969): B635-B649.

62. C. W. Churchman and A. H. Schainblatt, "The Researcher and the Manager: A Dialectic of Implementation," Management Science 11(February 1965): B69-B87; Thomas R. Dyckman, "Management Implementation of Scientific Research: An Attitudinal Study," Management Science 13(June 1967): B612-B620; and W. Jack Duncan, "The Researcher and the Manager: A Comparative View of the Need for Mutual Understanding," Management Science 20(April 1974): 1157-1163.

63. Jan H. B. M. Huysmans, "The Effectiveness of the Cognitive-Style Constraint in Implementing Operations Research Proposals," Management Science 17(September 1970): 92-104; Robert H. Doktor and William F. Hamilton, "Cognitive Style and the Acceptance of Management Science Recommendations," Management Science 19(April 1973): 884-894; and James

L. McKenney and Peter G. W. Keen, "How Managers' Minds Work," Harvard Business Review, May/June 1974, pp. 79-90.

64. Robert C. Ferber, "The Role of the Subconscious in Executive Decision-Making," Management Science 13(April 1967): B519-B526; William T. Morris, "Intuition and Relevance," Management Science 14(December 1967): B157-B165; and Bernard O. Koopman, "Intuition in Mathematical Operations Research," Operations Research 25(March/April 1977): 189-206.

65. Russell L. Ackoff, "Management MISinformation Systems," Management Science 14(December 1967): B147-B156.

66. Chris Argyris, "Management Information Systems: The Challenge to Rationality and Emotionality," Management Science 17(February 1971): B275-B292.

67. A. Charnes, G. Kozmetsky, and T. Ruefli, "Information Requirements for Urban Systems: A View into the Possible Future," Management Science 19(December, Part 2, 1972): 7-20.

68. Norman Johnson and Edward Ward, "Citizen Information Systems: Using Technology to Extend the Dialogue between Citizens and their Government," Management Science 19(December, Part 2, 1972): 21-34.

69. Richard O. Mason and Ian I. Mitroff, "A Program for Research on Management Information Systems," Management Science 19(January 1973): 475-487.

70. E. Burton Swanson, "Management Information Systems: Appreciation and Involvement," Management Science 21(October 1974): 178-188; Henry C. Lucas, Jr., "Performance and the Use of an Information System," Management Science 21(April 1975): 908-919; William R. King and David I. Cleland, "The Design of Management Information Systems: An Information Analysis Approach," Management Science 22(November 1975): 286-297; M. L. Bariff and E. J. Lusk, "Cognitive and Personality Tests for the Design of Management Information Systems," Management Science 23(April 1977): 820-829; Bert de Brabander and Anders Edstron, "Successful Information System Development Projects," Management Science 24(October 1977):

191-199; and Philip Ein-Dor and Eli Segev, "Organizational Context and the Success of Management Information Systems," Management Science 24(June 1978): 1064-1077, and "Strategic Planning for Management Information Systems," Management Science 24(November 1978): 1631-1641.

71. Gary W. Dickson, James A. Senn, and Norman L. Chervany, "Research in Management Information Systems: The Minnesota Experiments," Management Science 23(May 1977): 913-923.

72. Aharon G. Beged-Dov, "An Overview of Management Science and Information Systems," Management Science 13(August 1967): B817-B831.

73. Andrew Whinston, "Price Guides in Decentralized Organizations," in New Perspectives in Organization Research, ed. William W. Cooper, Harold J. Leavitt, and Maynard W. Shelly, II. (New York: John Wiley & Sons, 1964), pp. 405-448.

74. Timothy W. Ruefli, "A Generalized Goal Decompositon Model," Management Science 17(April 1971): B505-B518.

75. Dennis J. Sweeney, E. P. Winkofsky, Probir Roy, and Norman R. Baker, "Composition vs. Decomposition: Two Approaches to Modeling Organizational Decision Processes," Management Science 24(October 1978): 1491-1499.

76. Manfred Kochen and Karl W. Deutsch, "Decentralization by Function and Location," Management Science 19(April 1973): 841-856; and "A Note on Hierarchy and Coordination: An Aspect of Decentralization," Management Science 21(September 1974): 106-114.

77. Robert L. Swinth, "Organizational Joint Problem-Solving," Management Science 18(October 1971): B68-B79.

78. Stanley M. Davis, "Two Models of Organization: Unity of Command versus Balance of Power," Sloan Management Review, Fall 1974, pp. 29-40.

79. David O. Porter and Eugene A. Olsen, "Some Critical Issues in Government Centralization and Decentralization," Public Administration Review,

January/February 1976, pp. 72-84.

80. Norman Statland, "Computer Systems: Centralized or Dispersed," Administrative Management, March 1978, pp. 57-60, 62, 98.

81. Martin K. Starr, "Planning Models," Management Science 13(December 1966): B115-B141.

82. H. Igor Ansoff, "The State of Practice in Planning Systems," Sloan Management Review, Winter 1977, pp. 1-24.

83. George A. Steiner and John B. Minor, Management Policy and Strategy (New York: Macmillan Publishing Co., 1977), pp. 323-354.

84. Some examples include H. Igor Ansoff, Corporate Strategy (New York: McGraw-Hill, 1965); Russell L. Ackoff, A Concept of Corporate Planning (New York: Wiley-Interscience, 1970); Peter Lorange, "Divisional Planning: Setting Effective Direction," Sloan Management Review, Fall 1975, pp. 77-91; Richard F. Vancil, "Strategy Formulation in Complex Organizations," Sloan Management Review, Winter 1976, pp. 1-18; Peter Lorange and Richard F. Vancil, Strategic Planning Systems (Englewood Cliffs, N.J.: Prentice-Hall, 1977); Charles W. Hofer and Dan Schendel, Strategy Formulation: Analytical Concepts (St. Paul, Minn.: West Publishing Company, 1978); Danny Miller and Peter H. Friesen, "Archetypes of Strategy Formulation," Management Science 24(May 1978): 921-933; and Henry Mintzberg, "Patterns in Strategy Formation," Management Science 24(May 1978): 934-948. One of the few attempts at a "macro" mathematical model of strategy formulation is Dan Schenedel and G. Richard Patton, "A Simultaneous Equation Model of Corporate Strategy," Management Science 24(November 1978): 1611-1621.

85. Consider the word "organization" as example: "There is much written about organization without explicitly defining what is meant by the word. We have been puzzled by what we have read and have found very little consensus among different writers views. There seems to be too little in the way of general theory or in expression of concepts operationally defined." [S. B. Littauer, T. M. Yegulap, and G. K. Zaharlev, "A Framework for Optimizing Managerial Decision," OMEGA

4(1976): 43.]

86. Richard O. Mason, "A Dialectical Approach to Strategic Planning," Management Science 15(April 1969): B403-B414.

87. Ian I. Mitroff, "A Communication Model of Dialectical Inquiring Systems -- A Strategy for Strategic Planning," Management Science 17(June 1971): B634-B648.

88. Ian I. Mitroff and Frederick Betz, "Dialectical Decision Theory: A Meta-Theory of Decision-Making," Management Science 19(September 1972): 11-24.

89. Ian I. Mitroff, John Nelson, and Richard O. Mason, "On Management Myth-Information Systems," Management Science 21(December 1974): 371-382.

90. Melvin F. Shakun, "Management Science and Management: Implementing Management Science via Situational Normativism," Management Science 18(April 1972): B367-B377.

91. Melvin F. Shakun, "Policy Making Under Discontinuous Change: The Situational Normativism Approach," Management Science 22(October 1975): 226-235.

92. Paul C. Nutt, "An Experimental Comparison of the Effectiveness of Three Planning Methods," Management Science 23(January 1977): 499-511.

93. Richard A. Cosier, Thomas L. Ruble, and John C. Aplin, "An Evaluation of the Effectiveness of Dialectical Inquiry Systems," Management Science 24(October 1978): 1483-1490.

94. See, for example, Warren G. Bennis, Organization Development: Its Nature, Origins, and Prospects (Reading, Mass.: Addison-Wesley, 1969); Richard Beckhard, Organization Development: Strategies and Models (Reading, Mass.: Addison-Wesley, 1969); and Edgar H. Schein, Process Consultation: Its Role in Organization Development (Reading, Mass.: Addison-Wesley, 1969).

95. David A. Nadler, Feedback and Organizational Development: Using Data-Based Methods (Reading, Mass.:

Addison-Wesley, 1977).

96. Some relevant literature here includes Joseph Wolfe, "Effective Performance Behaviors in a Simulated Policy and Decision Making Environment," Management Science 21(April 1975): 872-882; Herbert H. Hand and Henry P. Sims, Jr., "Statistical Evaluation of Complex Gaming Performance," Management Science 21(February 1975): 708-717; James L. McKenney, Simulation Gaming for Management Development (Boston: Division of Research, Graduate School of Business Administration, Harvard University, 1967); John C. Porter, Maurice W. Sasieni, Eli S. Marks, and Russell L. Ackoff, "The Use of Simulation as a Pedagogical Device," Management Science 12(February 1966): B170-B179; Bernard M. Bass, "Business Gaming for Organizational Research," Management Science 10(April 1964): 545-556; and William R. Dill and Neil Doppelt, "The Acquisition of Experience in a Complex Management Game," Management Science 10(October 1963): 30-46. The latter article claimed that "learning derived more from interpersonal interactions with other players and with outside groups...than from interaction with the game model itself." (p. 30)

97. See, for example, Anatol Rapaport, Fights, Games, and Debates (Ann Arbor, Mich.: The University of Michigan Press, 1960); and William Riker, The Theory of Political Coalitions (New Haven, Conn.: Yale University Press, 1962).

98. James R. Emshoff, Analysis of Behavioral Systems (New York: The Macmillan Company, 1971).

99. A pilot study using a generalized gaming exercise, and dealing with consumerism policy, was conducted with top executives of a Philadelphia bank. The results pointed to a need for a richer theoretical framework. Laurence D. Richards and Robert J. Graham, "Identifying Problems through Gaming," Interfaces 7(May 1977): 76-79.

100. Raymond A. Bauer, "The Study of Policy Formation: An Introduction," in The Study of Policy Formation, ed. Raymond A. Bauer and Kenneth J. Gergen (New York: The Free Press, 1968), p. 2.

101. Edwin A. Murray, Jr. "Strategic Choice as a Negotiated Outcome," Management Science 24(May 1978): 960.

102. Keen, "Optimality," p. 52.

103. Keen and Scott Morton, Decision Support Systems , p. 87.

104. J. W. Botkin, "An Intuitive Computer System: A Cognitive Approach to the Management Learning Process," (Ph. D. dissertation, Harvard Business Scoool, 1973).

105. James R. Emshoff, "Experience-Generalized Decision Making: The Next Generation of Managerial Models," Interfaces 8(August 1978): 40-48.

106. Harold A. Linstone and Murray Turoff, "Computers and the Future of Delphi: Introduction," in Linstone and Turoff, pp. 489-496.

107. Magoroh Maruyama, "Heterogenistics: An Epistemological Restructuring of Biological and Social Sciences," Cybernetica 20(1977): 69-86.

108. Roger C. Conant and W. Ross Ashby, "Every Good Regulator of a System Must be a Model of that System," International Journal of Systems Science 1(1970): 97.

109. Herbert A. Simon, "Motivational and Emotional Controls of Cognition," Psychological Review 74(1967): 29-39.

110. Wendell R. Garner, Uncertainty and Structure as Psychological Concepts (Huntington, N.Y.: Robert E. Krieger Publishing Company, 1975).

111. Humberto R. Maturana, "Cognitive Strategies," unpublished manuscript (Cambridge, Mass.: Massachusetts Institute of Technology, undated).

112. K. A. Archibald, "Three Views of the Expert's Role in Policymaking: Systems Analysis, Incrementalism, and the Clinical Approach," Policy Science 1(1970): 79-80.

113. Simon, "Cognition."

114. G. A. Miller, E. Gallanter, and K. Pribram, Plans and the Structure of Behavior (New York: Holt, Rinehart, & Winston, 1960).

PART II

THEORETICAL FRAMEWORK

CHAPTER 5

PRELIMINARY CONCEPTS

The role of theory in scientific research is first, to provide guidance and direction to the conduct of the research; second, to be altered as a result of learning that occurs during the research; and third, to serve as a means of communicating ideas resulting from the research. If the assumptions underlying a theory or set of theories are not made explicit, communication is distorted and the mutual learning desired is impeded. Part II presents a framework of assumptions for the purpose of providing a basis for the approach to policy-level modelling developed in Part III. This framework is labelled "constraint theory."

This chapter discusses some preliminary concepts necessary as a precursor to Chapters 6 and 7. The first section is devoted to logic; we argue that mathematical structures and behavioral language are derivatives of the salient logic in a particular culture. The mathematics of cause and effect, probability, and optimization, and the language of rational decisionmaking, are traceable to a system of logic that deserves critical scrutiny. Recent and radical developments in logic provide the foundations for constraint theory. The mathematics proposed in this book, however, is not as radical, being presented primarily in set-theoretic terms. The second section of this chapter offers some basic mathematical definitions. The third section discusses some fundamental cybernetic principles which will be referred to often throughout the remainder of the book. They are presented here so that an appreciation of their implications will emerge as the framework unfolds. Conceptual simplicity has been one of the guiding criteria in preparing the following presentation of constraint theory.

5.1 LOGIC

In Chapter 3, the philosophical heritage which has provided the foundations for the two-valued logic which dominates mathematical thinking in the Western world

was presented. It is that logic that supports the
positive form of reasoning, the rational decisionmaking
paradigm, and the mathematics of statistical
probability and optimization. We suggested also that a
new logic was emerging in mathematical and systems
thinking which is supportive of the negative form of
reasoning. This logic was introduced in 1969 by George
Spencer Brown.[1]

A number of approaches to the problems of
two-valued logic, e.g., paradox and contradiction, are
possible. Early logicians simply ignored paradoxical
propositions "as cranks, as (syntactic) pathologies,
(semantic) freaks, in short, as aberrations (of
thought)."[2] A branch of abstract algebra, group
theory, "provides a valid framework for thinking about
the peculiar interdependence between persistence and
change,"[3] which the traditional logic of propositions
did not. Such a framework assists in understanding and
resolving paradox and contradiction. It does so by
specifying rules whereby changes can occur within a
system while the system as a whole remains invariant.
a distinctive characteristic of both traditional logic
and group theory is the independent identification of
operands, e.g., elements, components, objects, etc.
(i.e., things that persist), and operators, e.g.,
addition, multiplication, etc. (i.e., types of change).
This independence has allowed philosophers to postulate
an objective world of things separate from the
subjective world which perceives transformations on it.
The independence of operators also lends itself to a
linear concept of time, a concept culturally reinforced
by Newtonian mechanics. It should be obvious that
concepts of "time" play a central role in the emerging
logic.

The logic of fuzzy sets has also attempted to
circumvent the problems of two-valued logic by
postulating that the line of demarcation between
membership in and exclusion from a set of operands or a
set of operators may not be clear.[4] For example,
between the two operators and and or there is an entire
spectrum of operators, their membership to one of the
two extremes being fuzzified. Both group theory and
fuzzy set theory are major contributions to the logic
of first-order change. The difficulty arises in
transcending a particular frame of reference, that is,
examining changes in the rules that govern change
itself, (second-order change). Being able to transcend
a given frame of reference is essential to a

formalization of the subject/object relationship in mental models and self-reference. We contend that the metalogic required must ignore the operand/operator distinction and focus on the act of observation itself.

While fuzzy set theory is in the spirit of negative reasoning and will be used throughout our framework, an even more fundamental logic is necessary. The need was addressed by Whitehead and Russell[5] in their Theory of Logical Types, and further by Gödel[6] and Wittgenstein.[7] Spencer Brown's logic, however, is the cornerstone for the present work.

The logic takes as central, not a set of operands and a set of operators, but rather the boundary separating the elements included in a set from those excluded. The logic is based on this simplest of forms, a single mark, symbolized by:

$$\overline{}|$$

The mark is a symbol of an observation, a separation of one set of entities from another. Since an observation has no meaning in the absence of an observer, the logic is inherently self-referential. Furthermore, the mark can be thought of as the drawing of a "distinction" between that which is included and that which is excluded. A distinction implies both operand and operator; by focusing on the mark, the logic transcends the degenerate operand/operator dichotomy and all rules of the logic depend only on the mark.

There are two central axioms of the logic.

Axiom 1: Condensation (The law of calling)

$$\overline{}|\;\overline{}| \quad = \quad \overline{}| \qquad\qquad (5\text{-}1)$$

This axiom states that an observation involving two distinctions can be condensed to one. An individual who is male and is also tall, for example, is simply a "tall man."

97

Axiom 2: Cancellation (The law of crossing)

$$\overline{\overline{}} \quad = \quad \tag{5-2}$$

This axiom simply states that a distinction observed and then abandoned leaves no distinction. For such to occur, a second distinction must, in essence, be made on the original distinction. The hiring of an employee introduces a distinction; the firing of the employee is also a distinction superimposed on the first (i.e., the second would not be possible without the first). The result is the negation of the initial distinction, i.e., the employee is gone.

To illustrate how this logic treats paradox, let us take a statement that is equivalent to Russell's paradox:

$$f = f \; \overline{} \tag{5-3}$$

f is the argument, and the above statement is analogous to a statement like: "This statement is false." Spencer Brown resolves this paradox by introducing another logical dimension, "time." That is, the statement really represents an alternation between two states in time. Spencer Brown refers to the solution of (5-3) as an <u>imaginary</u> state, just as $\sqrt{-1}$ is an imaginary state, but one of course very useful in engineering dynamics. Varela states: "this interpretation is, in my opinion, one of his most outstanding contributions. He succeeds in linking time and description in a most natural fashion."[8]

Varela, however, extends Spencer Brown's logic even further. If one allows that time is not simply an alternation between states, but rather a sequence of distinctions, then the "imaginary" form above can be subjected to the rules of logic:

98

$$f = f$$

$$f = f$$

$$f = f$$

. .
. .
. .

(5-4)

Varela then postulates that the extension in time eventually results in "re-entry" into the form, symbolized:

$$f = f = f = f = \bullet \bullet \bullet \quad \square$$

(5-5)

This new symbol represents the autonomous state, i.e., self-awareness, self-consciousness, self-reflection, etc.; it is made possible in the observer through a complicated process of recursively circular operations.

> ...it is the reentry of an expression into its own indicative space that is the way to recover all the forms of circularity...Apparently our cognition cannot hold both ends of a closing circle simultaneously; it must travel through the circle ceaselessly. Therefore, we find a peculiar equivalence of self-reference and time, insofar as self-reference cannot be conceived outside time, and time comes in whenever self-reference is allowed.[9]

Much remains to be investigated in the logic and mathematics of time, a topic beyond the scope of this book.[10] The immediate need is to develop a modelling approach which operationalizes some of the concepts while maintaining consistency with the overall structure of the logic.

5.2 MATHEMATICAL DEFINITIONS

The task of this section is to summarize some of the basic mathematical concepts needed to operationalize the logic of the previous section, for the purpose of avoiding ambiguity and misunderstanding later. In this context, a legitimate question arises: why operationalize a logic that has its own built-in mathematics, and which, if institutionalized, would negate the need for the type of technology that it is being operationalized for? We do not claim to have a complete or a fully justifiable answer. However, the fact is that the logic is not institutionalized in the Western world, and many view the rationality-technology syndrome as a vicious circle that is steadily deteriorating our organizations and cultural values. One response to the question, then, is to argue for a need to reverse the trend. The role of a policy support system is in large part to infuse an alternative and complementary form of reasoning into policy formulation.

The negative form of reasoning does, however, raise doubts about the ethics of sophisticated management technologies. The decision scientist Sang Lee puts it this way: "in a society where limitation of desires is a respected way of life, it is unlikely that decision analysis will be important or even necessary."[11] The point is that if the logic is taken to the extreme, the type of policy support system proposed in this book should eventually negate itself. That is, such a system would be transcended through the restructuring of values, patterns of culture, and paradigms of thought and action. This altruistic dream, however, is not on the near horizon, so for now we must struggle with the problem of operationalization.

5.2.1 Distinctions and Relations

Commencing with the fundamental concept, a distinction is considered to possess "dimensionality." Each dimension is given a variable name, and each variable can assume a set of values or states. All the combinations of the states of the variable set being considered form a state space.

100

Definition 5.1: A variable (X,Y,...) is an abstraction of one of the characteristics (i.e., attributes) of the system under investigation.[12]

Definition 5.2: A state space (S) is the product set of all variables selected X × Y × ... .

Definition 5.3: The state (s) of a system at a point in time is the set of states of each variable (n-tuple) at that point in time (x_i, y_j, ...).

Definition 5.4: An action or alternative space (S^n) is a state space that includes at least the current perceived state of the system and possible alternative states that it could be transformed to over the time horizon under consideration.

Depending on the context, we signify variables by upper case letters (X,Y,...); lower case letters (x,y,...); or x's with subscripts (x_1,x_2,...). Since in this chapter subscripted letters represent states of a variable, we use (X,Y,...) to represent the variables.

The form of state space selected for the purposes of this book is n-dimensional Euclidean space (E^n). The major limitation of this selection is that it does not accommodate time as a variable in the form we think it ought to be treated. However, we take the existential point of view that treats a relation between variables as the perceived set of possible states over some subjective time horizon. To justify this point of view, the modelling approach proposed must be sufficiently flexible to allow continual change in perceived relations resulting from the dynamics of the policy formulation process (including shifts in time horizons). The classical method for treating the time dimension is simply to consider time as another variable in E^n. This may still be legitimate in systems in which variables are strictly mechanical; but in sociotechnical and other behavioral systems, we have argued that time, individual autonomy, and self-reference are inextricably interwoven and a linear treatment of time in E^n may misrepresent the mental modelling process.

Figure 5.1, then, provides, with these reservations, the basic mathematical framework (in two dimensions).

101

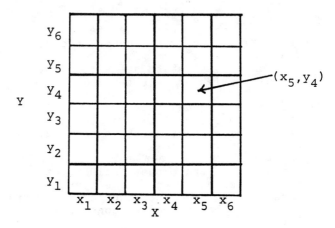

Figure 5.1   Two Dimensional State Space

Definition 5.5: A relation or relationship (R) is
a subset of states perceived as possible within a
defined state space.

This is a generalized notion of relation, first
proposed by Wiener;[13] it represents a concept
different from the one-to-one or many-to-one functional
relations that lead to cause and effect inferences.
This generalized definition accommodates the mutually
causative interrelationships characteristic of human
and social systems.

5.2.2 Constraint and Systems

Many factors contribute to the limitations on the
set of perceived possibilities; these are the set of
constraints. In addition to the type of constraint
considered in decision models, e.g., capacity
constraints, resource constraints, etc., systems of
knowledge, culture (e.g., traditions, taboos), values,
and organizational relationships also impose
constraint.

Definition 5.6: Constraint (N) is the complement
(negation) of a relation, representing the set of
states perceived as not reachable within a defined
state space.

Figure 5.2 depicts the concepts of relation and constraint.

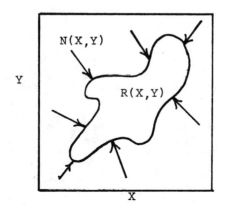

Figure 5.2 Relation and Constraint

Ashby discusses the nature and importance of the concept of constraint:

> The intensity of the constraint is thus shown by the reduction it causes in the number of possible arrangements. It seems that constraints cannot be classified in any simple way, for they include all cases in which a set, for any reason, is smaller than it might be...Constraints are of high importance in cybernetics...because when a constraint exists advantage can usually be taken of it...Consider as example the basic concept of a "thing" or "object," as something handled in daily life...the essence of the chair's being a "thing", a unity, rather than a collection of independent parts corresponds to the presence of the constraint. Seen from this point of view, the world around us is extremely rich in constraints. We are so familiar with them that we take most of them for granted, and are often not even aware that they exist.[14]

When an individual perceives an object or a relationship, then, he/she does not perceive all the

103

parts and their intricate interrelationships, but rather the whole as defined by the constraints.

To this point, we have been using the word "system" without defining it. Sachs presents a valid criticism to the traditional structural-relational approach to systems.[15] Hall and Fagen, for example, define a system as "a set of objects together with the relationships between the objects and between their attributes."[16] Under such a definition, a system is observed in its totality as a subset in an n-dimensional state space (a relation). What is missing from this definition is the operation by which the relation observed came to be selected in the first place. The operation of selective observation and the relation observed are inseparable. That is, the system observed is defined by the higher order act of observation.

Definition 5.7: An operation (ϕ) is the transformation (mapping) of a state or set of states to another state or set of states.

$$s_1 \xrightarrow{\phi} s_2$$

$$R_1 \xrightarrow{\phi} R_2$$

Definition 5.8: A process (P) is a set of operations, $(\phi_1, \phi_2, \ldots)$.

An operation or process may itself be one of the variables defining the set of states being operated on; we refer to operations on operations or processes as higher-order or meta-operations. Hence, irrespective of how encompassing we choose to define a set of elements and the relations among them, we can never completely specify the system. The relations themselves are being transformed by operations and those operations by still higher-order operations, ad infinitum. It is these second and higher order transformations which are of particular importance in policy issues and in the design of an interactive, policy support system.

The introduction of the concept of distinction provides some assistance, for by definition a distinction implies both observer and observed, operand and operator. A distinction, however, only provides a

104

line of demarcation, a boundary between the included
and excluded. To define a system as one side of the
boundary is to ignore the other, equally as important
side. The act of drawing a distinction defines both a
phenomenon <u>and</u> its opposite. That is, both sides are
necessary to define a system. Hence, we will not (and
need not) provide a formal definition of the word
"system." A system is whatever is being observed. Its
distinctiveness singles it out, and that cannot be
separated from the motives and interests of the
observer. The existence of a system implies constraint
in both the observed and the act of observation.

5.2.3 Behavior

A sequence of operations on a state describes a
line of behavior and the set of possible lines of
behavior is a field of behavior. These two concepts
represent perhaps the simplest way to distinguish the
positive form of reasoning from the negative form.

<u>Definition 5.9</u>: A <u>line</u> <u>of</u> <u>behavior</u> (L) is the
trajectory of a system specified by a succession
of states and the time intervals between them.[17]

$$L = \left\{ (s_0, t_0), (s_1, t_1) \ldots \right\} \qquad (5-6)$$

<u>Definition 5.10</u>: A <u>field</u> <u>of</u> <u>behavior</u> (F) is the
set of all lines of behavior possible by releasing
a system from all possible initial states in a
particular set of surrounding conditions and
within a particular time horizon, $(L_1, L_2, \ldots)$.[18]

Line of behavior and field of behavior are diagrammed
in Figures 5.3 and 5.4 respectively.

Under the broad conceptualization of policy formulation
that we are assuming, one of the many forms of policy
is the plan. A plan can be considered the design of a
desired line of behavior. The final state and time of
the line of behavior indicate the goal of the plan,
with each intermediate state and time indicating
intermediate goals. This represents the positive form
of reasoning. It assumes that if one collects "enough"
information, prevailing environmental conditions can be
forecast, and that if one "tries hard enough," he/she
can make events occur in some desired manner. The plan
is probably the most overrated form of policy in

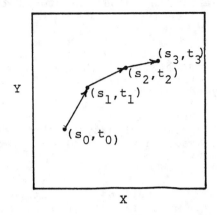

Figure 5.3   Line of Behavior

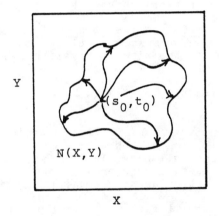

Figure 5.4   Field of Behavior

organizations today, for it can only be successful when
strict continuity is assumed.   As Ashby points out,
continuity is one of the most "powerful" forms of
constraint   and   is   exploited   in   virtually   all
technological innovation.[19]   But the social milieu in
which   both   private   and   public   organizations   must
operate   is   becoming   increasingly   characterized   by
discontinity[20] and turbulence.[21]   Ashby refers to
these social environments as "richly-joined"[22] and
Toffler has popularized the term "future shock."[23]

One response to this uncertainty has been the contingency plan, where more than one line of behavior is included in the plan. The line of behavior selected depends on conditions at that point in time. Often a contingency plan takes the form of best case, worst case, and most probable case forecasts. The contingency plan represents a hedge against risk, but is only appropriate when uncertainty can be expressed as probabilities of outcomes. In situations characterized by structural uncertainty, the contingency plan has the same deficiencies as the single trajectory plan.

Another response is to introduce feedback into the planning process, an approach Ackoff refers to as "adaptivizing."[24] This approach calls for continually updating and altering the plan as perceptions of the organization's present state, the efficiency of its course of action, and the relative value of the expected outcomes and goals change. Eilon points out that organizations, of course, do this anyway;[25] furthermore, it is not clear that the plan as an organizational artifact is any different from the single trajectory or contingency plan. The change is in the planning process. But if the nature of the plan has not changed, the process is still characterized by the positive, rational form of reasoning.

A more encompassing notion of policy is represented by "field of behavior." A field of behavior forms a relation consisting of the set of possible lines of behavior (courses of action) in the defined state space. The boundaries on this relation repesent the constraints on organizational behavior; the formulation of these constraints is the precise function of policy.[26] The plan also establishes constraints, but to a specific line of behavior. The field of behavior view of policy does not distinguish ends from means nor values from other constraints, and optimization as a concept has reduced significance. By concentrating on the states of behavior to be excluded, the negative form of reasoning is manifest. Eilon supports this perspective: "there is far more to be gained from scrutinizing and ranking constraints than in constructing a super utility function to delight the heart of the optimizer."[27]

107

5.3 CYBERNETIC PRINCIPLES

Recalling the suggestion of Chapter 2, that a synthesis of the literature on policy formulation requires a generalized concept of organizational communications and control, cybernetics, the science of communication and control, must assume a central role in our theoretical framework. This section discusses some basic principles of structure, communications, and modes of control, and their implications for policy formulation.

5.3.1 Variety

Ashby has shown that any generalization of the concepts of control and communication must consider the set of possible states available to a system.[28]

> Definition 5.11: Variety is the number of possible states represented by a relation.

Variety is associated with constraint in that the stronger the constraint, the less the variety. Variety as a quantity is sometimes measured in bits, i.e., the logarithm to the base two of the number of possibilities. It should be noted, however, that the significance of this measure is context dependent. Variety perceived by one observer may be very different from that perceived by another, depending on how each individual enumerates the possibilities and the frame of reference in which they are perceived.

Communication is impossible unless the variety exhibited by the communicating media, i.e., the channel of communication, is greater than one. Likewise, control is manifest only when a system has a variety of possible states. This variety represents the system's capability to respond to disturbances. This leads to what we consider to be the fundamental principle of communication and control.

> Principle 5.1: [Law of Requisite Variety] Only variety can destroy (absorb) variety.[29]

This law when applied to simple examples may seem trivial, but to understand the control of "organized complexity" it is an essential prerequisite.

5.3.2 Communication and Structure

Organization and communication are allied concepts in that a set of objects are "organized" when communication occurs between them.[30] "Communication is manifest when the behavior of the whole cannot fully be accounted for by the behavior of its components in isolation."[31] That is, communication implies some non-decomposable constraint in the set of possible states of the communicating objects, components, or variables.

> Thus, the presence of "organization" between variables is equivalent to the existence of constraint in the product space of possibilities. I stress this point because while, in the past, biologists have tended to think of organization as something extra, something added to the elementary variables, the modern theory, based on the logic of communication, regards organization as a restriction or constraint. The two points of view are thus diametrically opposed.[32]

Neither point of view is necessarily correct, but each will represent a different context for thinking about control in organizations.

Rather than formally defining either organization or communication, we will refer to the structure of the relation among the components. Ashby defines structure as a characteristic form or pattern.[33] It can be shown that the number of relations which can be formed from an n-dimensional state space, where each dimension (variable) can assume k discrete values, is:[34]

$$2^{k^n}$$

It does not take much imagination to realize that the number of relations, i.e., structures, which can be manifest in even very simple state spaces, rapidly exceeds any conceivable information processing capacity available to man.[35] Hence, in complex systems of the type characteristic of policy issues, it is usually fruitless to attempt to identify the precise pattern of relationships. However, it is sometimes worthwhile to identify amount of structure as measured by the strength of the constraint perceived.[36]

109

This approach is also consistent with the need to identify and maintain variety and flexibility in the face of uncertainty. Amount of structure is related to the decomposability, reducibility, or separability of an n-dimensional relation. The structure of a system remains unchanged by removing components or variables whose behavior can be accounted for independently of the behavior of the other components or variables. In such cases, the independent components exhibit maximum variety (freedom) with respect to the other components. Hence, the amount of structure of the remaining components (and sets of components) is also determined by the variety of their behavior with respect to the remaining components (and sets of components).

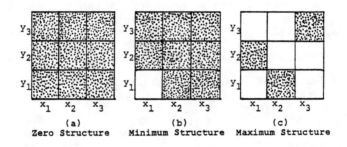

Figure 5.5   Amount of Structure[37]

Figure 5.5 depicts different amounts of structure in a two dimensional state space, where each variable (X and Y) can assume three discrete values (x_1, x_2, x_3, and y_1, y_2, y_3). A shaded cell indicates that the (x_i, y_i) pair is a member of the relation between the two variables. In (a) there is no structure because all states are possible, and the behavior of X can be explained independently of Y. Minimum structure is manifest in (b), where all but one (x,y) pair is possible. Maximum structure occurs when, for each x_i, and each y_i, one and only one y_i and x_i is possible. In (c), there is virtually no freedom in the behavior of X with respect to Y and vice versa. Information theory provides measures of constraint, and hence of structure and variety.[38] Again, however, these

110

measures are context dependent, their meaning being relative to the frame of reference of the observer.

5.3.3 Control

The last topic of this chapter is modes of control. There are many ways, of course, to classify organizational control. The discussion here is intended simply to distinguish the concept of control implied by policy formulation from the more technical concepts implicit in the mainstream management control and decision science literature. We identify four "modes" of control: error detection and correction, prediction, hierarchial decomposition, and variety amplification.

Figure 5.6 depicts the <u>error detection and correction</u> mode of control. This concept is represented by the simple feedback circuit commonly used to depict technological control systems. The establishment of performance measures or standards for individuals or units of an organization is one method of implementing this mode of control. If performance does not meet some threshold, management employs sanctions or takes some other form of action to counteract the deviation.

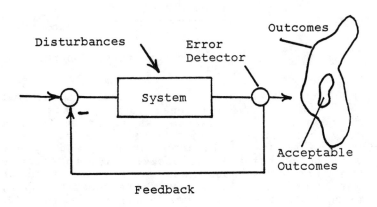

Figure 5.6   Error Detection and Correction

In the error detection and correction mode of control, a deviation must occur before corrective action can be taken. It may be possible, however, to collect information on surrounding disturbances prior to the occurrence of a deviation, i.e., to predict the conditions which cause disturbances. This predictive mode of control leads to what Ashby has termed "ultrastability."[39] The simple feedback circuit diagram is not adequate for depicting this concept. Figure 5.7 is a more generalized diagram which subsumes the error detection and correction concept as well as the prediction concept.[40] Planning and forecasting activities are manifestations of this mode of control.

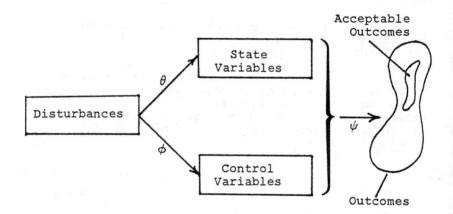

Figure 5.7 Generalized Concept of Control

Hierarchical control is not truly a separate category from the two mentioned above. It deserves special consideration, however, as it is employed in virtually all large organizations. In a complex system, the amount of information required by each subsystem to coordinate its activities with those of all the other subsystems may be greater than the information processing capacity of the subsystem (i.e., the manager of the subsystem). Figure 5.8 diagrams three subsystems which are linked in a chain. Using the simple feedback circuit concept, each subsystem has its own control mechanism. To coordinate the subsystems, a second feedback circuit is employed. Different schemes of hierarchical control are possible,

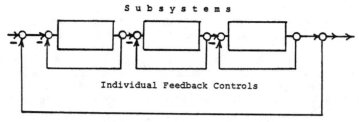

Subsystems

Individual Feedback Controls

Hierarchical Control

Figure 5.8   Hierarchical Control

depending on the method of aggregation selected. The
effectiveness of hierarchical control is related to the
nature of the technology being managed and to the
variation and intensity of disturbances from the
environment. As the disturbances become more intense
or unpredictable, i.e., the environment becomes more
richly-joined, hierarchies tend to grow, with
hierarchies becoming embedded within hierarchies. The
bureaucratic form of organization is the result.

Variety amplification subsumes the three modes of
control above, yet is a much broader concept. In
turbulent environments, characterized by high degrees
of uncertainty, the first three concepts offer little
relief. The law of requisite variety, however, states
that variety of response is what allows a system to
maintain control in the face of a variety of
disturbances. While the variety of a system can be
increased relative to its environment by collecting
information on the system and its behavior (error
detection and correction) and on environmental
distubances (prediction), and the information
processing capacity can be increased through
multiple-level processing (hierarchy), this does not
exhaust the possibilities. Another alternative is to
restructure the system and/or its outcome space, i.e.,
alter the constraints.

Organizations, however, have built-in mechanisms
that perpetuate the current structures and policies

113

which represent barriers to any restructuring process. Hence, one design feature that increases the variety amplification potential of organizations is flexibility, i.e., the capability to accommodate second-order change without prohibitive resistance. Flexibility, and variety amplification in general, cannot be had without a price. The price is a change in the outcome space, which in turn may require a change in values. In the management science literature this strategic concept is called "robustness," and is analogous to the colloquial phrase "keeping your options open."

The next chapter presents a language for formalizing the advanced concept of control. This language serves as a means for discussing the type of model useful in facilitating variety amplification.

NOTES

1. G. Spencer Brown, Laws of Form (New York: The Julian Press, 1972). See also, Robert A. Orchard, "On the Laws of Form," International Journal of General Systems 2(1975): 99-106.

2. Richard Herbert Howe and Heinz Von Foerster, "Introductory Comments to Francisco Varela's Calculus for Self-Reference," International Journal of General Systems 2(1975): 1.

3. Paul Watzlawick, John Weakland, and Richard Fisch, Change: Principles of Problem Formation and Problem Resolution (New York: W. W. Norton & Company, 1974), p. 5.

4. See A. Kaufman, "Fuzzy Logic," in Introduction to the Theory of Fuzzy Subsets, vol. 1: Fundamental Theoretical Elements, with a Foreword by L. A. Zadeh, trans. D. L. Swanson (New York: Academic Press, 1975), pp. 191-266.

5. Alfred North Whitehead and Bertrand Russell, Principia Mathematica, 2nd ed. (London: Cambridge University Press, 1925).

6. Kurt Gödel, "Ueber formal unentsheidbare Sätze der Principia Mathematica und verwandter Systeme I," Monatshefte fur Mathematik und Physik 38(1931): 173-198. (English translation: On Formally

Undecidable Propositions of Principia Mathematica and Related Systems I).

7. Ludwig Wittgenstein, Tractatus Logico-Philosophicus, with an Introduction by Bertrand Russell, trans. D. F. Pears and B. F. McGuiness (London and Henley: Routledge & Kegan Paul, 1922).

8. Francisco J. Varela, "A Calculus for Self-Reference," International Journal of General Systems 2(1975): 20.

9. Ibid.

10. Herbst has attempted to initiate a time-dependent behavioral logic based on Spencer Brown's Laws of Form, but at the present time it is in only rudimentary form. Ph. G. Herbst, Alternatives to Hierarchies (Leiden, The Netherlands: Martinus Nijhoff Social Sciences Division, 1976), pp. 84-106.

11. Sang M. Lee, Goal Programming for Decision Analysis (Philadelphia: Auerback Publishers, 1972), p. 5.

12. George J. Friedman and Cornelius T. Leondes, "Constraint Theory, Part I: Fundamentals," IEEE Transaction on Systems Science and Cybernetics 5(1969): 51.

13. Norbert Wiener, "A Simplification of the Logic of Relations," Proceedings of the Cambridge Philosophical Society 17(1914): 387-390.

14. W. Ross Ashby, An Introduction to Cybernetics (London: Chapman & Hall, 1956), pp. 128-131.

15. Wladimir M. Sachs, "Toward Formal Foundations of Teleological Systems Science," General Systems XXI (1976): 145-153.

16. A. D. Hall and R. E. Fagen, "Definition of System," General Systems I (1956): 18.

17. W. Ross Ashby, Design for a Brain (London: Chapman & Hall, 1960), p. 20.

18. Ibid., p. 23.

19. Ashby, Cybernetics, p. 133.

20. Peter F. Drucker, The Age of Discontinuity (New York: Harper & Row, 1968).

21. F. E. Emery and E. L. Trist, Towards a Social Ecology (London: Plenum Press, 1972).

22. Ashby, Design, p. 205.

23. Alvin Toffler, Future Shock (New York: Bantam Books, 1970).

24. Russell L. Ackoff, A Concept of Corporate Planning (New York: John Wiley & Sons, 1970), pp. 15-17.

25. Samuel Eilon, "Goals and Constraints in Decision-making," Operational Research Quarterly 23(March 1972): 8-9.

26. There is an interesting correspondence between this concept of field of behavior and Lewin's topological psychology, with its concepts of force field, life space, space of free movement, boundary zone, etc. This correspondence needs to be explored in more detail. See Kurt Lewin, Principles of Topological Psychology, trans. Fritz Heider and Grace M. Heider (New York: McGraw-Hill, 1936); and Field Theory in Social Science, ed. Dorwin Cartwright (Chicago: University of Chicago Press, 1951).

27. Eilon, p. 15.

28. Ashby, Cybernetics, pp. 121-123.

29. Ibid., p. 207. Beer prefers the word "absorb" to "destroy." Stafford Beer, Designing Freedom (London: John Wiley & Sons: 1974), p. 30.

30. W. Ross Ashby, "Principles of the Self-Organizing System," in Modern Systems Research for the Behavioral Scientist, ed. Walter Buckley (Chicago: Aldine Publishing Company, 1968), p. 109.

31. Klaus Krippendorff, "Communication and the Genesis of Structure," General Systems XVI (1971): 183.

32. Ashby, "Self-Organizing System," p. 109.

33. W. Ross Ashby, "The Set Theory of Mechanism

and Homeostasis," in _Automaton Theory and Learning Systems_, ed. D. J. Stewart (London: Academic Press, 1967), p. 44.

34. W. Ross Ashby, "Systems and Their Informational Measures," in _Trends in General Systems Theory_, ed. George J. Klir (New York: John Wiley and Sons, 1972), pp. 83-85.

35. For example, in a five dimensional state space where each variable has ten discrete values that it can be assigned, there are approximately 10^{50000} relations which can be formed.

36. Wendell R. Garner, _Uncertainty and Structure as Psychological Concepts_ (Huntington, N. Y.: Robert E. Krieger Publishing Company, 1962), p. 145.

37. Krippendorff, p. 175.

38. Shannon and Weaver's initial formulation of information theory considered only the binary relations between sender and receiver useful in communications technologies. For the purposes of psychological theory, Garner and McGill later extended the formulation to n-dimensional relations. Claude E. Shannon and Warren Weaver, _The Mathematical Theory of Communication_ (Urbana, Ill.: University of Illinois Press, 1949); W. J. McGill, "Multivariate Information Transmission," _Psychometrika_ 19(1954): 97-116; W. R. Garner and W. J. McGill, "The Relation between Information and Variance Analyses," _Psychometrika_ 21(1956): 219-228; Garner, _Uncertainty and Structure_.

39. Ashby, _Design_, pp. 80-99.

40. The diagram is adapted from Ashby, "Set Theory," p. 41. Ashby credits G. Sommerhoff, _Analytical Biology_ (London: Oxford University Press, 1950) with the formulation.

CHAPTER 6

MODELLING LANGUAGE

Different modes of control are appropriate for different types of organization. Hence, relatively stable manufacturing industries for which output can be measured with precision may successfully employ market (error detection and correction) or bureaucratic (hierarchical and predictive) modes of control. Market control mechanisms work through the reward of individual contributions as measured by output; bureaucratic control mechanisms work through rules, procedures, and the legitimization of authority. For many organizations in the public sector, in service industries, and in industries experiencing rapid technological change, the output is not easily measured nor is the output process stable.[1] We argue that in these organizations the formulation of policy and strategy is a critical concern, and that the more generalized concept of control -- variety amplification -- is particularly relevant. Furthermore, we recognize a trend toward the more complex and less stable types of organization in Western societies.

In organizations where market or bureaucratic modes of control are sufficient, single criteria decision models and forecasting models are valuable management tools. That the role of these models has changed, however, is evidenced by a survey of 346 corporations conducted by Social Systems, Inc. Seventy-three percent of these corporations were found to be using or developing some type of formal planning model; but, seventy-eight percent of those companies currently using models advocated them for generating a wider range of alternatives and perspectives, rather than for optimization and prediction, the roles for which they were originally designed.[2] As a consequence, the nature of the planning and policy formulation process has also changed. In place of a single organizational scenario, for example, Xerox now pits multiple scenarios against each other;[3] in place of most-probable-case forecasts, Exxon now develops more ambiguous "'envelopes' that include a range of possibilities;"[4] and in place if a single forward plan, American Telephone and Telegraph now formulates

multiple   contingency   plans   that   stress
"flexibility."[5]

6.1 OVERVIEW

We argue that not only does the role of formal
models change when applied to complex policy issues,
but that there is also a need for new types of model to
complement those currently in use. The characteristics
of these policy-level models, however, cannot be
adequately described with the language of rational
decision models and descriptive prediction models.
Table 6.1 compares the characteristics of the more
technical, operational-level models with those of the
proposed policy-level models. The well-structured
problems considered by operational-level management
concern technological systems which exhibit relatively
repetitive behavior. Hence, the alternative or outcome
space is relativley static, and uncertainty can be
treated with event probabilities. If these
probabilities cannot be developed from historical or
experimental event frequencies, they can be generated
subjectively. Whether the model is descriptive or
normative, however, its purpose is to assist the
decision-maker in searching for the best alternative,
i.e., the optimal solution.

The complex policy issues of top-level management,
on the other hand, concern sociotechnical systems which
exhibit a diversity of behavior, often innovative and
unpredictable. The set of possible outcomes is fuzzy,
primarily due to uncertainty in the dimensionality of
the set. The multidimensionality of the system and the
interconnectedness of the variables produce ambiguity
(fuzziness) with respect to whether outcomes are
possible or not. Furthermore, sociotechnical and
cultural relationships are dynamic, characterized by a
continually evolving value and knowledge base. Policy
models, of necessity, must rely on a generalized
structure and on subjective information. They must be
process-oriented in that their role is to assist in the
process of exposing information of a judgmental,
intuitive, or otherwise subjective nature and in
reconciling differences between individuals and between
groups of individuals.

A link between the language of traditional problem
solving and that of policymaking is provided by the
word   "constraint."   In   policymaking,   however,

Table 6.1   Comparison of Model Characteristics

Model Types

Model Characteristics	Operational-Level Models	Policy-Level Models
Purpose	Solving Technical Problems	Resolving Socio-Technical Issues
Structure	Well-Structured; Functional Relationships	Ill-Structured; Generalized Relationships
Focus	Goals and Objectives; Product-Oriented	Constraints (Perceptions and Values); Process-Oriented
Alternative Space	Well-Defined; Static	Fuzzy; Dynamic
Uncertainty Specification	Probabilities	Possibilities
Decision-Makers	One	Many
Decision Criteria	Few; Independent	Many; Conflicting
Search Rule	Optimization	Conflict Re/Dissolution
Primary Use	Selecting An Alternative	Generating Alternatives

constraint assumes a much broader and more significant role. The identification and manipulation of constraints is the key to generating alternatives. Keen[6] and Warfield[7] recognize the importance of this role. Bellman and Zadeh state that in fuzzy decisionmaking the distinction between goal and constraint is "erased";[8] and Simon concludes that the concept of organizational goal is best treated as a set of constraints.[9] In an operational-level model like linear programming, the constraints are well-defined, usually developed from resource and capacity measurements. A policy-level model needs to treat values and perceptions as constraints also. In the language we propose for policy-level modelling, we assume that each actor with a stake in a particular issue of policy/strategy (i.e., each "stakeholder") has a "mental" model of the situation, of the other actors in the situation, and of his/her own role in the situation. This mental model is represented by a set of constraints, i.e., a set of perceptions and values; it is individual and group differences with respect to these constraints that generate issues.

The need for a distinction between decision and descriptive models disappears at the policy-level; policy models must be descriptive of the policymaking process in order to filter information useful for policy decisions. Management becomes an integral part of the model, and the model of the management process. Starr and Zeleny make a distinction between "outcome-oriented" and "process-oriented" approaches. An outcome-oriented approach is "based on a view that one achieves an understanding of a process if one can predict its outcome accurately."[10] A process-oriented approach is "based on a notion that an understanding of the decision process, i.e., how the decisions are actually evolved, constitutes an alternative way of arriving at a correct prediction of choice while attempting to attain understanding of the underlying process as well."[11] In the process-oriented approach, much if not more knowledge is generated in the process of constructing the model as in the utilization of the final product.

The role of policy-level modeling, as Keen points out, is significantly different from the role of traditional models:

> Simon[12] summarizes the stages in the deci-
> sion process as Intelligence, Design, and
> Choice. The mainstream of optimization
> science has focused on Choice. The descrip-
> tively-based hybrid methodologies shift the
> emphasis to Intelligence and Design--the def-
> inition of relevant alternatives--and leaves
> the choice stage under the control of the
> decision maker's subjective judgement. Opti-
> mality is then a characteristic of the
> process rather than the solution and the role
> of the OR/MS analyst is to provide a suppor-
> tive and interactive methodology.[13]

Policy models must go even beyond Keen's statement above; to do so, however, requires a modelling language which supersedes terms like "decision maker" and "optimality."

6.2 MENTAL MODELS

In Chapter 4, we mentioned the work of Conant and Ashby who demonstrated that any good regulator of a system must possess a model of that system.[14] The implication is that the human mind being a regulator of human action both internally and externally, must possess a model of the self/environment system. The precise nature of this model we do not know; we only know that it must exist. However, we lean toward the Gestalt explanation—a dynamic distribution of stimuli, i.e., a pattern of stimulation resulting in organization.[15] Here the word "organization," while almost synonymous with the word "structure" defined in Chapter 5, takes on a slightly different connotation; the emphasis is on the relations that define a system as a whole, without reference to the nature of the system's components.[16] It is the pattern that is important, not the specific neurological components that form it. We will continue to use the word "structure," however, for in applying constraint theory to policy issues we will of necessity identify specific components or variables.

6.2.1 Background

A review of the psychological literature relevant to the topic of mental models reveals a wide diversity of terms, many of which seem arbitrary or unnecessary. We have, therefore, had to be highly selective in the terms we use and the distinctions we make. The intent is simply to clarify the language of mental models and to rigorously define a set of terms sufficient for communicating the concepts of policy formulation and the proposed mathematics of modelling. The process of definition, if carried to an extreme, can result in rigidification of the language, countermining our primary purpose for developing a modelling language.

The first distinction we make is between what Lewin calls topological problems and vector problems:

> In general one may say that topological tools allow us to determine which events are possi-

123

ble in a given life space and which are not
possible. Vector concepts are necessary to
determine further which of the possible
events will actually occur in a given
case.[17]

Lewin proceeded to develop the topological concepts --
boundary, region, psychological field -- concepts he
thought had been neglected in psychology. To "predict"
behavior, the traditional quest of psychology, requires
the vector concepts; but in complex situations
perceptions of boundary conditions and the flexibility
to adjust them are dominant factors. Alexander makes a
similar distinction, although the terms used are
culturally biased and misleading, between the
"unselfconscious" and "selfconscious" processes of
design. He argues that the selfconscious process, one
of attempting to predict and rationally plan
step-by-step, can result in reduced adaptive capability
in complex design problems.[18] Our focus is on the
topological concepts, on field of behavior and
constraint, and, hence, on the states excluded from the
alternative space or life space of the individual or
organization. In Western culture, this focus on
negative reasoning corresponds closely to Alexander's
unselfconscious process and perhaps to the process of
intuition.

While Lewin chose to describe his topological
concepts in what he called "hodological" space,[19] we
have chosen to define our terms in the mathematics of
set theory in Euclidean n-space. Representations in
Euclidean n-space have received substantial criticism
in recent years. For our purposes, however, these
representations are satisfactory as long as "time" is
not included as one of the n dimensions of the space.
This is consistent with Lewin's field theory, where
"behavior depends neither on the past nor on the future
but on the present field."[20] To study "lines" of
behavior over time, however, vector concepts are
needed, and Euclidean space may not be adequate for
this purpose. The exclusion of time as a variable
should not be interpreted as an intentional disregard
for the dynamics of behavior. To the contrary, it is
the complexity of this dynamics that leads necessarily
to the field approach.

The transformation of the field of behavior itself
is another issue; such a transformation is both the
result and intent of the participant-observer approach

124

to applied research. We do not know a priori what the outcome of participant-observer intervention will be; we know only that the process by which new fields are formulated involves adjustments in the perceptions and values of the organizational participants. Models of perceptions and values can facilitate communications in the policy formulation process, and possibly assist in generating creative policy alternatives.

Another distinction common in psychology is that between cognitive and affective processes. Varela prefers to consider a single "cognitive domain," defined by a pattern irrespective of whether the stimuli forming that pattern are electrical or chemical, mental or emotional.[21] Steinbruner combines his discussion of perceptions and values into the single topic of "cognitive processes."[22] Although we make a distinction between perceptions and values (and hence between cognitive and affective processes), we do so only for purposes of comparison with the means-ends distinction of the rational decisionmaking paradigm. In fact, perceptions and values are higly interdependent, each being conditioned by the other. We will use the term "constraint set"[23] to describe the cognitive domain as represented by the combination of both perceptions and values.

March and Simon also make a distinction between values/goals/attitudes and beliefs/perceptions/expectations in their concept of the "psychological set" of an individual.[24] "Frame or reference" is another term used to capture this concept.[25] One alternative for characterizing the distinction between perceptions and values is in terms of intrinsic and extrinsic constraint. Intrinsic constraint refers to the internal makeup of an individual and extrinsic constraint to the relationships in the external world. Values, then, are primarily intrinsic and perceptions are governed primarily by extrinsic constraint. But, as we discussed in Chapter 3, the self/environment distinction is not clearly delineated; "such a differentiation...is in a certain sense arbitrary."[26] Garner has a similar difficulty in isolating "internal" from "external" constraint:

It would be nice if there were perfect psychological performance counterparts of internal and external constraints, but there probably are not...the form of internal and

125

external constraint cannot be manipulated independently, since a given selection of
stimuli completely determines the form of
both types of constraint.[27]

Despite these limitations, the need for a clarification
of terms employed in modelling practice (e.g., "goals")
suggests that a distinction between perceptions and
values is useful.

6.2.2 Perception

Perception is distinguished from sensation in that
perception implies an internal pattern of activity,
i.e., an evoked response.[28] Sensation can occur
without such a response. Perception, then, is an
"adaptive updating of the state of orientation."[29]

The importance of perception has been articulated
by Taylor:

> It seems reasonable to assume...that the way
> in which a decision maker perceives a problem
> is a major determinant of the degree of un-
> certainty, complexity, and conflict he iden-
> tifies and hence the strategies he considers
> using. The influence of the decision maker's
> perceptual processes as a source of con-
> straints on problem-solving efforts, however,
> has received relatively little systematic
> attention in the literature of this
> field.[30]

We contend that in complex, ill-structured policy
situations, these constraints are of upmost importance.
In well-structured problems, rules exist for reaching a
solution within a set of given constraints. In
ill-structured issues, these rules do not apply and
adjustment of constraints is an appropriate heuristic
response.[31] The rules themselves are the subject of
policy formulation.

A policy situation consists of policy actors and
their constraint sets (mental models) and coalitions
and their constraint sets (culture).

Definition 6.1: A policy actor (A) is an individual with an active role in the policy formulation
process.

Definition 6.2: The _mental model_ or _image_ (G) of a policy situation (X) for actor i is the pattern of constraint (N_i) manifest on a set of policy variables ($x_1, x_2, \ldots x_n$).

$$G_i = N_i(x_1, x_2, \ldots x_n) \qquad (6\text{-}1)$$

If we decompose the constraint set of an actor into perceptions and values, perception corresponds to what in optimization theory is called the "feasible set of alternatives" and values to the "objective function."

Definition 6.3: _Extrinsic constraint_ (P_i) is the perception by actor i of the set of states or alternatives not reachable due to interactions in the actor's environment, including cultural relationships and values imposed by other actors.

Definition 6.4: _Intrinsic constraint_ (V_i) is the set of states or alternatives not acceptable to actor i as a result of interactions within the actor, including perceptual interactions.

The total constraint set is the union of extrinsic and intrinsic constraint:

$$N_i(X) = P_i(X) \cup V_i(X) \qquad (6\text{-}2)$$

Figure 6.1 is a two-dimensional diagram of extrinsic and intrinsic constraint. The shaded area is total constraint.

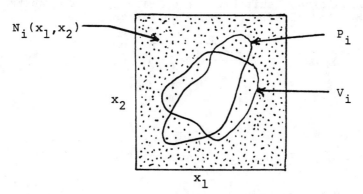

Figure 6.1 Extrinsic and Intrinsic Constraint

127

The limitations on human information processing imply that the number of policy variables perceived (i.e., the dimensionality of the alternative space) must be limited.[32] One does not perceive every aspect and detail of any situation. Rather, the mind selects for perception enough variables and relations among variables to be able to cope with the particular situation. If the information available is not sufficient, i.e., the situation is perceived to be too complex to manage, a process of either decomposing the relations perceived or searching for variables that enrich the perception of relations is undertaken.

In his discussion of visual perception and pattern recognition, Arbib makes a distinction between two strategies for identifying objects or patterns: straight-through analysis and nested analysis. In straight-through analysis, the strategy is to obtain as complete and precise a set of information as possible, and only then to attempt to identify the object or pattern. In nested analysis, the strategy is to hypothesize an object or pattern based on incomplete information, and then to search for additional information to confirm the hypothesis. Arbib claims that "humans use the nested analysis approach more than the straight-through approach: we see a contour, however ill defined, because we have recognized a cube, rather than recognize a cube because we have dutifully perceived all the contours."[33] (See Figure 6.2) In Chapter 7, we develop a mathematical approach to nested constraint analysis and generalized structural decomposition suitable for considering abstract patterns of constraint among policy variables.

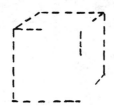

Figure 6.2   Contours of a Cube

6.2.3 Value Systems

We have defined individual values (attitudes) as an important aspect of intrinsic constraint. However,

128

values may also be shared by a group of individuals. In this context, the shared value system represents a "culture." Norms or standards of conduct are implicit in a value system, providing a set of social restraints on individual or group behavior. The "style" of an organization is also a reflection of its value system.

Definition 6.5: A value system is a set of constraints individually or culturally imposed on human behavior.

Vickers makes a distinction between "reality system" and "value system," as we have between perceptions and values:

> I will describe this system of schemata by means of which our world is ordered as a "reality system," although it is capable of representing the hypothetical, as well as the actual...Our world of reality is selected and structured by our interests and by the standards which our interests generate. I will comprehend these in the term "value"...They too are systematically organized, a value system, distinguishable from the reality system yet inseparable from it. For facts are relevant only by reference to some judgement of value and judgements of value are meaningful only in regard to some configuration of fact...I use the terms "reality system" and "value system" to describe the two complementary aspects of this organization, and "appreciative system" to describe them in the association in which they are always found.[34]

Vickers' "appreciative system," then, corresponds to our constraint set.

In the framework of rational decisionmaking, values are represented by goals and objectives and are considered independent of "means," the set of alternative courses of action. Multiple objectives are combined into a single objective function, and any conflict between the objectives of different policy actors is assumed to be resolved. The solution procedure for a decision problem so formulated is to find the most "efficient" alternative for achieving the specified goals and objectives. Vickers is highly critical of this approach to policymaking: "Policy does not consist in prescribing one goal or even one series of goals; but in regulating a system over time in such a way as to optimize the realization of many conflicting relations without wrecking the system in the process."[35] That is, the object of policy is the establishment of norms within which individuals can pursue their personal aspirations to the maximum extent possible without jeopardizing the social system as a whole. We refer to such policies as "value-rich."

The realization of value-rich policy, according to Vickers and others[36] is through participation and dialogue.

> A foreign policy, an educational policy, no less than a development plan, if they are to be more than a reaction to the most obvious pressing danger, need to display the charac-teristic qualities of a work of art--and call, in consequence, for common attitudes, as well as skills, in those who assess and support them, no less than in those who design them...The making of policy, especially in times of rapid change, involves continuing dialogue, based on readiness to question familiar assumptions and to consider the radical restructuring of problems.[37]

The need for participation and dialogue in policy formulation is one of the central premises of the modelling approach developed in Part III. The assumption of this need is itself a value judgment, one that the management scientist brings to a policy situation via his intervention in the organization.

Simon also recognizes the difficulty in treating the value system of an organization as an organizational "goal," and develops the notion of organizational goal as a set of constraints.[38] Building on Simon's concept, Taylor makes a distinction between explicit and implicit constraints. Explicit constraints are those that are formally recognized and promulgated, in written form or otherwise. "Implicit constraints are informally held by a decision maker, frequently without his awareness of their impact on his decision-making behavior."[39] In a culture, explicit constraints might include laws, rules, or written procedures, implicit constraints taboos, traditions, or rituals. In an individual, explicit constraints might include statements of preference, implicit constraints the broad set of relationships referred to as "personality."

The distinction between explicit and implicit constraints, however, is not always clear, just as the distinction between selfconscious and unselfconscious design processes is not clear. It is a useful distinction in that it allows us to create a spectrum of contrasting styles and personalities, and to demonstrate the limitations of certain classes of model with respect to different styles and personalitites. A linear programming model, for example, assumes a complete set of constraints; but the existence of implicit constraints could violate the assumptions of such a model, rendering its conclusions suspect. In their classification of managerial styles into "systematic" and "intuitive," McKenney and Keen point out that, for managers with a more intuitive style (perhaps more unselfconscious also), "the model must allow the manager to range over alternatives."[40] They contend that difficulties experienced in implementing management-oriented models stem in large part from the implicit constraints inherent in management behavior, particularly behavior characterized by the intuitive style. Yet, managerial intuition and judgment have proven to be vital factors in the resolution of complex policy issues.

6.3 GROUP PROCESS

As presented in Chapter 2, policy formulation involves the integration and reconciliation of the mental models of policy actors. The process of integration and reconciliation is characterized by negotiation, bargaining, compromise, persuasion, and cooperative learning. The relative power of the policy actors determines the extent to which they can influence the direction that process takes. As one means of altering the existing power structure, individual actors may form into groups or coalitions. The result of the policy formulation process is the resolution (or dissolution) of conflicting values and perceptions among the actors and coalitions.

6.3.1 Coalitions

Definition 6.6: A coalition (C) is a set of policy actors ($A_1, A_2 ...$) for which the difference between the constraint set for each actor [$N_1(X)$]

131

and that actor's perception of the shared constraint set of the coalition $\{G_i[N_c(X)]\}$ is within
an acceptable disagreement tolerance d_i.

The constraint set of a coalition is the constraint set
accepted by all members of the coalition for the
particular situation as defined on X. Notationally,
then:

$$C = \left\{ A_1, A_2, \ldots \middle| G_i[N_c(X)] - N_i(X) \subseteq d_i, \; \forall\, i \right\} \quad (6\text{-}3)$$

In Figure 6.3, a necessary condition for actor i to
join coalition k is that the shaded area be within the
acceptable limit d_i; d_i is the set of subsets in the
defined state space that actor i is willing to let
violate his constraint set in return for the leverage
he receives as a member of the coalition. The
characteristics of d_i reflect the relative power of
actor i with respect to the coalition and the perceived
impacts of policies resulting from the membership of
actor i in alternative coalitions (including a
coalition consisting of actor i alone). An actor may
alter a coalition's constraint set when he joins,
depending on his power relative to the coalition and
the other actors in it. The power of an actor derives
from his relative knowledge, persuasive skills,
personal friendships, access to resources and
sanctions, and recognized stature, prestige, and
authority.

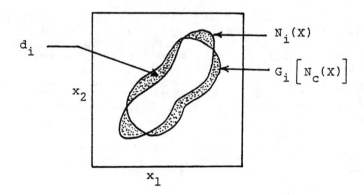

Figure 6.3   Coalition Formation

The perceptions of the constraint set of a coalition may not be identical for each member of the coalition. These perceptions may not even be defined on the same set of variables. In fact, ambiguity in the constraint set can serve the purpose of satisfying each actor, without acquiring total consensus of coalition members. The dynamics of coalition formation involve a set of complicated transactions. These transactions depend on the communicative proximity of the actors, on their knowledge and perceptions of each other, on their individual personalities and interpersonal styles, and on the presence of an organizing catalyst. Because the prevailing power structure of an organization is usually transformed by coalition formation, barriers to such processes are inevitable. The distortion or withholding of information and the physical separation of actors who represent a potentially threatening coalition are not uncommon practices in large organizations.[41] The sequencing of information can also affect the coalition formation process.[42]

The literature on power structure and coalition formation is not particularly useful in providing insights into the political process. A distinction is frequently made, for example, between power, authority, and influence, but "while power attaches to persons, authority to positions and statuses, and influence to ideas and ideologies, these concepts in reality are interrelated, and because of this do not ordinarily lend themselves to analysis on a separate basis."[43] Some efforts have focused on developing measures on the power of an individual or a coalition. These measures have a basis in game theory[44] and on the probabilities of influencing the outcome of a group decision.[45] We contend, however, that the power of an individual or a group is not the same for different policy issues and that it can change significantly in a short period of time. Hence, the value of measuring relative power at a point in time is limited.

The dynamics of coalition formation has been the subject of a number of studies. Recognizing the complex interactions possible in the process of coalition formation, Cyert and March simplify the process by postulating a "dominant coalition;" but they recognize that "drawing the boundaries of an organizational coalition once and for all is impossible."[46] Building on the Cyert and March formulation, Thompson develops a set of propositions.

For example:

> The more sources of uncertainty or contingency for
> the organization, the more bases there are for
> power and the larger the number of political
> positions in the organization.
>
> The more dynamic the technology and task environ-
> ment, the more rapid the political processes in
> the organization and the more frequent the changes
> in organizational goals.[47]

As the policy formulation process becomes more complex,
the notion of a dominant coalition that embodies the
constraint set of the organization becomes an
abstraction. That is, a dominant coalition is a
representation of the outcome of the policy formulation
process, not an entity per se.

Our view is that as policy situations become more
complex, more sophisticated informal political
structures evolve.[48] These structures reflect the
bargaining process among coalitions and subcoalitions
and sub-subcoalitions. This bargaining process
involves negotiation across the policy variables in an
issue, across domains that intersect different policy
situations, and across policy issues themselves. The
result of this process is the formation of new
coalitions--some homogeneous, others heterogeneous.
The number of possible combinations is simply too great
to permit prediction of the outcome of the process.

The role of the management scientist in these
situations does not require prediction of the outcome.
The model is a vehicle for facilitating dialogue and
participation among the policy actors. Hence, the
management scientist is himself a participant in the
policy formulation process, bringing to it his own
mental model of the conditions that, in his opinion,
assist in directing the process toward value-rich
policy. In addition, we believe that improved dialogue
and participation can lead to the generation of
creative alternatives, and hence, on occasion, avoid
the fate of disjointed incrementalism.

6.3.2 Conflict Resolution

In Chapter 2, we defined a policy issue as a
complex system of problems and as a situation of
inherent conflict.

<u>Definition 6.7</u>: A <u>policy issue</u> is imminent when
the difference between a coalition's shared constraint set $[N_k(X)]$ and its shared perception of
the constraint set of another coalition q,
$\{G_k[N_q(X)]\}$, is greater than some acceptable conflict threshold (f_k).

$$
I_{k,q} = \begin{cases} 1 & \text{if } G_k[N_q(X)] - N_k(X) \supset f_k \\ 0 & \text{otherwise} \end{cases} \qquad (6\text{-}4)
$$

Conflict between <u>at least</u> two coalitions is a minimal
condition for the generation of an issue, although only
one coalition needs to recognize the conflict. That
is, a particular situation may be an issue for one
coalition but not for another, depending on the
perception of difference and the conflict threshold
levels of the coalitions involved. As with
disagreement tolerances, conflict threshold levels
reflect both the relative power of a coalition and its
shared perception of the possible impacts of
alternative policies.

The modelling of conflict situations has been
dominated by the game-theoretic framework. Classic
game theory lends itself particularly well to zero-sum
games, where a gain by one actor is an equal loss to
another. As Deutsch points out, "this concept is
particularly convenient for the analysis of situations
of merciless interest antagonism in two-person
games."[49] But actual conflict situations involve
many actors and combinations of actors that "have not
only antagonistic interests but also significant
interests in common."[50] This area of mixed interest
games is explored by Schelling.[51] The strategies
employed in mixed interest situations are much more
sophisticated than those in antagonistic games. Some
of these strategies include bluffs, delay tactics,
threats, and promises.[52] Deutsch suggests that
limiting consideration to these more "rational"
strategies is to ignore an important category: "It is
known that repeated frustrations increase the
probability of an 'irrational' or 'spiteful' response,
and frightened and overstrained men may react
aggressively."[53]

135

In a gaming experiment conducted with top executives of a bank, for example, Richards and Graham observed that the behavior of a team, playing the role of a consumer advocacy group, was erratic; this behavior was perceived by the other team, playing the role of the bank's planning committee, to be irrational.[54] The point is that erratic behavior is a viable strategy, particularly when a coalition perceives itself in a position of relatively little power. Classic game theory does not treat these types of strategy.

MacMillan[55] formulates the process of political negotiation in terms of the minimum and maximum acceptable levels of policy variables for the actors involved. Figure 6.4 diagrams this formulation for the case of two actors, A and B, and a single variable, x_1. The shaded area represents the zone in which negotiations will occur. While we accept this basic formulation, it should be pointed out that, when many variables and many actors are involved, there may be no mutually acceptable negotiating zone, and that perceptions of the negotiating zone may be quite different for the different actors.

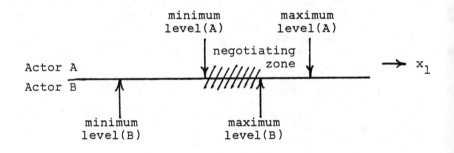

Figure 6.4   Negotiating Zone

Definition 6.8: Conflict resolution is the trans-
formation of the difference between a coalition's shared constraint set $[N_k(X)]$ and its shared perception of the constraint set of another coalition $\{G_k[N_q(X)]\}$ from greater than to equal to or less than the conflict threshold (f_k).

Resolution of conflict can result from a change in

perception of the situation or of the constraint sets of the other coalitions (learning); a change in the values of one or more of the coalitions involved (persuasion); a change in the conflict threshold levels (bargaining or compromising); or a change in the constraint sets or conflict threshold effected through the direct exercise of power (coercion). Conflict resolution, or course, is an ongoing and continuous process. Evidence that some conflict has been resolved takes the form of statements of policy or strategy.

> Definition 6.9: Organizational policy is an explicit statement of guidance reflecting the outcome of conflict resolution and designed to constrain the behavior of the members of the organization.

Writing policies that reflect the outcomes of conflict resolution is not always a straightforward task. Issues that arise from differences between written policy and the resolution of conflict may require a metapolicy.[56] Ambiguity in policy, however, is not necessarily the result of poor policy writing; it may reflect the nature of a particular issue and how it was resolved.

6.4 SOME POLICY CONSIDERATIONS

In this chapter, we have attempted to clarify some of the language associated with policy formulation, and to develop it with sufficient rigor to accommodate the mathematical concepts to be discussed in Chapter 7. The need for this development derives from the barriers that the language of rational decisionmaking pose to the design of new model structures and roles. Two additional terms associated with the rational decisionmaking approach to modelling, and also commonly used in everyday conversation, need clarification -- probability and optimization.

6.4.1 Uncertainty

"Probability" is a term that has come to be used almost synonymously with "uncertainty." The rational decisionmaking paradigm for modelling assumes that uncertainty can be specified in terms of probabilities.[57] Dror, however, is critical of contemporary decision analysis and its reliance on probabilistic uncertainty, observing that it:

...has difficulties dealing with "irrational"
phenomena, such as ideologies, charisma, high-risk
commitments, martyr tendencies, and unconventional
styles of life.
...is unable to deal with basic value issues and
often inadequately explicates the value assumptions of analysis.
...deals with identifying preferable alternatives
among available or easily synthesized ones. In-
vention of radically new alternatives is beyond
its scope, although it can probably help by
showing the inadequacy of available alternatives.
...requires some predictability in respect to
alternatives. Situations of primary uncertainty
cannot be handed by systems [decision]
analysis.[58]

By "primary uncertainty," Dror is referring to
situations where one is ignorant not only of the
probability distributions of possible outcomes but also
of the dimensions of possible outcomes. The
implication is not that decision models have no
usefulness for policy analysis, but rather that they
need to be placed in a conceptual framework that is
more consistent with the complex characteristics of the
social systems being modelled.

In reference to the probabilistic specification of
uncertainty, Steinbruner states:

Though this conception of uncertainty is an
exceedingly important one, it is too narrow to
capture the meaning of uncertainty for the complex
policy problem, for it assumes that a great deal
of inferential structure can be imposed on the
decision problem with complete confidence. It
assumes that the range of possible outcomes is
known and thereby eliminates the possibility than
an outcome might occur which was not even
visualized in advance. It assumes that the
operating characteristics of the game are known--
i.e., that its rules are specified and stable.
For complex problems neither of these assumptions
can be held.[59]

Steinbruner uses the term "structural uncertainty" to
refer to uncertainty in the ability to impose enough
structure on a situation so that possible outcomes can
even be described.

138

Definition 6.10: Structural uncertainty (u) is a characteristic of a constraint set referring to lack of complete confidence that the necessary and sufficient variables (dimensions) of a situation have been considered or that sets of variables have been adequately decomposed (structured).

The result of structural uncertainty is ambiguity with respect to whether a state or alternative is or is not a member of the constraint set. Fuzzy set theory provides a treatment of structural uncertainty by assigning a membership grade to each element in a set.[60] The grade assigned, then, depends on an individual's confidence that a state or alternative is excluded from the set of possible states. Figure 6.5 is a diagram of a fuzzy constraint set. For each n-tuple defined on the state space, X, there is assigned a grade of membership:

$$N_i(X) = \left\{ [n_1, u_i(n_1)], [n_2, u_i(n_2)], \ldots \right\} \qquad (6-5)$$

where $n_1, n_2 \ldots$ are n-tuples in $N(X)$. The grades of membership do not carry information about the probabilities of the states, only subjective ambiguity with respect to whether states are even reachable within the specified time horizon.

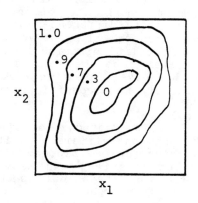

Figure 6.5 Structural Uncertainty

139

Friend and Jessop refer to three types of uncertainty: "uncertainties in knowledge of the external environment, uncertainties as to future intentions in related fields of choice, and uncertainties as to appropriate value judgements."[61] While the ability to separate these types of uncertainty in a policy situation may not exist, the important point is the recognition of uncertainty of more than the first type. In fact, "It is through a perception of our second kind of uncertainty -- uncertainty as to intentions in related fields of choice -- that the process of decision first begins to become one of planning or strategic choice."[62] Reduction of this type of uncertainty requires an expansion of the decision field, i.e., adding relevant variables or integrating and restructuring fields previously separated. Since we have argued that perceptions and values are difficult to separate, we also choose not to separate decision fields from value judgments.[63] Furthermore, there is a role for probabilities and decision analysis within the context of policy guidance and strategic choice. Our focus is on the process of providing that context.

6.4.2 Policy Criteria

In situations where (1) the preferences and values of individual policy actors can be reduced to a single preference or utility function; (2) there is either little disagreement among the actors or specified procedures for resolving differences among actors; and (3) uncertainty in the alternative space can be specified with probability distributions, optimization is an appropriate concept for selecting among alternatives. We have tried to make the point, however, that none of these conditions prevail in many policy situations.

Thompson, in his "paradox of administration," distinguishes between the efficiency criterion and the flexibility criterion.[64] Efficiency lends itself to the concept of optimization, and is an appropriate criterion for solving technical problems at the operational levels of an organization. Flexibility, on the other hand, is an essential criterion for ensuring an organization's capability to respond to unanticipated disturbances. Bateson defines flexibility "as uncommitted potentiality for change."[65] The dilemma of policy-level management is one of finding the correct balance between efficiency (an achievement or goal orientation) and flexibility (a survival or constraint orientation.)

Myers makes a similar distinction in his comparison of Holling's concept of "resilience" (a measure of the ability of a system to absorb changes and still persist[66]) with the policy formulation and planning concepts advanced by Lindblom, Ackoff, and Argenti.[67] Lindblom argues that by taking a satisficing orientation and by relying on a political process for resolving issues, adaptability to unexpected events is enhanced.[68] Ackoff contends that a satisficing orientation does not permit an organization to realize its potential for excellence, and that organizations that seek an ideal do not necessarily lose flexibility.[69] Argenti, in his study of corporate failure, suggests that organizations ought to seek both achievement and resilience, but that the latter is more often neglected.[70]

Our view is that the need for "achievement" is an individual attribute, and that an organization provides a structured arena within which the achievement aspirations of an organization's members are accommodated. Certain achievements, of course, require coordination of individual efforts, which require compatible aspirations. When conflicts occur, the role of policy is to provide guidance with respect to permissable pursuits. The appropriate criterion for policy formulation is to permit the members of an organization maximum latitude in pursuing their aspirations while ensuring that the organization itself persists. In this context, achievement is not separate from, but rather intrinsic to, the survival orientation. That is, the survival orientation transcends and incorporates the achievement orientation. Furthermore, providing flexibility with respect to individual achievement accommodates creativity and the generation of innovative responses to unanticipated events. Too much flexibility, however, can result in disturbances from within the organization that may threaten its survival.

The implication is that some fluctuation in organizational performance is desirable. The amount of fluctuation to permit, however, depends on perceptions of the amount of complexity and uncertainty confronting the organization and of the organization's capability to appropriately respond to it. Eoyang has shown that, up to a point, variability in corporate performance

141

measures results in higher performance over the long-run. Corporations that exhibit relatively small or relatively large amounts of variability do not fare as well.[71] There is apparently a critical balance between stability and flexibility.

In the management science literature, flexibility as a decision criterion has been operationalized and given the name "robustness."[72] Robustness refers to the amount of constraint imposed on future decisions as a result of commitments made in the present. The larger the decision field (i.e., policy domain) remaining, the more robust the decision.[73] "All decisions limit the future by committing the present."[74] But the present must be committed, even if no action is taken; and there is a cost associated with selecting commitments based on robustness. "It may be necessary to weigh the apparent loss of value involved in adopting a robust decision, against the loss in flexibility in adopting the 'optimal' decision."[75]

> Definition 6.11: Robustness is the degree to which policy constrains the field of behavior of an organization.

Robustness, as a response to shared perceptions of uncertainty, is related to the concepts of requisite variety and variety amplification. In Chapter 7, we develop the concept of robustness more rigorously and attempt to generalize it for use not only in selecting among a set of commitments but also in formulating the policies that limit the set of commitments considered.

NOTES

1. William G. Ouchi, "A Conceptual Framework for the Design of Organizational Control Mechanisms," Management Science 25(September 1979): 833-848.

2. "Piercing Future Fog in the Executive Suite," Business Week, April 28, 1975, p. 48.

3. Ibid.

4. Ibid., p. 47.

5. Ibid.

6. Peter G. W. Keen, "The Evolving Concept of Optimality," in Multiple Criteria Decision Making, ed. Martin K. Starr and Milan Zeleny (Amsterdam: North-Holland Publishing Co., 1977), p. 53.

7. "Perhaps the most powerful way to approach such issues (behavioral issues involved in policymaking) is in terms of constraints on human behavior." John N. Warfield, Societal Systems: Planning, Policy, and Complexity (New York: John Wiley & sons, 1976), pp. 110-111.

8. R. E. Bellman and L. A. Zadeh, "Decision-Making in a Fuzzy Environment," Management Science 17(December 1970): B-147.

9. Herbert A. Simon, "On the Concept of Organizational Goal," Administrative Science Quarterly 9(June 1964): 1-22.

10. Martin K. Starr and Milan Zeleny, "MCDM-State and Future of the Arts," in Multiple Criteria Decision Making, ed. Starr and Zeleny (Amsterdam: North-Holland Publishing Co., 1977), p. 25.

11. Ibid.

12. Herbert A. Simon, The New Science of Management Decision (New York: Harper and Row, 1960).

13. Keen, p. 52.

14. Roger C. Conant and W. Ross Ashby, "Every Good Regulator of a System Must be a Model of That System," International Journal of Systems Science 1(1970): 89-97.

15. Wolfgang Kohler, Gestalt Psychology (New York: The New American Library, 1947), p. 97.

16. Humberto R. Maturana, "Cognitive Strategies, " unpublished manuscript (Cambridge, Mass.: Massachusetts Institute of Technology, undated).

17. Kurt Lewin, Principles of Topological Psychology, trans. Fritz Heider and Grace M. Heider (New York: McGraw-Hill, 1936), p. 85.

18. Christopher Alexander, Notes on the Synthesis of Form (Cambridge, Mass.: Harvard University Press,

1964), Chapters 4 and 5.

19. Kurt Lewin, Field Theory in Social Science, ed. Dorwin Cartwright (Chicago: University of Chicago Press, 1951), p. 25.

20. Ibid., p. 27.

21. Francisco J. Varela, Principles of Biological. Autonomy (New York: Elsevier North-Holland, 1979), pp. 260-265.

22. John D. Steinbruner, The Cybernetic Theory of Decision (Princeton, N. J.: Princeton University Press, 1974), Chapter 4.

23. The term "constraint set" is used similarly in Thomas P. Ferrence, "Organizational Communications Systems and the Decision Process," Management Science 17(October 1970): B83-B96.

24. James G. March and Herbert A. Simon, Organizations (New York: John Wiley & sons, 1958), p. 11.

25. Paul Watzlawick, Janet Helmick Beavin, and Don D. Jackson, Pragmatics of Human Communication (New York: W. W. Norton & Company, 1967), Chapter 1.

26. Gregory Bateson, "Information and Codification: A Philosophical Approach," in Jurgen Ruesch and Bateson, Communication: The Social Matrix of Psychiatry (New York: W. W. Norton & Company, 1968), p. 188.

27. Wendell R. Garner, Uncertainty and Structure as Psychological Concepts (Huntington, N. Y.: Robert E. Krieger Publishing Company, 1962), p. 174.

28. Donald M. MacKay, Information, Mechanism and Meaning (Cambridge, Mass.: The M.I.T. Press, 1969), p. 68.

29. Donald M. MacKay, "The Informational Analysis of Questions and Commands," in Modern Systems Research for the Behavioral Scientist, ed. Walter Buckley (Chicago: Aldine Publishing Company, 1968), p. 205.

30. Ronald N. Taylor, "Perception of Problem Constraints," Management Science 22(September 1975):22.

31. Ibid., pp. 25-27.

32. See George A. Miller, "The Magical Number Seven Plus or Minus Two," Psychological Review 63(1956): 81-97.

33. Michael A. Arbib, The Metaphorical Brain (New York: John Wiley and Sons, 1972), pp. 110-111.

34. Geoffrey Vickers, Value Systems and Social Process (Middlesex, England: Penguin Books Ltd., 1968), pp. 197-198.

35. Geoffrey Vickers, Freedom in a Rocking Boat: Changing Values in an Unstable Society (Middlesex, England: Penguin Books Ltd., 1970), p. 116.

36. For example, John Friedmann, Retracking America: A Theory of Transactive Planning (Garden City, New York: Anchor Press/Doubleday, 1973).

37. Vickers, Value Systems, p. 104.

38. Simon, "Organizational Goal."

39. Taylor, pp. 24-25.

40. James L. McKenney and Peter G. W. Keen, "How Managers' Minds Work," Harvard Business Review, May/June 1974, p. 88.

41. In his discussion of bureaucratic behavior in government operations, Stockfisch states that "manipulation of data, including avoidance of collecting important kinds of data, becomes a feature of a bureau's 'management'." J. A. Stockfisch, Analysis of Bureaucratic Behavior: The Ill-Defined Production Process, P-5591 (Santa Monica, Calif.: The RAND Corporation, January 1976), pp. 15-16.

42. Ian C. MacMillan, Strategy Formulation: Political Concepts (St. Paul, Minn.: West Publishing Company, 1978), p. 61.

43. William R. Sherrard and Richard D. Steade, "Power Comparability--Its Contribution to a Theory of Firm Behavior," Management Science 13(December 1966): B-187.

44. Michael Maschler, "The Power of a Coalition," Management Science 10(October 1963): 8-29.

45. Sherrard and Steade; Raini Hofshi and James F. Korsh, "A Measure of an Individual's Power in a Group," Management Science 19(September 1972): 52-61.

46. Richard M. Cyert and James March, A Behavioral Theory of the Firm (Englewood Cliffs, N. J.: Prentice-Hall, 1963): 27.

47. James D. Thompson, Organizations in Action (New York: McGraw-Hill, 1967), p. 129.

48. See MacMillan, pp. 63-64.

49. Karl W. Deutsch, The Nerves of Government (New York: The Free Press, 1966), p. 66.

50. Ibid., p. 67.

51. Thomas C. Schelling, The Strategy of Conflict (Cambridge, Mass.: Harvard University Press, 1960).

52. See MacMillan, Chapter 3.

53. Deutsch, p. 70.

54. Laurence D. Richards and Robert J. Graham, "Identifying Problems Through Gaming," Interfaces 7(May 1977): 76-79.

55. MacMillan, pp. 29-32.

56. Warfield, p. 103.

57. See Ralph L. Keeney and Howard Raiffa, Decisions with Multiple Objectives (New York: John Wiley & Sons, 1976), pp. 5-7.

58. Yehezkel Dror, "Prolegomena to Policy Sciences," Policy Science 1(1970): 140.

59. Steinbruner, pp. 17-18.

60. Bellman and Zadeh, p. B-143.

61. J. K. Friend and W. N. Jessop, Local Government and Strategic Choice, 2nd Edition (Oxford: Pergamon Press, 1977), p. 106.

146

62. Ibid., p. 108.

63. We refer to conjunctions of decision fields and value systems as constraint or policy domains.

64. Thompson, pp. 148-150.

65. Gregory Bateson, "Ecology and Flexibility in Urban Civilization," in Steps to an Ecology of Mind (New York: Ballantine Books, 1972), p. 497.

66. C. S. Holling, "Resilience and Stability in Ecological Systems," in Evolution and Consciousness: Human Systems in Transition, ed. Eric Jantsch and Conrad Waddington (Reading, Mass.: Addison-Wesley, 1976), p. 83.

67. Kent C. Myers, "Rationale for a Corporate Resilience Strategy," Proceedings of the Twenty-Fourth Annual North American Meeting of the Society for General Systems Research, 1980, pp. 540-547.

68. C. E. Lindblom, Politics and Markets: The World's Political-Economic Systems (New York: Basic Books, 1977).

69. Russell L. Ackoff, A Concept of Corporate Planning (New York: John Wiley & Sons, 1970).

70. John Argenti, Corporate Collapse: The Causes and Symptoms (New York: John Wiley & Sons, 1976).

71. Carson Eoyang, in presentation of "Requisite Variety in Organizations," Proceedings of the 22nd Annual North American Meeting of the Society for General Systems Research, 1978, pp. 369-378.

72. Shiv K. Gupta and Jonathan Rosenhead, "Robustness in Sequential Investment Decisions," Management Science 15(October 1968): B18-B29.

73. Friend and Jessop, p. 237.

74. Jonathan Rosenhead, Martin Elton, and Shiv K. Gupta, "Robustness and Optimality as Criteria for Strategic Decisions," Operational Research Quarterly 23(1972): 418.

75. Ibid., p. 427.

CHAPTER 7

MODELLING MATHEMATICS

The constraint-theoretic approach to modelling has implications not only for the language of policy formulation but also for the mathematical analysis used in the research and modelling process. The key concepts in the mathematics of constraint theory are nested constraint analysis, structural decomposition, structural uncertainty, and robustness. These concepts provide an integrating framework for the modelling approach developed in Part III. Constraint theory does not replace the mathematics of decision and predictive models, but rather complements and generalizes it. It does, however, have significant implications for the interpretation of the assumptions and outputs of those models when applied to policy formulation.

This chapter presents these mathematical concepts, thus providing a basis for a rigorous treatment of system structure, mental models, and issue analysis.

7.1 CONSTRAINT ANALYSIS

Ashby may have been the first to take Wiener's generalized notion of relation and constraint[1] and develop an analytical framework from it.[2] Friedman and Leondes developed it further for the purpose of determining the computability and consistency of a set of large-scale mathematical models.[3] Klir,[4] Broekstra,[5] and Krippendorff[6] have applied constraint analysis to the problem of structure identification; the latter two use information-theoretic measures as indications of amount of structure, where structure and constraint are equivalent concepts. We rely primarily on Ashby's original development, although we do use a measure of disagreement developed by Krippendorff as an indication of amount of structural uncertainty. That measure is presented in a later section of this chapter.

149

7.1.1 Relational Projections

A fundamental assumption of our representation of mental models is that the human mind does not perceive or process simultaneously all the variables and relations among them when structuring a complex situation. Rather, it selects for attention certain variables and subrelations, although it may connect subrelations with a "metastructure." Examples of these metastructures are discussed in the next section. We refer to the subrelations as "projections" of the higher order relation.

> Definition 7.1: A projection (Pr) of an n-dimensional relation (R) is the set of m-tuples (m<n) in a subspace with m dimensions such that each element of the set satisfies the m dimensions of R.[7]

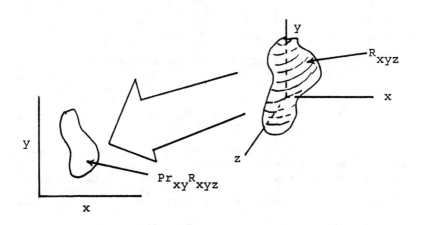

Figure 7.1 Projection

Figure 7.1 depicts the projection of a three-dimensional relation (R_{xyz}) onto the two-dimensional xy subspace ($Pr_{xy}R_{xyz}$). Projection is, then, a dimension reducing operation.[8]

If $i \in I$ is an index for the dimensions of an Euclidean state space, S^n, ($i = 1,...,n$); $j \in J$ is an index for the dimensions of a subspace of S^n, S^m, ($j=1, ...,m$ and $J \subset I$); and a_i is any n-tuple (element) composed of one component from each dimension i, the

150

notation for the projection of a_i from S^n to S^m is:

$$Pr(a_i)_{i \in I} = (a_i)_{i \in J} \qquad (7\text{-}1)$$

For a relation, R_I, with elements r_i,

$$Pr_J R_I = (r_i)_{i \in J} = \bigcup_{i \in J} a_i \in R_I \qquad (7\text{-}2)$$

For two sets A and B, some properties of their projections include the following:

$$(1) \quad \text{If } A \subset B, \ Pr_J A \subset Pr_J B \qquad (7\text{-}3)$$

$$(2) \quad Pr_J(A \cap B) \subset (Pr_J A) \cap (Pr_J B) \qquad (7\text{-}4)$$

Property (2) implies that the intersection of the projections of two sets encompasses or bounds the projection of the <u>actual</u> intersection of the sets.[9]

To accurately collect the data necessary to construct a relational projection, the focus needs to be on identifying the states <u>excluded</u> from the set of possibilities rather than on the most likely states. If these data are generated subjectively, as was the case in the issue analysis performed for the MFS Finance Corporation, the structure of the data collection instrument must reflect this focus. The questionnaire we used, for example, explicitly asked respondents to specify the acceptable and feasible <u>limits</u> (i.e., the constraints) on the variables of concern. These limits represent one-dimensional projections of the relations among the variables. We propose the development of higher order projections by taking advantage of the different perspectives of the individuals participating in the exercise. By superimposing the various perspectives, multidimensional shape begins to emerge in the relationships apparent in the data.

7.1.2 Cylindrical Closure

The inverse of the projective operation is extension. That is, if a projection in m-space is extended into n-space, a cylinder is formed with the m-dimensional projection as its base and the other n-m variables being unrestricted. Figure 7.2 illustrates the extension of a two-dimensional set (M_{xy}) into three dimensions (xyz).

151

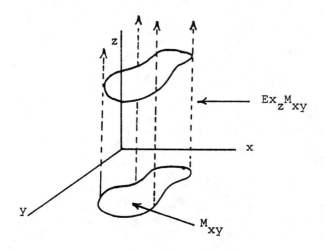

Figure 7.2 Extension

Definition 7.2: The extension (Ex) of an m-dimensional set (M_J) into n dimensions (n>m) is the set of all n-tuples containing as components the elements of M_J.[10]

Sometimes the notation used for extension is the inverse projection symbol, Pr^{-1}. We use Ex.

The notation for the extension of a set (M_J) defined on the subspace S^m to the space S^n (where m<n) is:

$$Ex_{I-J}M_J = M_J \times \prod_{i \in I-J} S^i \qquad (7-5)$$

We refer to this extension as the cylindrical set on M_J. The intersection of the cylindrical sets on all p-dimensional projections (p m) of a relation R_n is called the cylindrical closure of order p for R_n.

Definition 7.3: The cylindrical closure (C_p) of order p (p≤n) on an n-dimensional relation R_I, forming all cylinders in S^n with these projections as bases, and then taking the intersection of all cylinders.[11]

$$C_p R_I = \bigcap_k Ex_{I-K}Pr_K R_I \qquad (7-6)$$

152

where K is the set of all p-dimensional subspaces in S^n. The number of projections of dimension p in an n-dimensional space is easily found as the combination of n variables taken p at a time:

$$\frac{n!}{(n-p)!p!} \qquad (7-7)$$

Some important properties of cylindrical closure include the following.[12]

$$(1) \quad C_0 R_I = S^n \qquad (7-8)$$

$$(2) \quad C_n R_I = R_I \qquad (7-9)$$

$$(3) \quad C_p R_I \subset C_m R_I, \text{for } m \leq p \qquad (7-10)$$

Property (3) implies that the set of cylindrical closures of a relation, R_I, form a nested set. That is, as p increases from zero to n, the respective cylindrical closures lose elements and increasingly approximate the actual relation. The relation is bounded by the constraints as defined by the cylindrical closures. The significance of this property is that a very complex relation can be studied in lower than full dimensionality. If the approximations to the relation as represented by the lower dimensional projections is not sufficient for the purposes of the study, the dimensionality can be increased sequentially until the information about the relation is adequate.

The nested constraint analysis performed for MFS Finance and described in Chapter 10 took precisely this approach. Examining the data first in one dimension, then in two, etc., a point was eventually reached at which there was sufficient information to form some hypotheses about the nature of the relationships. The relations that were more "complex" were indicated by a requirement for analysis in higher dimensionality.

7.1.3 Cylindrance

An important observation of the set theoretic framework above is that, in general:[13]

$$Ex_{I-J}(Pr_J R_I) \neq R_I \qquad (7-11)$$

That is, we cannot reconstruct a relation simply by

153

extending a lower dimension projection of the relation. Krippendorff argues that this is precisely what many statistical techniques do, and that the relationships formed may be greatly distorted as a result.[14] Multiple regression, for example, treats only one variable as dependent while assuming the others independent. Correlation and factor analysis treat only binary relations, i.e., two-dimensional projections. This is not to say that statistical techniques are useless tools, but only that their applicability is limited. A more generalized framework of analysis is needed. The set-theoretic framework developed by Ashby (primarily in response to the ill-structured relations observed in biology) provides this generality.

As its concepts are initially quite free from any implication of either continuity, or of order, or of metric, or of linearity (though in no way excluding them), the method can be applied to the facts of biology without the facts having to be distorted for merely mathematical reasons.[15]

To treat all relations in their full dimensionality, however, is not practical. "The Law," for example, consists of thousands of variables. "Yet, it can, in fact, be dealt with piecemeal; for it is built by the intersection of such subrelations as: Drivers of age x may drive only automobiles of class y."[16] The concepts of cylindrance and irrelevant variable are introduced to specify the conditions under which a multi-dimensional relation can be treated as a set of subrelations.

> Definition 7.4: The cylindrance (cyl) of a rela-
> tion (R_I) is the smallest p for which the cylin-
> drical closure $C_p R_I$ is equal to R_I.

That is,

$$\text{cyl } R_I = \min(p: C_p R_I = R_I) \qquad (7\text{-}12)$$

Cylindrance, then, is a measure of the intrinsic complexities of a relation.[17] However, two relations that have the same cylindrance may not be equivalently complex, for complexity depends on the purposes of the observer or modeller as much as on the relation observed. Hence, a relation may be treated in lower dimensionality simply because the information provided in the lower dimensional representation is sufficiently approximate for the use to be made of it. That is, the effort required to obtain information in higher dimensionality is not justified by the value of the information obtained.

Reducing the dimensionality of an n-dimensional relation to p dimensions is always justified when the cylindrance (p) of the relation is less than n. The following theorem justifies a further reduction in dimensionality (if the implications of the theorem are properly understood).

Theorem 7.1: Every relation is contained in all its cylindrical closures.[18]

$$R_I \subset C_p R_n \ \forall \ p \leq n \qquad (7-13)$$

The proof follows from equation (7-10).

This theorem guarantees that the elements of the constraint set of the projections of a relation and of the intersection of the cylinders formed with those projections as bases are elements of the constraint set of the relation itself. The implication is that, while the lower dimensional representation bounds the relation, the relation itself may contain subtle complexities of which the modeller or analyst might be unaware. Reliance on a plan of action based on lower dimensional information could lead to unanticipated consequences if the subtle complexities are not detected in time. Establishing a rigid line of behavior based on incomplete information reduces the ability of an organization to react and adapt to these unanticipated consequences. However, the role of policy formulation we prescribe is simply to establish the limits necessary to accommodate the values of the individuals in an organization while maintaining the organization as a viable entity. We contend that information on constraint sets, i.e., the limiting values and perceptions, is useful for this purpose.

Definition 7.5: An irrelevant variable is one that does not alter a constraint set sufficiently to justify adding it to the dimensionality of the analyses being performed.

This is, y is an irrelevant variable if for a three-dimensional relation, R_{xyz}:

$$Ex_y(Pr_{xy}R_{xyz}) \cong R_{xyz} \qquad (7-14)$$

155

The determination of sufficient approximation depends, of course, on the judgment of the analyst or modeller.[19]

The analysis and interpretation of these multi-dimensional representations of mental models in not as straightforward as the statistical analysis of binary relations. The analytical procedure is one of pattern recognition and is, therefore, as much an art as a science. We develop some heuristic procedures and apply some measures of multidimensional variability in the analysis described in Part III.

7.2 STRUCTURAL DECOMPOSITION

The concept of cylindrance leads to that of decomposition. By decomposing a complex system or policy situation into a set of subrelations, analysis of the system is simplified. Decomposition, however, does not imply total independence; there are still linkages among the subrelations that permit the whole to be defined as a system. We refer to the form or pattern of these linkages as a "macro" or "meta" structure. The development of a macrostructure in our approach precedes the analysis of issues. We presented the mathematics of analysis first because it is important that the mathematics of structure be consistent with it. The form selected for a macrostructure can have a strong influence on the interpretation of management information of all types. This section begins with a discussion of the concepts of independence and conditional independence, and then describes the logic and limitations underlying hierarchical, directed graph, and bipartite graph structures.

7.2.1 Conditional Independence

A complex relationship among a large set of variables can be decomposed if the variables or subsets of variables are independent. Independence implies that the set of states of a variable or subset of variables is not constrained by the set of states of another variable or subset of variables. In a closed system of variables, a variable or subset of variables is considered <u>totally</u> independent if another variable or subset of variables of the independence relation between them remains the same irrespective of changes

156

in the states of all other variables and subsets of variables in the system. When total independence occurs, a system can be decomposed into two systems, and each can be analyzed separately without loss of information. Figure 7.3 depicts an independence relation (R_{xy}) between two variables, x and y. Notice that x and y are independent if:

$$Ex_y Pr_x R_{xy} \cap Ex_x Pr_y R_{xy} = R_{xy} \qquad (7\text{-}15)$$

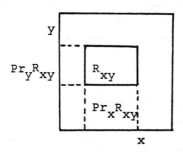

Figure 7.3   Independence Relation[20]

If a variable or subset of variables remains independent of another variable or subset of variables, but the independence relation between them changes as another variable or subset of variables changes, they are said to be conditionally independent.

Definition 7.6: Conditional independence is manifest when two or more variables or subsets of variables in a system exhibit independence, given the values of all other variables in the system.

Figure 7.4 illustrates conditional independence between the two variables x and y, given a value of the variable z. Notice that x and y are conditionally independent given z if the relation R_{xyz} can be decomposed as follows:

$$Ex_x Pr_{yz} R_{xyz} \cap Ex_y Pr_{xz} R_{xyz} = R_{xyz} \qquad (7\text{-}16)$$

7.2.2   Hierarchical Structures

Conditional independence or "near decomposability" is the basis for hierarchical structures.[22]   The

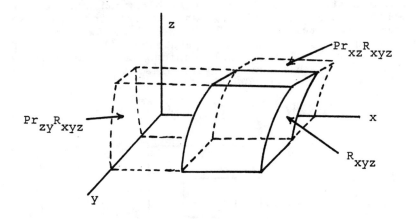

Figure 7.4   Conditional Independence[21]

relation depicted in Figure 7.4, for example, could be
hierarchically structured as in Figure 7.5. Analyzing
the relations between two variables is considerably
simpler than analyzing relations among three or more
variables.   The power of hierarchical decomposition
becomes more evident when the number of variables is
increased, because the number of possible relations in
a state space increases as the "exponential of an
exponential."[23]   The danger in hierarchical
structuring is that sets of variables that are not
conditionally independent will be decomposed, and the
relations among them distorted as a result;   or
conversely, that sets of variables will be aggregated
as though they are conditionally independent, again
resulting in distortion of the aggregate relations if
in fact they are not.   We contend that this is
precisely what is done in aggregate statistical

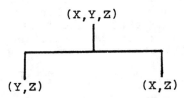

Figure 7.5 Hierarchical Decomposition of Variable Sets

158

analysis and that the applicability of statistical techniques is, therefore, limited.[24]

We make use of a hierarchical structure in the Department of Defense study for clarifying the language of defense objectives and for establishing priorities on those objectives representative of the values of defense administrators. It proved impossible to construct a perfect hierarchy, but the exercise did reduce some of the confusion and ambiguity associated with terms used to represent military objectives. We used a scaling and prioritization scheme developed by Saaty to establish priorities on the elements in the hierarchy.[25] This was valuable in assessing the perceived importance of issues in logistics policy and in narrowing the scope of the subsequent analysis performed. However, the assumptions of independence required to formulate the hierarchy limited the applicability of the priorities generated; that is, we do not believe that they can be used to quantitatively represent the values of the administrators or the perceived tradeoffs among policy variables.

The principle of hierarchical structuring of objectives or values is depicted in Figure 7.6. If the three variables of Figure 7.4 represent policy variables or objectives upon which priorities are to be established, and Z dominates X and Y, the value of Z can be determined first, and then the values of X and Y independently. However, if Z changes then X and Y need to be reevaluated.

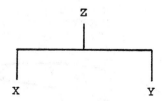

Figure 7.6   Hierarchical Decomposition
of Policy Variables

All classification schemes are hierarchical and have a basis in Aristotelian logic. Taxonomies, then, are also hierarchical. The absence of complete conditional independence is often treated by introducing some structural uncertainty into the taxonomy. The theory of fuzzy sets has been used for this purpose.[26] While a hierarchy can be useful for qualitatively structuring the variables of a complex policy situation, the quantitative analysis of a hierarchy suffers from certain limitations. A hierarchical structure is a static structure; structural changes or changes in the values of variables in a hierarchy as a result of some interdependence among variables are not easily isolated and analyzed. The next two subsections discuss structures that can accommodate limited analysis of dynamic behavior.

7.2.3 Directed Graph and Matrix Structures

Directed graphs and matrices are used in a number of ways. We discuss only a few here.[27] We consider the state transition or kinematic graph as the fundamental form of directed graph.[28] Figure 7.7 depicts a state transition graph; each node represents a state of the system being modelled ($s_1, s_2, s_3 \ldots$), and each arc represents the transition from one state to another. When the number of states is easily enumerable, and when the transitions occur with relative predictability, this method of structuring a complex relationship is very powerful. However, in the general case where there are a large number of possible states and the transition times are erratic, such a model becomes very difficult to construct and analyze.

One application of the kinematic graph is to the flow of concrete entities, e.g., material, people, money, or information, within a sociotechnical system or organization. We used flow graphs in both the

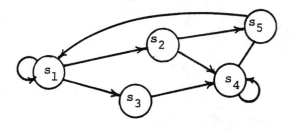

Figure 7.7 State Transition Graph

160

Department of Defense and MFS Finance Corporation studies, for example. The states of the system are the locations of the entities at a point in time. The transitions are determined by the flow processes and the capacities of the flow channels. When policy variables are superimposed on a flow graph, the constraint-theoretic approach focuses on the potentiality or capacity constraints that determine the amount of structure in a flow process. However, the relations between policy variables and flow capacities may be modelled better with a bipartite graph as discussed in the next subsection.

Another form of directed graph that has become quite popular models a linear system by representing variables with the nodes and the relationships between pairs of variables with the arcs. The form of graph, therefore, models binary relations between variables. Harary, Norman, and Cartwright have applied this type of directed graph to simple models of social interaction.[29] Warfield has applied it to a computer-assisted group process he refers to as "interpretive structural modeling."[30] Roberts has applied weighted digraphs and double weighted digraphs to a number of complex problems, most notably problems involving large-scale environmental and energy systems.[31] The double weighted digraph incorporates time leads and lags and hence permits some limited analysis of the dynamic behavior of a system.

Any digraph can be converted into a matrix of some type. Often, a matrix is a more convenient form for collecting and displaying data. The cells of a matrix correspond to the relationships between the variables represented by the rows and columns. A tool called cross impact analysis uses a matrix structure and has been applied to problems of technology assessment and the impacts of policy decisions.[32] The quantification of these digraph and matrix structures has generally relied heavily on the subjective judgments of experts. Delphi techniques are often used to refine initial assessments.

The difficulty with this form of directed graph or matrix is that only systems that can be decomposed into sets of binary relations are suitable for analysis. We contend that it is precisely the multidimensionality of relationships in sociotechnical systems that renders them complex. To assume that such systems can be decomposed into binary relations can lead to considerable distortion in the indicated characteristics of these systems and to dilemmas in applying the resulting information to the formulation of management policy.

7.2.4 Bipartite Graphs

A bipartite graph, or model graph as it is sometimes called, contains two types of vertices: nodes correspond to the relations in a system and knots correspond to the variables of the system.[33] Figure 7.8 is a bipartite graph; the squares are nodes and the circles are knots. The arcs connecting knots to nodes indicate that a variable is relevant to a particular relation. For purposes of computation the information in Figure 7.8 can be stored in a constraint matrix as in Figure 7.9. From this matrix we can see that $\propto$ and β are two-dimensional relations and γ is a three-dimensional relation, a "1" indicating that a variable is relevant to a relation and a "0" indicating that it is not. This matrix is useful for "computer manipulation of the model graph's topology."[34] Some topological properties of bipartite graphs are discussed in Friedman and Leondes, and Friedman; these properties represent rich opportunities for further mathematical development. Connectivity, trees, and circuits are examples of useful topological characteristics of bipartite graphs.[35]

The types of analysis that can be applied to a bipartite graph depend on the class of relationship being represented by the graph. Friedman identifies three classes of relation: the discrete relation, the continuum relation, and the interval relation.[36] If we let λ be any line through any point in the relation R, the Pr_λ R is the projection of R onto the line λ.

Definition 7.7: (a) R is a discrete relation if both $R \cap \lambda$ and Pr_λ R are point sets of measure zero;
(b) R is a continuum relation if $R \cap \lambda$ is a point set and Pr_λ R is an interval set of non-zero measure; and
(c) R is an interval relation if both $R \cap \lambda$ and Pr_λ R are interval sets.

Figure 7.10 provides examples of each type of relation. Friedman develops analytical tools for treating bipartite graphs and constraint matrices consisting of

162

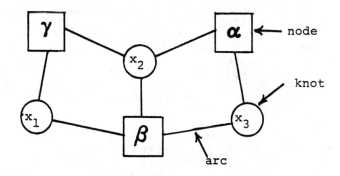

Figure 7.8 Bipartite Graph

	α	β	γ
x_1	0	1	1
x_2	1	1	1
x_3	1	1	0

Figure 7.9 Constraint Matrix

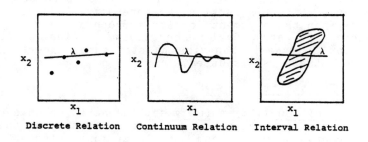

Discrete Relation Continuum Relation Interval Relation

Figure 7.10 Classes of Relation

continuum relations. His purpose is to determine the consistency and computational allowability of a set of mathematical equations all purporting to model the same system, but not all employing the same variables. The equations are consistent if there exists at least one point that satisfies all equations. A computational request is allowable if there exists at least one point that satisfies all equations when the variables identified by the request are held constant or limited to specific ranges.[37]

Richards has argued that a notion of relation more generalized than the continuum relation is often appropriate for modelling complex social systems.[38] The relations analyzed in Chapter 10, for example, are interval relations. The mathematics employed is not as clean as the mathematics that can be applied to continuum relations; heuristic procedures are more appropriate. Also, for purposes of measuring the structural uncertainty and disagreement inherent in a set of data, we approximate an interval relation with a discrete relation.

7.3 UNCERTAINTY AND ROBUST POLICY

The concept of structural uncertainty was introduced in Chapter 6. We stated at that time that the theory of fuzzy sets offered a rigorous mathematical treatment of structural uncertainty. The first topic of this section is that of fuzzy sets and of a measure of the amount of structural uncertainty represented by a set of data. Robustness as a criterion in policy formulation was also introduced in Chapter 6. In this section, we generalize that concept and develop the argument for its appropriateness in the presence of structural uncertainty. Finally, the relation of dynamic behavior to structural uncertainty and robustness is discussed.

7.3.1 Fuzzy Sets

Definition 7.8: A fuzzy set is one in which each element is assigned a grade of membership on the interval [0,1], and at least one element is assigned a grade other than 0 or 1.[39]

As discussed in Chapter 6, we use the concept of fuzzy set as one mathematical representation of structural uncertainty. There is a substantial body of literature on fuzzy logic and mathematics,[40] but applications to policy issues are scarce. The computational problem is one of operationalizing the concept with measures of fuzziness. The method of Saaty[41] has been declared an operational measure of fuzziness,[42] but as discussed under hierarchical structures (subsection 7.2.2) the method requires certain assumptions of independence that significantly limit its applicability.

Figure 7.11 is a fuzzy set of the type we use for the analysis of policy-level issues in MFS Finance

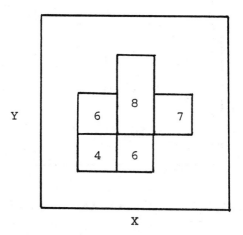

Y

X

Figure 7.11   An Interval Fuzzy Set

(Chapter 10). Each number corresponds to the number of individuals who include that region in their acceptable and feasible set of states in X x Y. These regions, then, represent the values and perceptions of the individuals in the participating group. To convert the numbers in Figure 7.11 to the interval [0,1] we simply divide by the total number of respondents. The assumption is that disagreement among the policy actors is an indication of structural uncertainty. Again, we take advantage of the different perceptions and priorities of the actors in single dimensions in order to develop a multi-dimensional representation of the situation.

The measure of fuzziness or disagreement that we use was developed by Krippendorff, but has not yet been

165

published.[43] It was developed for use with variables whose states are nominally defined, although we take the liberty of applying it to variables defined on a discretized ratio scale. The interval relation shown in Figure 7.11 is first converted to the discrete relation of Figure 7.12. Again, the numbers correspond to the number of respondents including that point in their acceptable and feasible set of states.

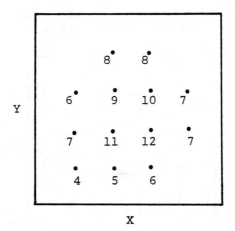

Figure 7.12   A Discrete Fuzzy Set

The measure of fuzziness or disagreement (D) is:

$$D = 1 - \frac{n^2}{n-1} \left[\frac{\sum_i \left(\frac{n_{i1}\, n_{i0}}{r-1} \right)}{\left(\sum_i n_{i1} \right) \left(\sum_i n_{i0} \right)} \right]$$

(7-17)

where,

$n = m \times r$
m = number of states being observed
r = number of participating individuals
n_{i1} = number of individuals who included point i
n_{i0} = number of individuals who excluded point i

166

The development of (7-17) is presented in Krippendorff.[44] It should be emphasized that this is only one measure of fuzziness and that other measures are possible and may prove superior for certain applications. For our purposes, however, this measure was adequate.

It is important at this time to recognize that structural uncertainty and probabilitistic uncertainty are not contradictory, but rather complementary, concepts. Clark and Pipino demonstrate that utility functions are a special case of fuzzy membership functions, and propose that both types of function can be useful for evaluating "hedonistic" values, while a fuzzy membership function is useful for evaluating more ethical or altruistic values. Hedonistic values derive from individual desires and tend to focus on relatively few variables; the relationships among the variables are perceived as sufficiently structured to accomodate subjective probability assessments. Ethical values derive from the perceived relationshilp of an individual to the social and natural milieu of which he/she is a part. This involves a more complex, unstructured set of relationships among a significantly larger set of variables. The structural uncertainty inherent renders inappropriate the use of subjective probabilities.

Clark and Pipino combine the two types of function into a single analysis as in Figure 7.13. Note that the utility function, v(x), is monotonically increasing, i.e., the more of x (e.g., profit) the

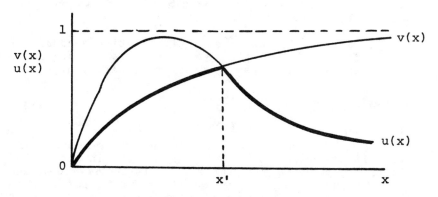

Figure 7.13   Structural Uncertainty and Utility[46]

better. The fuzzy membership function, u(x), indicates that the individual perceives his acquisition of x to be socially acceptable up to the point x'. Above that point, uncertainty with respect to social or environmental impact make additional x less desirable despite the still increasing personal utility. The combined effect of the two functions is indicated by the heavy line representing min [v(x),u(x)].

This is a very simplistic formulation of the tradeoff between individual achievement and social adaptability and responsibility. Furthermore, since both types of function are subjectively generated, the formulation can only represent the tradeoffs as perceived by a single decisionmaker. In policy formulation, it is the conflicts that exist within a group of actors that are of primary concern. These conflicts themselves contribute to the structural uncertainty in a policy issue, making the fuzzy membership function the dominant of the two. However, the distinction between utility functions and fuzzy membership functions serves to introduce the next topic, robustness as distinct from optimality.

7.3.2 Robustness

The concept of robustness was defined in a policy context in Chapter 6 (Def. 6.11). Its mathematical development, however, was originally designed for evaluating a finite set of sequential investment decisions.[47]   We propose generalizing this mathematics to the policy formulation process by using a constraint-theoretic approach.

As applied to the problem of selecting a course of action from a finite set (S) of alternative sequences of decisions, robustness is defined mathematically as:

$$\rho_i = \frac{n(S_i)}{n(S)} \qquad (7-18)$$

where ρ_i is the robustness of an initial decision; $n(S_i)$ is the number of elements remaining in the set of alternatives after the initial decision is made; and $n(S)$ is the total number of elements in the set of alternatives prior to the decision.[48]   The reduction in S resulting from a strategic decision represents the

168

commitment of resources made by the decision, where a null decision is itself a commitment that forecloses on certain future options.

The advantages of robustness over more conventional investment criteria are in the reduction of the need for subjective estimation--only a range of likely variation in outcome, rather than a set of subjective probability distributions; and in the formal abandonment of the search for an unknowable future optimality in favour of the more modest and practical goal of future flexibility.[49]

The limitation on this formulation of robustness is that it assumes a complete and ennumerable set of alternatives. When completeness cannot be assumed or when there is ambiguity associated with the feasible and acceptable set of alternatives, the measure (7-18) becomes imprecise and possibly misleading.

We propose focusing, not on the number of elements in the set of alternatives, but rather on the states excluded from the set as defined in a specified state space. This permits a comparative evaluation of alternative "policies" relative to that state space, where a policy serves the role of constraining the set of alternatives considered and hence of providing strategic guidance. We do not develop an absolute measure of robustness, but this formulation does accomodate a quantitative evaluation which can include consideration of incompleteness and structural uncertainty.

In Figure 7.12 of Subsection 7.3.1, the relative robustness represented by the pattern of data presented would be:

$$\rho = \sum_i 1 - \frac{n_{i0}}{r} \tag{7-19}$$

where n_{i0} is the number of individuals who exclude the point i, and r is the total number of individuals participating. Of course, a policy is not likely to be as fuzzy as indicated by Figure 7.12; in the process of formulating policy, greater agreement on allowable variability should be reached. Furthermore, resolving conflict through a widening of the acceptable amount of variability to accommodate a larger number of

169

organizational members results in more value-rich <u>and</u> robust policy. As pointed out by Rosenhead,[50] however, robustness cannot be had without a price. Pye attempts to formalize the tradeoff between robustness and optimality and to estimate the cost of flexibility in terms of the short-term gains sacrificed.[51] The price that a decisionmaker or a group of policy actors is willing to pay depends on their perception of the uncertainty facing their organization. The argument leads necessarily to the conclusion that participation and cooperation are desirable characteristics of the policy formulation process in the face of highly uncertain and dynamic environments.

7.3.3 System Dynamics

The topic of time as a variable has appeared a number of times in previous chapters. Some of the more popular modelling techniques include time explicitly as a variable in a policy model.[52] In these models, the dynamic characteristics of a system are one aspect of the system. Our viewpoint, however, is best summarized by Ashby:

> Among the variables recorded in an observation of a system will almost always be "time", so one might think that this variable should be included in the list that specifies the system. Neverthe-less, time comes into the theory in a way funda-mentally different from that of all the others... Experience has shown that a more convenient classification is to let the set of variables be divided into "system" and "time". Time is thus not to be included in the variables of the system.[53]

The <u>relationships</u> among the variables of a system determine its dynamic characteristics. Different perceptions of uncertainty with respect to these relationships, as well as different time-related values, lead to different treatments of the time dimension in mental models. These different perceptions of time are themselves sources of conflict in the social process of policy formulation.

We propose considering the time dimension by modelling the perceptions of <u>relationships</u> and the values imposed on those relationships rather than explicitly including "time" as a variable. This point of view is supported by Hanssmann, who argues that by

dispensing with dynamic detail more meaningful
operational detail can be added to a static model.

In fact, we believe that the burden of dynamic detail necessarily connected with the typical corporate simulation model is a basic cause of its
weaknesses...The simulation in time of a large
system severely taxes computing capacity. Model
development and preparation of input data also
require considerable effort. Since these
resources are always limited the possibility of
detailed simulation in time must be paid for by
strong simplifications of other aspects of the
model.[54]

Hanssmann defends the case for static models in
situations of high uncertainty. Not surprisingly, he
advocates robustness as a criterion for evaluating an
uncertain future as it is perceived in the present.[55]
Rosenhead, et al., also claim that robustness provides
a criterion that treats time in a manner very different
from most operations research models:

Time frequently enters as a variable in O.R.
models, but its effect on decision criteria has
been almost exclusively through the concept of
time discounting of future benefits...The role of
time in the structure of the decision process
itself has not been embodied in modifications of
existing criteria. This is of particular importance for long-range planning problems, where both
the time dimension and the prevailing uncertainty
are of the essence.[56]

He proposes, as we do, incorporating the criterion of
robustness through a continuous and adaptive process.
The process of Hanssmann and Rosenhead is a strategic
planning process involving a sequence of decisions;
ours is the more encompassing policy formulation
process involving the establishment of the constraints
on decision alternatives.

The process orientation is necessary not only for
dealing with dynamic uncertainty but also for dealing
with the methodological problem of self-reference. The
management scientist brings to the policy formulation
process his own perception of time which may itself
conflict with those of other participants in the
process. The process orientation permits the
management scientist to participate in the process and

to contribute his knowledge and expertise without requiring that his mental model dominate the process. This process, of course, has a dynamics of its own. We do not explore this dynamics in this book, but the approach developed in Part III would accommodate such an investigation, particularly if applied in a structured group or computer conferencing context.

NOTES

1. Norbert Wiener, "A Simplification of the Logic of Relations," Proceedings of the Cambridge Philosophical Society 17(1914): 337-390.

2. W. Ross Ashby, "Constraint Analysis of Many-Dimensional Relations," General Systems 9(1964): 99-105.

3. George J. Friedman and Cornelius T. Leondes, "Constraint Theory, Part I: Fundamentals," IEEE Transactions on Systems Science and Cybernetics SSC-5 (January 1969): 48-56; "Constraint Theory, Part II: Model Graphs and Regular Relations," SSC-5 (April 1969): 132-140; "Constraint Theory, Part III: Inequality and Discrete Relations," SSC-5 (July 1969): 191-199.

4. G. J. Klir, "Identification of Generative Structures in Empirical Data," International Journal of General Systems 3(1976): 89-104.

5. G. Broekstra, "Constraint Analysis and Structure Identification," Annals of Systems Research 5(1976): 67-80; "Constraint Analysis and Structure Identification II," Annals of Systems Research 6(1977): 1-20; "Structure Modelling: A Constraint (Information) Analytic Approach," in Applied General Systems Research: Recent Developments and Trends, ed. George J. Klir (New York: Plenum Press, 1978), pp. 117-132.

6. Klaus Krippendorff, "On the Identification of Structures in Multivariate Data by the Spectral Analysis of Relations," Proceedings of the 23rd Annual North American Meeting of the Society for General Systems Research, 1979, pp. 82-91.

7. George J. Friedman, "Constraint Theory: An Overview," International Journal of Systems Science 7(1976): 1122.

8. Ibid.

9. Ashby, p. 100.

10. Friedman, p. 1123.

11. Ashby, pp. 100-101.

12. Ibid., pp. 101-102.

13. Friedman, p. 1123.

14. Krippendorff, p. 82.

15. W. Ross Ashby, "The Set Theory of Mechanism and Homeostasis," in Automaton Theory and Learning Systems, ed. D. J. Stewart (London: Academic Press, 1967), p. 24.

16. Ashby, "Constraint Analysis," p. 99.

17. Gerrit Broekstra, "(Non)Probabilistic Constraint Analysis and a Two-Stage Approximation Method of Structure Identification," Proceedings of the 23rd Annual North American Meeting of the Society for General Systems Research, 1979, p. 76.

18. A proof is provided in Ashby, "Constraint Analysis," p. 102.

19. The term "relevant variable" is defined in Friedman, p. 1124.

20. Figure 7.3 is adapted from David E. Boyce, Chris McDonald, and Andre Farhi, "Constructing Procedures for the Design of Alternatives," Appendix A, An Interim Report on Procedures for Continuing Metropolitan Planning, Federal Highway Administration Contract FH-11-7068 (Philadelphia: Regional Science Department, University of Pennsylvania, 1970), p. A-3.

21. Ibid., p. A-4.

22. Herbert A. Simon, "The Architecture of Complexity" in The Sciences of the Artificial (Cambridge, Mass.: The M.I.T. Press, 1969), pp. 99-107.

23. Ashby, "Constraint Analysis," p. 100.

173

24. "many statistical techniques in the social sciences are arbitrarily set to a cylindrance of two and are therefore unable to recognize higher order dependencies if they exist. A peculiarity of such techniques is that without variability in ordinality, their own inadequacy becomes unrecognizable". (Krippendorff, p. 83)

25. Thomas L. Saaty, "A Scaling Method for Priorities in Hierarchical Structures," Journal of Mathematical Psychology 15(June 1977): 234-281.

26. Lofti A. Zadeh, "Outline of a New Approach to the Analysis of Complex Systems and Decision Processes," in Multiple Criteria Decision Making, ed. J. L. Cochrane and M. Zeleny (Columbia, S.C.: University of South Carolina Press, 1973), pp. 686-725.

27. A thorough treatment of digraphs with applications is provided in Fred S. Roberts, Discrete Mathematical Models (Englewood Cliffs, N.J.: Prentice-Hall, 1976).

28. W. Ross Ashby, An Introduction to Cybernetics (London: Chapman & Hall, 1956), p. 22.

29. F. Harary, R. Z. Norman, and D. Cartwright, Structural Models: An Introduction to the Theory of Directed Graphs (New York: John Wiley & Sons, 1965).

30. John N. Warfield, Societal Systems: Planning, Policy, and Complexity (New York: John Wiley & Sons, 1976).

31. F. S. Roberts, Weighted Digraph Models for Energy Use and Air Pollution in Transportation Systems, R-1578-NSF (Santa Monica, Calif.: The RAND Corporation, December 1974).

32. See, for example, Mitchel F. Bloom, "Designing a Time-Dependent Technology Assessment Model: Problems and Pitfalls," Proceedings of the XXIst Annual North American Meeting of the Society for General Systems Research, 1977, pp. 238-242; and Murray Turoff, "An Alternative Approach to Cross Impact Analysis," in The Delphi Method: Techniques and Applications, ed. Harold A. Linstone and Murray Turoff, with a Foreword by Olaf Helmer (Reading, Mass.: Addison-Wesley, 1975), pp. 338-368.

33. Friedman, p. 1124.

34. Friedman and Leondes, p. 198.

35. Ibid.

36. Friedman, pp. 1130-1131.

37. Ibid., pp. 1125-1127.

38. Laurence D. Richards, "Cybernetics and the Management Science Process," OMEGA 8(1980): 71-80.

39. R. E. Bellman and L. A. Zadeh, "Decision-Making in a Fuzzy Environment," Management Science 17(December 1970): B-143.

40. See, for example, A. Kaufmann, Introduction to the Theory of Fuzzy Subsets, vol. 1: Fundamental Theoretical Elements, with a Foreword by Lofti Zadeh (New York: Academic Press, 1975).

41. Saaty, "Hierarchical Structures".

42. Jean-Marie Blin, "Fuzzy Sets in Multiple Criteria Decision-Making," in Multiple Criteria Decision Making, ed. Martin K. Starr and Milan Zeleny (Amsterdam: North-Holland Publishing Co., 1977), p. 131.

43. Klaus Krippendorff, "Reliability, The Case of Binary Attributes," unpublished manuscript (Philadelphia: The Annenberg School of Communications, University of Pennsylvania, June 1, 1978).

44. Ibid.

45. R. H. Clark and L. L. Pipino, "Fuzzy Sets and Utility Theory," working paper # 74-47 (Amherst, Mass.: School of Business Administration, University of Massachusetts, 1974).

46. Ibid., pp. 9-11.

47. Shiv K. Gupta and Jonathan Rosenhead, "Robustness in Sequential Investment Decisions," Management Science 15(October 1968): B18-B29.

48. Jonathan Rosenhead, Martin Elton, and Shiv K.

175

Gupta, "Robustness and Optimality as Criteria for Strategic Decisions," Operational Research Quarterly 23(1972): 419.

49. Gupta and Rosenhead, p. B-21.

50. Rosenhead, Elton, and Gupta, p. 427.

51. Roger Pye, "A Formal, Decision-Theoretic Approach to Flexibility and Robustness," Journal of the Operational Research Society 29(1978): 215-227.

52. For example, Jay W. Forrester Industrial Dynamics (Cambridge, Massachusetts: The M.I.T. Press, 1961).

53. W. Ross Ashby, Design for a Brain: The Origin of Adaptive Behavior (London: Chapman and Hall, 1960), p. 16.

54. Fred Hanssmann, "The Case for Static Models in Strategic Planning," in Studies in Operations Management, ed. Arnoldo C. Hax (Amsterdam: North-Holland Publishing Co., 1978), p. 123.

55. Ibid., pp. 122-123.

56. Rosenhead, Elton, and Gupta, p. 417.

PART III

MODELLING APPROACH

CHAPTER 8

DEVELOPMENT OF APPROACH

In Part I, we motivated the need for an approach to policy-level modelling by reviewing the literature on policy formulation concepts and on methodological approaches being used to perform research in support of policy formulation. We also argued that the link between modern concepts of the policy formulation process and the modelling methods integrated into that process requires a critical assessment of the philosophical foundations underlying the methodology of management science. However, this critical assessment should not be interpreted as a rebuke of current management science techniques; we have found considerable application for many existing tools. Rather, the need is for a framework that integrates the information acquired from numerous sources, including the more traditional ones.

In Part II, we proposed such a framework. That framework builds on the philosophical foundations previously introduced and includes a logic, language, and mathematics for modelling at the policy level of an organization. We argued that the nature of typical policy issues requires a heavy reliance on subjective sources of information, and that the complex structure of those issues requires a heuristic approach to their analysis.

In Part III, we develop an approach for employing management science in the investigation and service of policy formulation. The approach builds on both the synthesis of the literature of Part I and the theoretical framework of Part II. It is an integrated approach in that each step of the approach is consistent with the other steps. This is made possible by the provision of a language for describing the behavioral aspects of policy formulation that is consistent with the mathematics of policy issue analysis. The more qualitative, structural aspects of the approach, then, directly complement the more quantitative, analytical aspects. We describe the evolution of the approach through the research performed on policy-level logistics management in the

179

Department of Defense and on organizational policies in the MFS Finance Corporation.

It is important to point out that the modelling approach was not conceived prior to the research projects described here. Rather, it evolved from those projects in response to the research needs experienced. In fact, many of our preconceived notions were to eventually be discarded. These projects, therefore, should be regarded as demonstrations of aspects of the modelling approach, not as proof of their utility. That proof can only come through repeated application and further development.

In this chapter, we provide an overview of the evolution of the modelling approach, including the design of the two research projects and the methods employed during the conduct of that research. The integrated approach that emerges will provide the basis for presenting the results of the respective projects in Chapters 9 and 10.

8.1 EVOLUTION OF RESEARCH DESIGN

The research issues confronted in the two organizations were briefly described in Chapter 1. The extreme differences that characterize these organizations made each an excellent forum for developing the separate steps of the modelling approach. The Department of Defense (DoD) is an extremely large and complex government agency characterized by multiple objectives that are very difficult to quantify; the MFS Finance Corporation is a medium-sized private sector firm that provides primarily one service, personal loans.[1] The size and scope of DoD logistics required that substantial effort be put into simply describing and structuring policy-level logistics objectives in terms of an aggregate view of logistics operations. In the MFS Finance Corporation, while the process of description and structural analysis was important, it was not as complicated. This, by design, permitted focusing of the research on specific policy domains and issues. These final steps of the approach are also applicable to the analysis of issues in the Department of Defense. Unfortunately, DoD officials were not interested in participating in research involving the collection and analysis of the subjective type of information we believe necessary for issue analysis. We were, however, able to make limited use of some of the more formal sources of information available in DoD, namely computerized inventory and simulation models.

8.1.1 Structural Analysis: Department of Defense

The DoD project began as an effort to develop a policy-level management support system, or simply "policy support system," for the logistics arm of the Office of the Secretary of Defense (OSD). The research was divided into three phases. The first phase was to provide a broad description of logistics operations, organizations, management procedures, and accounting, budgeting, and reporting systems throughout the DoD. The second phase was to identify the policy-level information needs of the Assistant Secretary of Defense for Installations and Logistics [now the Assistant Secretary of Defense for Manpower, Reserve Affairs, and Logistics--ASD(MRA&L)], and to determine the availability of the appropriate information. The third phase was to develop an analytical framework for using this information in the formulation of DoD logistics policy.

The research was originally designed on the assumption that aggregate trend indicators could serve as the basis for a comprehensive policy support system. While we expressed considerable skepticism with respect to the extent that such indicators could be used in providing quantitative insights, DoD officials were convinced that previous efforts did not reflect the true potential of this form of information and that a more comprehensive and rigorous investigation was therefore worthwhile. Our skepticism was to prove well-founded to the extent that the application of statistical techniques to aggregate trends developed from historical performance data revealed little in the way of significant correlations and insights. In fact, even trends that one would logically expect to be correlated often did not exhibit the behavior anticipated.

Emerging from this effort at indicator development, however, were some conclusions about the role of trend indicators, the nature of required supplemental information, and the methods needed for collecting and interpreting this information. These conclusions serve as some of the central premises of our modelling approach.

181

Premise 1: The description of an organization and its operations is an extremely important aspect of policy-level research in that it provides the context for all further intervention, interaction, and analysis. The management scientist must have a sufficient knowledge of the conduct of business in an organization before he has any chance of successfully contributing to its policy formulation process. We believe that this process of description has not received the attention it deserves in the management science and operations research profession. In particular, the behavioral and political processes of an organization are often neglected.

Premise 2: Aggregate trend indicators can serve a valuable role in the descriptive phase of policy-level research. These indicators raise questions with respect to relationships within an organization's operations, and hence provide an agenda for constructive interaction. In general, however, the relationships cannot be derived through quantitative analysis of the trends. The answers to the questions raised must come from other sources of information.

Premise 3: The single most valuable source of policy-level information is the institutional knowledge of an organization's stakeholders. This institutional knowledge is embodied in individual values, perceptions, judgments, and intuitions. We believe that the technology for facilitating the transfer of this type of information has not been adequately developed. There is therefore a need for new mechanisms of communication within an organization and between an organization and its social environment.[2]

Premise 4: The link between the qualitative description of an organization and its operations and the quantitative analysis of issues arising in that context can be provided by a rigorously developed macrostructure. The structure selected, while presented in qualitative form, represents certain mathematical assumptions about the nature of the relationships among the variables of the structure. These mathematical assumptions provide the basis for the subsequent quantitative analysis of policy issues. If the participants in a group process can agree that a structure is representative of the aggregate relationships in the organization and its operations, that structure can serve as a forum for identification and discussion of issues. Perhaps more significantly, the evaluation of the structure itself and the strategic assumptions implied by it are facilitated. We contend that one of the primary roles of policy is the establishment or adjustment of organizational constraints and, hence, structure; adjustment of the states of individual variables is secondary.

Premise 5: A macrostructure can provide an integrating framework for the design of a policy support system. We refer to this framework as an "interpretive structural framework" and use it to integrate information from many sources, but most particularly from the more informal channels of communication where institutional knowledge resides.

The conceptual design of a policy support system for DoD logistics incorporated a number of tools exhibiting different structural characterisitics. The integration of these different tools, including traditional operations research models, represents an eclectic approach to the design. It is not unlike the municipal simulation laboratory proposed by Bauer, Ruppert, and Wegener; they propose combining system dynamics, multiattribute utility theory, and conflict analysis through gaming into an integrated, computerized planning tool.[3] Our research with the MFS Finance Corporation was designed to develop and demonstrate a structure for the last of those three tools, as conflict (issue) analysis is the key to a successful integration. Friend and Jessop also propose an eclectic approach to the use of quantitative techniques in strategy formulation. They include mathematical programming, decision analysis, risk analysis, cost-effectiveness evaluation, and robustness analysis in their repertoire.[4]

To demonstrate the process of structural analysis, the logistics support of Air Force aircraft was selected for preliminary development of an interpretive structural framework.

8.1.2 Issue Analysis: MFS Finance Corporation

The structural analysis of Air Force aircraft logistics led to the identification of logistics policy issues and a procedure for evaluating the priorities on strategic directions that administrators believe should be reflected in logistics policy. Analysis of conflict within a specific policy domain, however, was not performed in the Department of Defense for the reason previously cited. The next course of action in our research, then, was to identify another organization that would support the demonstration of issue analysis. MFS Finance Corporation became that organization.

MFS Finance provided an excellent arena for the demonstration because the time required for performing the first steps of the approach--description, structure, and issue identification--was minimal compared to the monumental task required in the Department of Defense. Furthermore, the President and Chairman of the Board of MFS indicated a particular strategic area he wanted to have investigated, namely organizational strategy as opposed to growth or market strategy. The interrelationships between these three strategy areas, however, required that some analysis be done on each.

The organizational strategy that MFS was intending to implement was embodied in the term "management by planning." The intent was to develop management skills, reduce employee turnover, and stimulate creative thinking among MFS personnel. The implementation of this strategy, however, was perceived to require the resolution of certain conflicts that were bound to surface with the establishment of relevant policy guidance. The selection of a policy domain with well-defined, quantifiable variables that would reflect some of the potential conflicts was not easy. However, the results of interviews and of a preliminary questionnaire led to the selection of loan office "task structure" as a policy domain, with the percentages of time spent in six task-related activities serving as the variables defining that domain.

Most of the central premises of the modelling approach demonstrated in MFS Finance have been previously mentioned in this book. We now summarize them.

Premise 6: The assumptions implicit in strategic priorities are manifest in the structure of the mental models of the individuals establishing those priorities. The implication of this premise is that the process of developing a macrostructure and establishing strategic priorities can serve to elucidate underlying assumptions and, hence, bring conflicts into sharper focus. In fact, the process of assumption surfacing and debate is the central theme of

184

an approach developed by Emshoff, et al.[5] We use a process of establishing strategic priorities in our approach to narrow the scope of the subsequent modelling effort.

Premise 7: The presentation of multiple perspectives on a policy issue, in the form of individual perceptions and values, provides information that can enrich the policy formulation process. The exposure to multiple perspectives, according to Lombard, is an intermediate stage in the development from dualism (two-valued logic) to relativism (multi-valued logic).

> At the stage of relativism a student is aware of the internal structure of his views, and he has the capacity to examine hitherto unstated basic assumptions in his thinking and thus to change them (and his behavior). Not only does he perceive events differently from the way he did earlier, but he can also perceive the same event from different perspectives.[6]

We contend that in the policy formulation process this relativistic frame of reference leads to mutual understanding and robust policy. Relativism, by the way, is consistent with the philosophy of modern existentialism described in Chapter 3.

Premise 8: The collection and analysis of data on individual perceptions and values should emphasize variability in the relationships among the relevant variables. Most data collection methods currently employed use measures of central tendency (means or medians) or linearly scaled measures.[7] The need is for mechanisms that can elicit responses on permissable variety, and hence constraint, in a policy domain. The instrument we use to demonstrate such a mechanism is a questionnaire. However, the generic structure of the questionnaire could easily be adapted for use in a structured group process, a gaming exercise, or computerized conferencing. The focus on variability is particularly relevant in the policy context, as another primary role of policy is control of variability.

Premise 9: A primary role of the quantitative analysis of policy issues should be to stimulate the generation of creative alternatives and to facilitate particpation in the policy formulation process. The latter is necessary for ensuring value-rich (robust)

185

policy. The point here is that issue analysis itself is not designed to find the best resolution of the issue, nor is it intended to generate a consensus. It is "a forum for ideas,"[8] a medium for cooperative interaction. Through the feedback of information on individual perceptions and values, organizational learning is possible.

The MFS Finance research led to models that required the introduction of new methods of analysis. These methods included the application of a measure of disagreement and a heuristic procedure for assessing relational tendencies in the data. As a demonstration of the novelty and viability of the modelling approach, the research was successful. The determination of its value to an organization or to the study of policy formulation will require an extensive series of applications, involving continuous monitoring.

8.1.3 An Integrated Approach

The foci of the above research projects were on two aspects of the proposed modelling approach: structural analysis in the case of DoD and multidimensional issue analysis in the case of MFS. The primary theoretical contribution is the development of a mathematics of structure and of an analytical approach to multidimensional relationships expressed in terms of variabilities (i.e., interval relations). This development required consistency with behavioral aspects of policy formulation. This consistency is provided through the rigorous development of a language for policy-level modelling.

The total modelling approach is formulated into six steps; each of these steps was performed, at least conceptually, in both projects. Integration of the six steps is accommodated by the consistency inherent in the modelling language and mathematics. The following is a summary of each step in the integrated approach.

1. Description. This step takes on the characteristics of a case study. In the DoD logistics
study, it resulted in the publication of a
large volume describing the operation and
management of logistics systems in the
Department of Defense.[9] In the MFS study,
it resulted in a "scenario" describing the
strategic direction MFS is committing itself
to. This scenario prefaced the second ques-

186

tionnaire, and was essential for providing a context within which partipicants could formulate their responses. Another way of viewing this step is as the formulation of an organizational "story" similar to the approach used by Mitroff and Kilmann.[10] Such a story represents a vehicle by which policy guidance and constraints can be promulgated through the informal communication channels of an organization.

2. Structural Analysis. This step requires assessing the organization and its operations as a whole. The management scientist must ensure that the macrostructures that result are mathematically consistent with the perceived complexities of the relationships among the subsystems identified. The structures should also be displayed in a form meaningful to the policy actors in the organization. If a consensus cannot be reached with respect to the representativeness of the structures, they become themselves the subject of conflict. Since these structures represent fundamental assumptions about the role and purpose of an organization, conflict is symptomatic of ambiguity with respect to what the organization is all about.

3. Issue Identification. Broad issues can be identified during the process of description, the process of structural development, or any other step in the approach. There is little in the way of formal procedures for identifying issues. They generally emerge as intuitive insights on the part of single individuals or as manifestations of conflict between individuals or groups of individuals. This step can benefit from the type of skills possessed by an "artist" or a "psychotherapist." These skills are often neglected by the professional modeller or management scientist. The result of this step should be the delineation of some major areas of conflict and a listing of some strategic alternatives for addressing them.

4. Strategic Prioritization. The process of quantitatively weighting or ranking a set of strategic alternatives can be a valuable step in further highlighting areas of conflict and

187

narrowing the focus of the modelling effort.
When the establishment of priorities is conducted as a group process, we have found that
constructive discussion ensues and individual
assumptions and perspectives are clarified.
This step could be bypassed, particularly in a
project sponsored by an administrator who has
already determined the appropriate strategic
thrusts for his organization, and who is simply
interested in discovering what conflicts those
thrusts might provoke.

5. Policy Domain Selection. With areas of potential conflict identified, the next step is to
   select policy domains in which that conflict
   may become manifest. Policy domains are specified by the Euclidean product of the variables
   that define them. The difficulty encountered
   in this step is one of identifying concrete,
   quantitative variables to which organizational
   participants can relate and sets of variables
   that can be treated as relatively autonomous.
   One of the roles of structural analysis is to
   enhance awareness of relationships between
   policy domains. The identification of policy
   domains, then, should emerge from Steps 1-4.

6. Issue Analysis. The final step of the approach
   is the collection and analysis of data representative of the perceptions and values of
   participating policy actors. The intent of
   this step is to identify regions of conflict as
   well as creative alternatives. That is, an
   individual whose responses are in total disagreement with all other policy actors may have
   an innovative perspective on the issue that no
   one else has. We also take advantage of the
   different perspectives represented to develop
   relationships among the variables. When incorporated into a dynamic and continuous group
   process, the proposed analysis would facilitate
   the development of tradeoffs between the variables and between policy domains. The process
   of data collection, analysis, and feedback is
   similar to that used by Nadler in organizational development.[11]

8.2 RESEARCH METHODS

As already stated, an eclectic approach was taken to the selection of research methods. This selection was by no means exhaustive; other methods could also be used and in some situations might prove superior. There is also substantial room for development of new tools and for using the tools in new organizational communications and control technologies. The methods we selected for each step of the modelling approach are described below. Step 3, Issue Identification, and Step 5, Policy Domain Selection, did not involve any formal methods.

8.2.1 Description

In both DoD and MFS, extensive interviews and review of relevant documents were used to develop a description of the organizations and their operations. The interviews were not structured interviews, but did involve predetermined questions, both open- and closed-ended. The intent of these interviews was to identify key policy actors and issues, the relative power of the actors with respect to each issue, sources of conflict and constraint, perceptions of structural relationships and relevant variables, etc. The descriptions had to be sufficiently comprehensive to establish our credibility with respect to the structures presented and the questionnaires distributed.

We also examined historical trends relevant to each organization. In the DoD study, this investigation became a major undertaking, resulting in a 300 page volume with displays and interpretations of these trends for the Air Force alone.[12] To assist in interpreting the historical data, we used trend analysis techniques with time lags, correlation analysis, and multiple regression. The results of this analysis, however, provided little in the way of new insights. Of significant value, however, was the discussion stimulated within the Air Force as a result of the displays and our tentative interpretations of them. In the MFS study, industrial and market trends proved useful in the descriptive process.

The type of information acquired from this step of the approach is the type that any modeller would want to acquire prior to structuring and quantifying his model. However, we believe that this step is so important to a process-oriented approach that it should be guided by accepted principles of documentation. We found Diesing's development and critique of the case study method to be particularly useful.[13]

8.2.2 Structural Analysis

The types of structure used in the DoD study included flow graphs, bipartite graphs, and hierarchies. Flow graphs were used to represent the operations of Air Force logistics; bipartite graphs were used to display the resource constraints on the flow graphs; and a hierarchy was used to structure the broad objectives of logistics policy. In the MFS project, a flow graph was used to structure the operations of a loan office and a hierarchy was used to display the relationships between levels of management (i.e., an organization chart). These structures were relatively simple compared to those developed for Air Force logistics.

A number of modelling tools proved useful in providing conceptual insights into the DoD structures. In the case of flow graphs, maximal flow algorithms[14] and system dynamics techniques[15] pointed out the importance of flow capacity and the difficulty in developing quantitative relationships from historical data. In the case of bipartite graphs, goal programming methods[16] highlighted the importance of treating resource and policy variables as constraints on organizational operations. Multiattribute utility theory methods were useful in the hierarchical structuring of objectives.[17]

8.2.3 Strategic Prioritization

In the policy support system designed for DoD logistics management, we included a hierarchical prioritization scheme for evaluating logistics policy objectives.[18] However, that procedure was never tested by DoD logistics administrators. The project team did experiment with the procedure, but its value requires an operational assessment. The procedure involves pairwise comparisons of the elements at each level of the hierarchy on a scale of relative importance. An eigenvalue technique is used to calculate priorities from the weighted elements.

The first questionnaire administered to MFS personnel was designed to determine the strategic

190

inclinations of managers at different levels of the
organization. The questionnaire asked respondents to
rank a set of alternative responses to a particular
issue. A consensus ranking for each level of
management was calculated using a distance measure
similar to that developed by Kemeny and Snell.[19] The
procedure minimizes the sum of the distances between
each individual ranking and the consensus group
ranking. This sum is used as an indication of the
amount of disagreement exhibited by the responses.

8.2.4 Issue Analysis

The second questionnaire administered to MFS
Finance personnel asked for an indication of the
minimum and maximum feasible and acceptable limits that
should be placed on the percentage of time spent, at
various levels of management, on selected task-related
activities. The questions asked respondents to put
themselves in the position of establishing guidelines
for the management of time in the appropriate
managerial position. The responses were superimposed
and the resulting patterns analyzed.

The analysis involved, first, the identification
of relevant variables in the spirit of nested
constraint analysis. That is, analysis of one, then
two, then three, etc., variables was performed. The
analysis in higher order dimensions was terminated when
a judgment was made that the "relevant" variables had
all been included.

The techniques employed next included examination
of "prominent points" and measurement of disagreement.
A prominent point is one that a substantial number of
respondents include within their acceptable limits.
The examination of these points led to some hypotheses
about the nature of the relationships among the
variables. The measure of disagreement was described
in Chapter 7 (Equation 7-17).

The incorporation of this analysis into the policy
formulation process requires some form of feedback to
participants. In the MFS study, this feedback involved
simply a presentation to the Executive Planning
Committee and a report to the President and Chairman of
the Board. We recommend that an actual application of
the approach use media that permit rapid feedback.
Computer-assisted methods are particularly well-suited
for this purpose. Rapid feedback also permits

repetition of the exercise following group interaction. Changes in amount of disagreement and robustness (see Equation 7-19) would provide valuable information on the nature of the group process.

8.3 SUMMARY OF APPROACH

Table 8.1 presents a summary of the modelling approach. While each step of the approach has a product, the approach as a whole is process-oriented. The methods listed in the table are those we used; others could also be included. The results of the research projects presented in the next two chapters focus on two pivotal steps of the approach: structural analysis and issue analysis. In the design of a policy support system, the result of structural analysis is an "interpretive structural framework"; the result of issue analysis is accessibility to "institutional knowledge," i.e., a collection of mental models.

NOTES

1. The difference between government and corporate organizations is also discussed in Herman L. Weiss, "Why Business and Government Exchange Executives," Harvard Business Review, July/August 1974, pp. 129-140; and Hal G. Rainey, Robert W. Backoff, and Charles H. Levine, "Comparing Public and Private Organizations," Public Administration Review, March/April 1976, pp. 233-244.

2. This point of view is supported by Eastman, et al., in their criticism of the census type of information and their proposal for an urban information system based on "continuous 'transaction' and 'encounters' between groups and individuals." [Charles Eastman, Norman J. Johnson, and Kenneth Kortanek, "A New Approach to an Urban Information Process," Management Science 16(August 1970): B-738.]

3. Volker Bauer, Wolf-Reiner Ruppert, and Michael Wegener, "Simulation, Evaluation and Conflict Analysis in Urban Planning," in Portraits of Complexity, ed. H. Baldwin (Columbus, Ohio: Battelle Memorial Institute, 1975), pp. 179-193,

4. J. K. Friend and W. N. Jessop, Local Government and Strategic Choice, 2nd. ed. (Oxford, England:

192

Table 8.1   Summary of Approach

	Task	Product	Methods	Process-Oriented Role
1.	Description	Case Study Scenario (Story) Trends	Interviews Document Search Trend Analysis	Ensure Common Context (Qualitative Perspective)
2.	Structural Analysis	Interpretive Structural Framework	Flow Graphs Bipartite Graphs Hierarchies	Provide Structured Context (Link Qualitative And Quantitative Perspective)
3.	Issue Identification	List of Issues Alternative Strategic Responses	Subjective Pattern Recognition	Develop Agenda
4.	Strategic Priortization	Weightings Rankings	Eigenvalue Technique Consensus Ranking Analysis of Disagreement	Concentrate Efforts
5.	Policy Domain Selection	Sets of Quantitative Variables	Subjective Pattern Recognition	Establish Quantitative Perspective
6.	Issue Analysis	Institutional Knowledge	Analysis of Prominent Points Analysis of Disagreement Analysis of Robustness	Facilitate Participation and Communications Stimulate Creative Thinking

Pergamon Press, 1979), p. 238.

5. James R. Emshoff and Arthur Finnel, "Defining Corporate Strategy: A Case Study Using Strategic Assumptions Analysis," Sloan Management Review, Spring 1979, pp. 41-52; also, Ian I. Mitroff, James R. Emshoff, and Ralph H. Kilmann, "Assumptional Analysis: A Methodology for Strategic Problem Solving," Management Science 25(June 1979): 583-593.

6. George F. F. Lombard, "Relativism in Organizations," Harvard Business Review, March/April 1971, p. 57.

7. See, for example, the questionnaire structures in David A. Nadler, Feedback and Organization Development: Using Data-Based Methods (Reading, Mass.: Addison-Wesley, 1977), pp. 177-197; and Rensis Likert, The Human Organization: Its Management and Value (New York: McGraw-Hill, 1967), pp. 196-211.

8. Murray Turoff, "The Policy Delphi," in The Delphi Method: Techniques and Applications, ed. Harold A. Linstone and Murray Turoff, with a Foreword by Olaf Helmer (Reading, Mass.: Addison-Wesley, 1975), p. 101.

9. Murray A. Geisler, Mary J. Hutzler, Robert D. Kaiser, Myron G. Myers, and Laurence D. Richards, A Macro Analysis of DoD Logistics Systems, vol. I: Logistics Systems in the Department of Defense (Washington, D. C.: Logistics Management Institute, December 1976).

10. I. I. Mitroff and R. H. Kilmann, "On Organizational Stories: An Approach to the Design and Analysis of Organizations Through Myths and Stories," in The Management of Organization Design, ed. R. H. Kilmann, L. Pondy, and D. Slevin (Amsterdam: North-Holland Publishing Co., 1976), pp. 189-207.

11. Nadler, Feedback.

12. Murray A. Geisler, Mary J. Hutzler, Robert D. Kaiser, Myron G. Myers, and Laurence D. Richards, A Macro Analysis of DoD Logistics Systems, vol. II: Structure and Analysis of the Air Force Logistics System (Washington, D. C.: Logistics Management Institute, September 1977).

13. Paul Diesing, "The Practical Use of Case

Studies" and "Weaknesses and Problems of Case Study Methods" in Patterns of Discovery in the Social Sciences (Chicago: Aldine-Atherton, 1971), pp. 259-285.

14. L. R. Ford, Jr. and D. R. Fulkerson, Flows in Networks (Princeton, N.J.: Princeton University Press, 1962).

15. Jay W. Forrester, Principles of Systems (Cambridge, Mass.: The M. I. T. Press, 1968).

16. Sang M. Lee, Goal Programming for Decision Analysis (Philadelphia: Auerbach Publishers, 1972).

17. Ralph L. Keeney and Howard Raiffa, "The Structuring of Objectives," in Decisions with Multiple Objectives: Preferences and Value Tradeoffs (New York: John Wiley and Sons, 1967), pp. 31-65.

18. Thomas L. Saaty, "A Scaling Method for Priorities in Hierarchical Structures," Journal of Mathematical Psychology 15(June 1977): 234-281.

19. J. G. Kemeny and J. L. Snell, Mathematical Models in the Social Sciences (New York: Blaisdell Publishing Co., 1962), pp. 9-23.

CHAPTER 9

POLICY SUPPORT: INTERPRETIVE STRUCTURAL FRAMEWORK

In this chapter, we discuss the results of a research project directed toward the design of a policy support system for the now Office of the Assistant Secretary of Defense for Manpower, Reserve Affairs and Logistics--ASD(MRA&L). The methodological issues faced in this project led to the specification of some preliminary steps that we believe are extremely important to the success of any policy-level modelling effort. Of these steps, structural analysis presented the most difficulty. However, it also provided the major theoretical contribution to our conceptual design of a policy support system, namely the inclusion of an "interpretive structural framework." This framework should not be confused with Warfield's "interpretive structural modelling,"[1] although it serves a similar purpose in that it provides a structured context for quantifying institutional knowledge. However, our modelling language and mathematics are different, resulting in different structures.

The first section of this chapter describes our preliminary investigation of Department of Defense (DoD) logistics and its management. In particular, an extensive effort was put into the identification and analysis of aggregate trends. Aggregate trend indicators, however, failed to provide the type of insights necessary for them to serve as the primary content of a policy support system. The next section discusses the structural analysis performed in response to this inadequacy. Most of the structural analysis effort was focused on one Military Department, the Air Force. The result of this effort was the specification of an interpretive structural framework as one aspect of a DoD logistics policy support system. In the third section, we describe the conceptual development of additional aspects we believe a policy support system should incorporate. The final section presents our total integrated concept for such a system.

9.1 PRELIMINARY INVESTIGATION

In two separate volumes, we documented our findings of the descriptive phase of this research. The first volume is a description of the organization, management practices, and control mechanisms used in DoD logistics management.[2] It resulted from interviews with over fifty top-level DoD administrators and policy analysts and an extensive review of documents, studies, and other reports concerning logistics operations. Of particular interest are the modes of management control manifest in logistics systems and the associated role of policy-level management.

The second volume is a compendium of aggregate historical data relevant to Air Force aircraft logistics management.[3] It resulted from an extensive examination of existing data collection and reporting systems. Of particular interest is the effort to develop a set of management indicators for use by policy management, and the difficulty encountered in our attempt to analyze and interpret those indicators.

9.1.1 Management Control

Figure 9.1 depicts the basic hierarchical relationship of the Office of the Secretary of Defense (OSD), the Military Departments, and the Joint Chiefs of Staff. One principle of Department of Defense organization is that civilian administrators should have ultimate policy control. Hence, the Secretary of Defense sits on top of the organization, with each Military Department reporting to him. Within each Military Department, the Office of the Secretary provides civilian control, with the Military Services-- Army, Navy, Air Force, Marine Corps --responsible to those Offices. The Joint Chiefs of Staff (JCS) is responsible for the preparedness and coordination of all the Military Services in the event of an emergency. This is achieved through the Unified and Specified Commands. In addition, there are a number of defense agencies, e.g., the Defense Logistics Agency, that provide DoD-wide services.

Within virtually every organizational entity in Figure 9.1, there is a designated logistics arm. In the Offices of the Secretary of Defense and the Secretaries of the Military Departments, logistics policy is the responsibility of an Assistant Secretary.

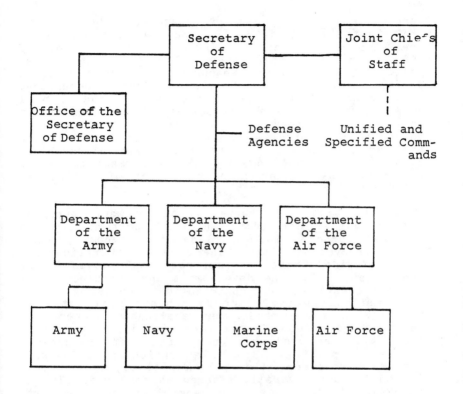

Figure 9.1   Basic Organization of the
Department of Defense

Within the Military Services, a Deputy Chief of Staff
or Deputy Chief of Naval Operations has logistics
responsibility. In addition, there are large logistics
organizations in each service that perform intermediate
and operational-level management functions -- the Army
Development and Readiness Command (DARCOM), the Chief
of Naval Materiel (CNM), and the Air Force Logistics
Command (AFLC).   JCS and all military commands also
have logistics organizations.

The management control of DoD logistics is
two-sided. On the one hand, there is the day-to-day
monitoring of the status of military combat units and
of the capability of the available logistics systems to
support them.   If a major deficiency surfaces,

corrective attention can be focused on the problem. This is the error detection and correction mode of control and is, of course, appropriate for the role of JCS. On the other hand, there are the broad policymaking and annual resource allocation functions performed by OSD and its Military Department counterparts. These functions involve the complex determination of the directions that progress in logistics technology and management should be moving. The modes of control espoused for these functions are the rational modes of prediction and hierarchical control. In fact, however, the policymaking process exhibits many of the characteristics of disjointed incrementalism.

As mentioned in Chapter 1, the primary mechanism for embedding rationality into the policymaking and budgeting process is the Planning, Programming, and Budgeting System (PPBS). The adoption of rationality as a desired mode of control has provided the justification for the development and construction of many predictive and optimization models and for detailed analysis of aggregate historical data. A majority of these models and analyses, however, are never used in PPBS. The results of models or analyses that have been used are often those that support the opinion or point of view of a particular individual. "Optimal" resource allocation decisions derived from DoD models are generally altered at some point in the process, whether by DoD administrators, Federal budgeters, or Congress. The point is that the PPBS process is not the rational process it portends to be, but is rather a political process involving negotiation, compromise, and power plays. Furthermore, the rules of that political game are in continual flux, changing as the policy actors change and as new issues emerge.

While in theory the ASD(MRA&L) has civilian control over DoD-wide logistics policy, in fact the distribution of power in the policy formulation process does not necessarily follow hierarchical lines. Hence, while OSD has responsibility for the preparation of the Consolidated Guidance, the primary statement of DoD-wide policy in PPBS, the content of that document is greatly influenced by contradictory opinion and political factors outside OSD. This point is well made in Levine's description of the politics of the cruise missile.[4] Levine, in fact, uses Steinbruner's[5] cybernetic paradigm to conclude that:

200

...enormous evidence has been accumulated that does in fact show that weapons are initiated not as a result of objective value maximization from a global perspective, but rather as the output of standardized and parochial processes proceeding from within the military services. These processes are interfaced with only rarely, when unusual circumstances prompt Congressional or White House intervention.[6]

The result is that OSD logistics administrators and analysts devote substantial time to routine tasks and the operational-level details of Service programs and budgets, rather than to broad logistics policy guidance.[7] This mode of management is reinforced by demands for operational-level detail placed on OSD by the Office of Management and Budget (OMB), the General Accounting Office (GAO), Congressional staffs, and others. It is often referred to as a "firefighting" mode of management. This is actually an error detection and correction mode of control, although the organization is certainly not designed with this in mind.

The firefighting mode of management and the search for rationality within OSD have had certain consequences on the policy formulation process and the nature of the policies that result. The size and complexity of DoD logistics operations are such that a rational treatment of the whole would be awesome. Hence, logistics management is subdivided into a number of specialized functions and categories. Each Service is treated separately; the logistics system of each Service has supply, maintenance, and transportation functions; the supply and maintenance functions are provided through a multi-echelon system consisting of at least a central or depot level (wholesale), an intermediate or base level (retail), and an organizational or unit level (users); the material processed through the logistics system is categorized into end items (major weapon systems and equipments), ordnance, repairable spare parts, and consumable spare parts and supplies. These subdivisions serve as areas for management specialization. In OSD, the first subdivision is by function -- supply, maintenance, and transportation. Within these functions, there are subdivisions by Service and by class of material. Traditionally, OSD has focused its attention on the central or depot echelon of logistics, ignoring the other echelons. This has perhaps contributed to OSD's advocacy for more centralization of logistics operations.[8]

As long as the focus of OSD policymaking is on operational-level detail, the specialization of functions serves its needs well. Furthermore, as long as demands for operational-level detail continue to be made by OMB, GAO, Congress, etc., there is little reason to expect that the present organizational form will change. However, without an integrated view of DoD logistics systems, the ability of OSD or any other agency within or external to DoD to formulate policy with respect to logistics philosophy, new logistics concepts, or a "vision" for DoD logistics organization and management is greatly limited.[9] Formulation of these broad policies requires a view of DoD logistics as a whole, highlighting the interrelationships among functions, echelons, and classes of material.

The interrelationships among logistics functions do receive some visibility in the dialogue and debate that accompanies the review of programs and budgets. However, this is not a structured process, and there is, therefore, no assurance that the most significant relationships will receive consideration. Again, the process is a political one and the result is generally disjointed incrementalism. We contend that a view of the logistics system as a whole requires an explicit macrostructure, and that the assumptions behind such a structure provide some of the primary topics for DoD-wide logistics policy. That is, the structural assumptions should be given more attention than the specific states of variables within the structure.

It was, in fact, the candid admission of the Assistant Secretary of Defense, that he did not have an adequate understanding of DoD logistics --as a whole-- to perform the broad policymaking role he believed he should be performing, that led to our study. However, another consequence of the search for rationality is the presumption that objective information should be employed in policymaking, and that analysis of this type of information will lead to rational policy insights. Hence, the initial thrust of our study was to be on the identification, aggregation, and analysis of logistics data that could serve as policy-level management indicators. Of course, our findings were not encouraging with respect to this line of reasoning. Rather, we concluded that the most valuable source of information in support of robust policy was that of institutional knowledge; that this form of information is consistent with the variety amplification mode of control; and that an interpretive structural framework provides a structured context for collecting and analyzing such information.

9.1.2 Management Indicators[10]

Our investigation of management indicators for the ASD(MRA&L) began with an investigation of the history of logistics indicator systems in DoD. First, it is important to realize that many of the OSD assistant secretaries have corporate backgrounds, and even those that do not would like to pattern their management practices after those in the private sector.   In general, they perceive corporate operations as being more "efficient" than government operations.   Hence, they view themselves in the role of a "Chairman of the Board" or "Chief Executive Officer" of a large, integrated organization, and would like to receive periodic reports similar to the financial reports received by their corporate counterparts.

The most recent indicator system used in the Office of the ASD(MRA&L) was the Logistics Performance Measurement and Evaluation System (LPMES). It was established in 1969 and suspended in early 1976. LPMES consisted of formal reports submitted by each service on a quarterly basis. The reports contained indicators of performance for the various logistics functions.[11] While some OSD analysts claimed the information was useful, the Services were not pleased with the reporting requirements and perceived little benefit from them. The Services became lax in their reporting, sometimes submitting the reports as much as six months late. Eventually the system was cancelled.

Our primary conclusions about the failure of LPMES are twofold. First, the type of indicator included in LPMES did not adequately represent the ultimate criteria of DoD-wide logistics decisions and policies. While we stated in Chapter 1 the difficulty in defining and measuring such criteria, the focus on logistics functions is simply too narrow and operational level oriented.   Decisions or policies based on such indicators cannot ensure consistency in logistics management as a whole. This "micro" view of logistics is, we think, a major reason why the Services were skeptical of the value of LPMES.

Second, the interrelationships among the indicators in LPMES were ignored. That is, it was assumed that one direction of a trend was good and the other, bad. This was evident in the method used to monitor the indicators; goals were established for each quarter and were used as standards of performance for the Service logistics systems. The goals were, however, assumed independent. There was no consideration for the possibility that, if one indicator improved, it might negate the need for improvement in another, or that improvement in one would be of little value without improvement in others. This substitutability or complementarity among indicators is only one manifestation of interrelationships. This difficulty is one of the principal reasons for the inappropriateness of the error detection and correction mode of control in complex systems.

Our response to these two deficiencies of LPMES was to focus our attention on "readiness" as a policy criterion and to emphasize the need for a macrostructure to assist in at least qualitatively evaluating the relationships among logistics variables. Our next step, then, was to collect logistics data and to attempt to relate logistics variables to measures of readiness. To conduct a thorough study of the entire Department of Defense would have been overwhelming. We, therefore, selected Air Force aircraft logistics for our initial investigation.

There are currently two major readiness reporting systems used throughout the DoD. The first is the Unit Status and Identity Report (UNITREP). This system is monitored primarily by JCS. The measure of readiness used takes the form of a scale with four ratings: a rating of <u>one</u> meaning fully ready, <u>two</u> meaning minor deficiencies, <u>three</u> meaning major deficiencies, and <u>four</u> meaning not ready. While there are some rigid guidelines for selecting the appropriate rating, the measure must rely to a large extent on the subjective assessment of the commander making the rating. The result is lack of complete uniformity in the reporting of readiness. Also, some bias enters into the measures reported, for the ratings are used to evaluate the commanders making them.

While UNITREP is a valuable tool for the role of JCS, the subjective content renders it of little value in broad policymaking and resource allocation. This is an important lesson, for it seems to contradict one of our premises -- the importance of institutional knowledge. We believe that the method of extracting institutional knowledge for the purpose of policy formulation should not be one involving a rating scale. Furthermore, the organizational climate must be such that the participants in the process are not intimidated by the reporting system, but rather participate freely and in the spirit of cooperation.

The second reporting system used to measure readiness in DoD is more narrow in scope than UNITREP in that it does not attempt to assess the wartime capability of military units; it measures only the peacetime condition of military systems and equipments. Because this system is regarded by OSD as more "objective," it is more widely used in PPBS than UNITREP; it is also the measure of readiness used in the annual readiness report to Congress that supports DoD program and budget requests. Hence, most of our effort at developing management indicators focused on this measure.

Figure 9.2 shows the aggregate trend of this measure, Operational Readiness (OR),[12] for all Air Force aircraft. The graph indicates that the percentage of Air Force aircraft Not Operationally Ready (NOR) has increased over the period of time depicted. Furthermore, the percentage Not Operationally Ready due to Supply (NORS) has remained relatively constant while the percentage Not Operationally Ready due to Maintenance (NORM) has increased.

In attempting to interpret these readiness indicators and relate them to other factors, it became apparent that the trends can be very misleading. There are many subtle aspects to the reporting system and the events which occurred over the period of time studied that must be understood in order to draw any conclusions. For example, a change in the OR reporting system occurred in the period 1973-74. While the definition of OR and NOR did not change, we believe that the change in the <u>discipline</u> by which it was reported had a significant impact on the trend. Other factors affecting the interpretation of this trend included a change in the mix of aircraft types, with more sophisticated aircraft being introduced and simpler, easier to maintain aircraft being retired, and

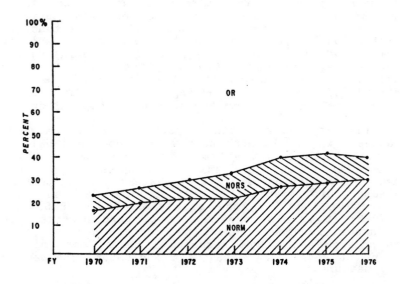

Figure 9.2   Operational Readiness Rate
Trend for Air Force Aircraft[13]

the end of the Viet Nam conflict in 1973. With all
these and other factors entering the picture, it
becomes difficult to even determine if a trend is
favorable or unfavorable. Furthermore, information
that is particularly relevant at this high level of
aggregation, information on variability, is not
available.

A good example of how a trend can be misleading is
provided by the NORS rate in Figure 9.2. While the
NORS rate appears relatively constant, the number of
incidents for which a spare part was not available in
the local supply system increased dramatically over the
latter portion of the time period depicted. One reason
why the NORS trend remained fairly constant was that
the incidents were satisfied, and hence the NORS
condition terminated, by unconventional means. One of
these was the increased use of War Reserve Materiel
(WRM). Hence, what appears to be a favorable action in
terms of the peacetime OR rate, may in fact be

detrimental in terms of wartime capability. The point is that Operational Readiness is only one reflection of the total concept of readiness, and a rather weak and

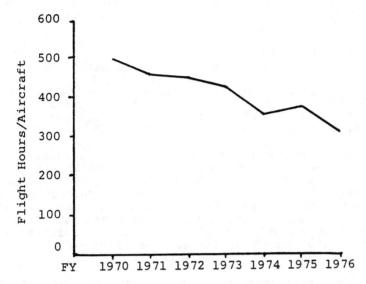

Figure 9.3 Air Force Flight Hours per Aircraft[14]

distorted one at that. There are many other aspects that OR rate does not capture.

An example of the problem encountered in relating trends in OR rates to other trends is evident from Figure 9.3. This graph shows the trend in the average number of flight hours flown by Air Force aircraft in the respective years. The downward trend is indicative of a reduction in the Air Force flight hour program due to the increasing cost of flying and the reduction in the number of pilots trained since Viet Nam. Flight simulators are being used as a substitute for actual flying. The question raised by this trend is: If the aircraft are flying less, should they not be failing less, and should not there be more time to properly maintain them, resulting in decreased NORM rate? The two trends do not coincide with our logical expectations. What is happening is that aircraft that are not immediately needed for training or for emergency alert are having their maintenance deferred in favor of other activities. Also, the slack in

207

aircraft utilization provides an opportunity to perform preventative maintenance that might otherwise be ignored, but which temporarily places the aircraft in a NORM condition. We had similar difficulties with other trends that should logically be related but which we could not statistically correlate.

Most administrators and managers, when presented with a trend, have a tendency to immediately draw a conclusion about it or to extrapolate it. Our experience with management indicators, at the level of aggregation appropriate to policy-level management, suggests that this tendency should be avoided. This does not mean, however, that there is no role for management indicators in policy management, but only that that role should not be one of error detection and correction or of prediction. Rather, the trends serve to raise questions. Virtually all the insights apparent in the discussion above were acquired through a process of questioning DoD officials, analysts, and logistics managers about the various trends. Hence, information about policy criteria (i.e., readiness) and relationships among variables came from what we are calling "institutional knowledge."

The importance of the subjective assessments inherent in institutional knowledge is recognized by Rockart in his approach to management indicators for chief executives. In particular, he states that at least one-fifth of the indicators should be subjectively derived.[15] The implication of any indicator system, however, is that each indicator represents a criterion upon which goals can and should be established. In the political process characterizing policy formulation, goals are elusive and arise after the identification of feasible and acceptable means (i.e., programs and policies). Our view is similar to that of Hoffenberg who, in his critique of the social indicators approach to public policy,[16] states:

> As a theory, the "science of muddling through" would I believe, exclude goals analysis as a meaningful exercise. I won't go into it here, but I do not consider "muddling through" as either an immutable or a complete description. I do believe in the importance of analysis in the public policy area. The problem here as with goals analysis and social indicators, is to ex- pand the role of analysis in what is basically

208

a political process. What can be done is to
illuminate and bound the political adversary
conditions through quantification and analysis,
and provide a more quantified framework for
conflict resolution.[17]

Our approach to readiness as a policy criterion is
to treat it as a concept, a concept that is value-laden
and that cannot be completely captured in any set of
measures irrespective of how many factors are included.
Measures that can serve as reflections of different
aspects of readiness represent variables that overlap
and that are completely interrelated.[18] The result
is disagreement and confict over the proper emphasis to
put on the various factors. The resolution of this
confict can be assisted through a structural framework
that provides a common ground on which to debate
individual assumptions.

9.2 STRUCTURAL ANALYSIS

Structural analysis involves the identification of
key variables and a qualitative assessment of the
relationships among them. This qualitative assessment
should, however, be consistent with the mathematical
assumptions implicit in the various representations of
structure. The product of structural analysis is a set
of visual displays representing the relationships among
the variables selected. These displays should be
compatible with the mental models of policy management;
if agreement on displays cannot be reached by policy
management, the structures themselves generate issues
in the policy formulation process.

The structural representations selected for
display should exhibit certain characteristics. First,
they should, at least collectively, represent the macro
structure of the system for which policy is being
formulated. This is necessary to provide a perspective
of the system as a whole. It does not, however, imply
a need for inclusion of excessive detail. Second, the
form of structure selected should be sufficiently
generalized to accommodate a variety of different
conceptualizations of intrasystem relationships.   In
particular, the relations among the aggregate variables
of a macrostructure are typically interval relations.
Third, the visual displays should be sufficiently
simple to be comprehended and used by the policy actors
themselves, i.e., not developed for the management

209

scientist alone. This is necessary for successful implementation of the modelling approach and again requires that excessive detail be avoided.

Chronologically, our structural analysis of DoD logistics began with the development of a macrostructure for Air Force aircraft logistics operations. Next, we added policy variables that constrain the operational variables of that macrostructure. Finally, we structured the policy criteria and logistics objectives that guide policy and resource allocation decisions. However, the fundamental importance of policy criteria, and of the conflicts that inevitably arise over "appropriate" criteria, suggests that we discuss this structure first.

The hierarchical structure we selected for policy criteria provides a basis for strategic prioritization. The structure we selected for logistics operations is the flow graph, with an emphasis on capacity constraints. The structure we selected for policy variables is the bipartite graph, emphasizing resources as constraints on logistics capability. These latter two structures provide a basis for selecting policy domains.

9.2.1 Policy Criteria

The ubiquitous nature of the term "readiness" was briefly discussed in Chapter 1. The problem of measuring readiness was discussed in Chapter 3. We have concluded that the lack of uniformity and clarity in using the word "readiness" stems in large part from its value content as opposed simply to the complexity of DoD operations.[19] To highlight the value conflicts inherent in readiness as a policy criterion, we determined that it would be useful to structure the language of readiness and of associated policy criteria terms. Figure 9.4 is the result.

The selection of a hierarchical structure for policy criteria was based not on an assessment that distinct boundaries exist between the terms, but only that the terms tend to be used in reference to different concepts and entities. The concepts and entities themselves, however, are highly interrelated. The construction of the hierarchy served to narrow the focus of subsequent analysis while maintaining a systemwide perspective.

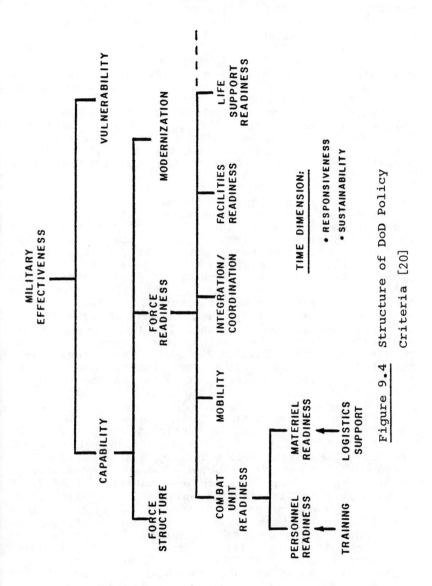

Figure 9.4   Structure of DoD Policy
           Criteria [20]

211

We will not define each term in Figure 9.4 here.[21] It should suffice to point out, first, that "military effectivess" is the term we found used most often to represent the overall objective of DoD policy, and second, that "capability" is subdivided into three components of which readiness is only one. "Force readiness" is subdivided into functional categories, and associated with each unit performing these functions are "personnel readiness" and "materiel readiness." An unique feature of this hierarchy of policy criteria is the inclusion of a time dimension. The terms associated with this dimension are "responsiveness" and "sustainability" (i.e., persistence) and each term in the hierarchy contains both these aspects.

Rather than include training and logistics operations as functions comparable to combat, mobility, etc., we chose to treat them as directly supportive of the personnel and materiel readiness of the units performing the other functions. Again, this permitted a narrowing of the focus on DoD policy criteria specifically for the purpose of performing issue analysis in support of logistics policy. However, the hierarchy should serve to emphasize that materiel readiness is only one small aspect of overall DoD policy criteria; the fact that logistics policies are obviously interrelated with other defense policies points out the limitations of the hierarchical structure and the need for interaction between logistics policy actors and other defense policy actors.

We took the hierarchical structure one step further for purposes of prioritization of the directions in which Air Force logistics policy might proceed (to be discussed in Section 9.3.2). Figure 9.5 takes as its starting point "materiel readiness," subdividing it into "peacetime materiel readiness" (responsiveness) and "sustainability." The next level of the hierarchy consists of the basic Air Force logistics activities, i.e., functions and support echelons. For purposes of policy formulation, we determined that combining intermediate and unit-level functions into a single echelon, "base" level, was a reasonable simplification, resulting in a two echelon system. This is the point in the hierarchy at which the ambiguous policy criteria terms begin to assume a concrete identification. Under each logistics activity is a set of quantifiable policy variables expressed in

212

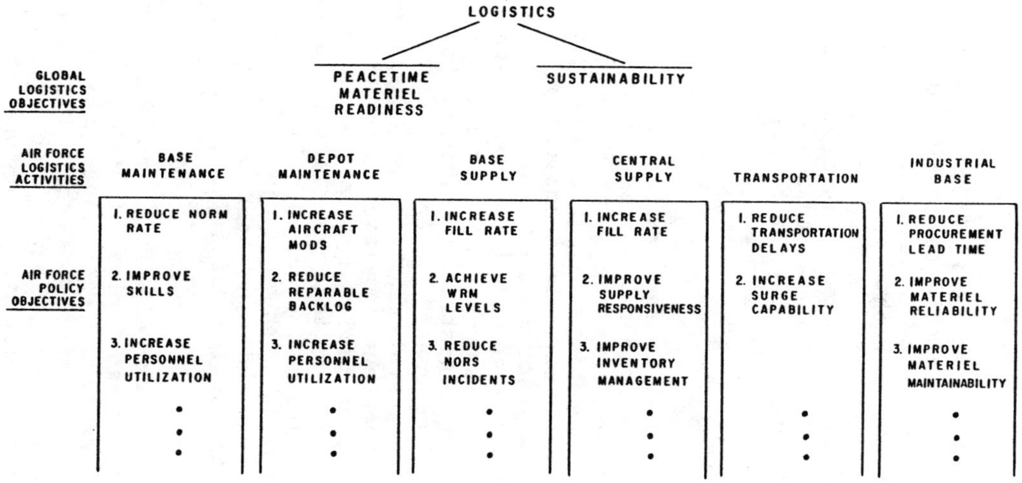

Figure 9.5 Structure of Air Force Logistics Policy Variables [22]

213

terms of possible changes in those variables (i.e.,
policy objectives). These changes serve as indications
of alternative strategic thrusts for Air Force
logistics policy.

It is important to emphasize once more that the
hierarchical structuring of logistics activities and
policy objectives is misleading in that these entities
are in fact highly interrelated. We attempt to
structure some of these relationships in the flow
graphs and bipartite graphs of the next two
subsections. The primary use of Figure 9.5, then, is
in providing a means, through a ranking or weighting
procedure, of concentrating attention on certain
logistics activities and variables and selecting policy
domains.

9.2.2 Capacity Constraints

The operations of any organization or system can
be structured as a flow process. Whether this is worth
devoting substantial effort to or not depends on the
complexity of these operations. In the case of DoD, we
concluded that the intrinsic complexity of the
logistics systems warranted a thorough structural
examination. Furthermore, while there are many
logistics managers who have a comprehensive knowledge
of a certain aspect of logistics operations, there are
few who have an adequate understanding of the
macrostructure of these systems. Such an understanding
is, we contend, an important provision for constructive
discussion and debate on policy issues. It is also an
essential step in introducing quantitative analysis
into the policy formulation process. In the case of
MFS Finance (Chapter 10), the relative simplicity of
loan office operations made the task of developing a
flow process structure of less significance than in the
DoD project.

Figures 9.6 through 9.9 show the flow graphs
developed for various categories of material in Air
Force aircraft logistics. Each node in the graphs
represents an aggregate logistics activity; each arc
represents a flow of material from one activity to
another. The flows of material and the stocks of
material residing at an activity can serve as one type
of policy variable. The policy variables in Figure
9.5, for example, are various measures of stocks and
flows. The nodes and arcs are, of course, abstractions
in that each represents an aggregation of many

214

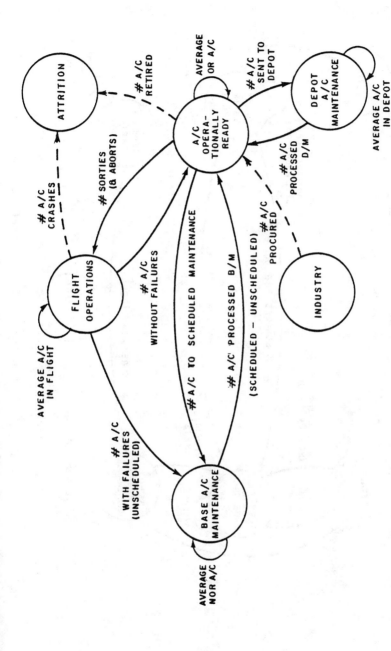

Figure 9.6 Flow Graph for Air Force Aircraft [23]

215

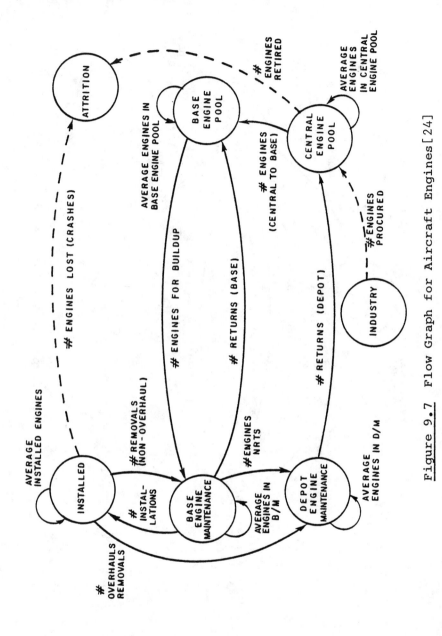

Figure 9.7 Flow Graph for Aircraft Engines[24]

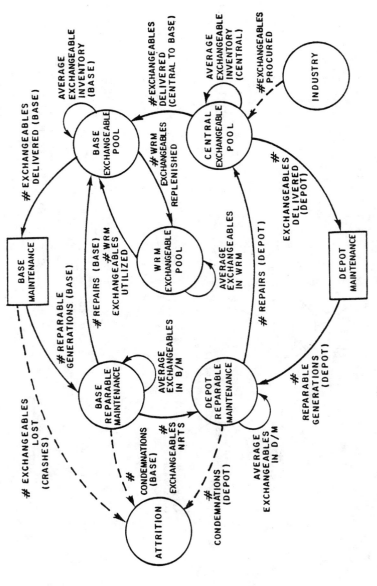

Figure 9.8 Flow Graph for Exchangeable Spare Parts [25]

217

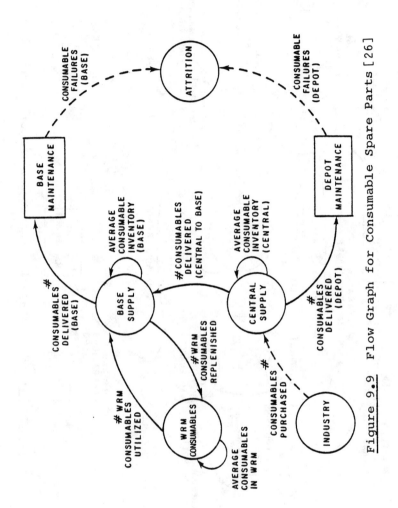

Figure 9.9 Flow Graph for Consumable Spare Parts [26]

218

activities and flows. The variation among activities is an important policy consideration.

The four flow graphs are interelated through the common logistics activities. We will not describe these graphs in detail here,[27], except to say that the selection of the four categories of material was based on the fact that each has its own distinct management system. The end items, of course, are aircraft; aircraft engines are separately managed and are always repaired when a failure occurs; repairable spare parts (also called exchangeables, reparables, or recoverables) are investment items in that if possible they are repaired and returned to inventory when a failure occurs; and consumable spare parts are expense items that are always discarded when a failure occurs.

When the flow graphs are combined into a single diagram, the result is as depicted in Figure 9.10, with the addition of another category of material, munitions. Also, the industrial base (i.e., industry) is omitted. In the report submitted to OSD, nodes and arcs corresponding to different categories of material in Figure 9.10 were depicted in different colors. We believe that the mode of display is extremely important to the effectiveness of structural representations in an interpretive structural framework.

We found the work of Forrester of use in structuring the flow graphs.[28] However, his mathematics, and in fact the mathematics of flow graphs in general, does not capture adequately the concept of the readiness of a logistics system. Forrester's emphasis on stocks and flows(i.e., levels and rates) is useful for looking at the history of a system's performance, and may be useful at the operational level where technological systems are designed to exhibit repetitive behavior; but, at the policy level it is the potential of the system, i.e., its capability, that is of prime concern. This is represented not by average stocks and flows, but by the range of variability possible and allowable in these stocks and flows. It is this notion of the capacity of the system under varying circumstances (and uncertainty) that we concluded best captures the concept of readiness.

The focus on capacity, however, requires a different perspective on the mathematical structure of the flow graphs, namely a constraint-theoretic perspective. This has implications for how one

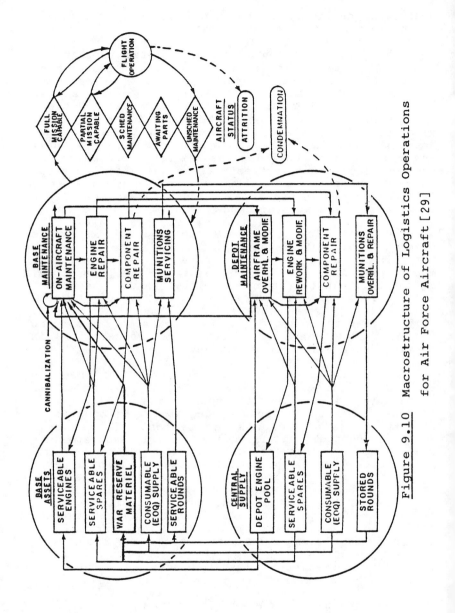

Figure 9.10   Macrostructure of Logistics Operations
for Air Force Aircraft [29]

220

interprets the flow graph structures and the information relevant to them. Capacity is seldom directly measureable except where very rigid conditions exist. Hence, it requires subjective assessment in terms of perceived uncertainty and values (i.e., acceptable variability).

In this context, the use of the flow graphs as tools for prediction or optimization is of limited value. The focus is not on most probably states of the system, but rather on the states excluded from consideration whether because they are unacceptable or because they are simply not feasible. They can serve, however, as a context for highlighting conflicts in values and perceptions, with the minimum and maximum acceptable stocks and flows defining the policy domains. We also found them useful in assessing the structure and assumptions of operational-level inventory and simulation models. The process of assumption surfacing itself led to some insights with respect to how the outputs of optimization and prediction models might be useful in policy formulation. Namely, if the assumptions and inputs of a model are best case or worst case, i.e., the constraining cases, then the output of the model represents a limiting value for the variable being optimized or predicted. The interpretation of model output in this way, however, represents the negative form of reasoning, to which the culture of bureaucratic organizations is not necessarily accommodating.[30]

9.2.3 Policy Constraints

Capacity constraints provide a reasonable approach for assessing the relationships among logistics activities. But each capacity itself can also be viewed as a relationship among a set of policy variables. For purposes of structuring these relationships, we selected resources (funding) levels as the policy variables and used a bipartite graph structure. The choice of resource levels as the variables was based on the emphasis on funding in PPBS, the principal policy vehicle of our sponsor for this project. Other variables, e.g., measures of stocks and flows, could also have been selected. Figure 9.11 is the basic form of this structure; when a bipartite graph is assembled for all the activities of a flow graph, it appears as in Figure 9.12, which is the bipartite graph for the logistics activities in Figure 9.6. Such graphs for the other categories of material

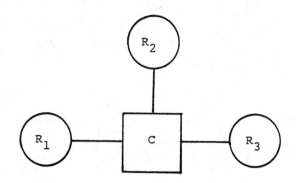

Figure 9.11   Structure of Policy Variables

were also developed. The circles (knots) in these
graphs correspond to the relevant variables (R_1, R_2...)
and the squares (nodes) correspond to the relations
among those variables in terms of an acceptable system
capacity (C). The relations will, in general, be
interval relations representing the range of
variability in the flow through the respective
activity. As with the flow graphs, the structure of
policy variables in terms of interval relations
suggests a constraint-theoretic approach to evaluating
a bipartite graph. That is, the relations among policy
variables should be interpreted as constraints on the
capacities. This is, of course, different from the
conventional view that the specification of a
one-to-one correspondence between resources and
readiness is desirable and can be achieved if enough
data are collected, i.e., that they are functionally
related (a continuum relation).[31]

Figure 9.13 adds to Figure 9.10 the set of policy
variables indicated by the dollar signs. An arrow from
a policy variable indicates that the level of that
resource constrains the capacity of the activity to
which it is pointing. In some cases, the resource is
identified to a specific category of material. These
resource variables are at the level of aggregation with
which OSD and policy-level Air Force administrators
generally deal in the PPBS, although in some instances
additional detail is available as well. The use of
cost estimating relationships for evaluating the impact
of a resource variable on an activity is the means of

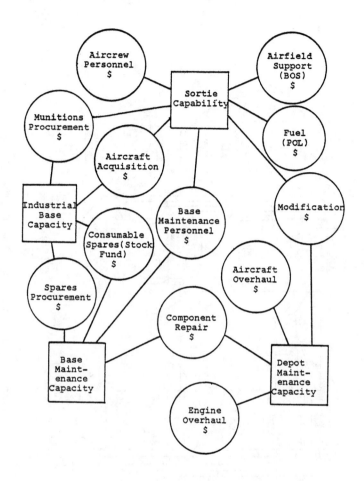

Figure 9.12   Bipartite Graph for Air Force
Aircraft Logistics

223

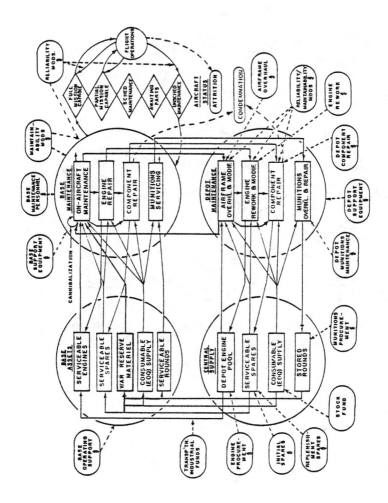

Figure 9.13   Resource Constraints on Air Force Logistics Operations [32]

224

analysis typically employed. These cost estimating relationships are usually developed by applying linear regression techniques to historical data. As a result, they do not capture the capacity of the activity nor can they account for higher order relations among the variables.

DoD logistics policy itself will not necessarily be formulated in terms of the policy variables. Rather, policy issues will be reflected in the policy variables. The variables serve to define policy domains within which quantitative analysis can be performed and conflicting perceptions and values surfaced.

9.3 FURTHER DEVELOPMENT

The macrostructures that evolved from the above structural analysis provide the basic elements of an interpretive structural framework. The next step of the approach would have been to use that framework to develop some quantitative insights into specific policy issues. This would have involved the tapping of institutional knowledge in some structured manner. The project as originally conceived, however, was considered complete with the development of the structural framework, and we were unable to stimulate interest for research involving subjective sources of information. DoD officials continued to express the opinion that "objective" sources of information could serve the purposes of policy formulation adequately, and that subjective judgments and perceptions could be of only limited value in an organization like DoD. We agree that the structured use of institutional knowledge requires a climate of cooperation and genuine dedication to the principle of participation, and that this is not currently widespread in DoD. We were fortunate to find the organizational climate of the MFS Finance Corporation, to be discussed in the next chapter, to be conducive to such a research project.

Our final step in the DoD project was to specify how our modelling approach would have been carried forward if it had been supported. In this section, then, we describe hypothetical examples of issue identification, strategic prioritization, policy domain selection, and issue analysis as they might have followed from structural analysis.

225

9.3.1 Issue Identification

A number of policy issues surfaced during our interviews with DoD administrators and as the result of comments on our interpretation of the trend indicators. Many of these issues were parochial and expressed in the vernacular of specific logistics functions. However, most had much broader implications. We found the interpretive structural framework useful for clarifying the broad policy content of these issues.

The first such issue is that of short-term versus long-term priorities. This is manifest in Figure 9.5 as a tradeoff between responsiveness (usually referred to in the logistics arena as peacetime materiel readiness) and sustainability. The issue also gets reflected in shifts of emphasis on logistics activities. For example, short-term priorities would result in an emphasis on the base-level activities and on central-level spare parts availability. Long-term priorities would result in emphasis on the industrial base and depot aircraft maintenance. Shifts in policy variables would also reflect a change in priorities. An emphasis on war reserve materiel, for example, reflects an emphasis on sustainability.

Another issue is that of centralized versus decentralized logistics operations. A shift to a more centralized system would be manifest in an emphasis on the central and depot activities, and the corresponding resource levels, whereas a decentralized system would be indicated by an emphasis on base-level activities.

There is also disagreement over the issue of whether military logistics systems should be more labor intensive or more capital intensive. A more labor intensive system would place emphasis on the maintenance activities, a more capital intensive system on the supply activities.

These issues are, of course, all interrelated just as Friend and Jessop's "decision fields" are interrelated.[33] One of the factors connecting these and other issues is the type of technology (i.e., design and complexity of weapons systems) that the logistics system is expected to support. This in itself is an issue that to a certain extent overrides the others.[34]

226

9.3.2 Strategic Prioritization

Strategic prioritization can take a number of forms, but its intent is to determine which issues should be given priority and the degree of disagreement inherent in them. It thus serves to narrow the focus of subsequent analysis. In the DoD project, we proposed using a technique developed by Saaty[35] to prioritize the logistics activities and policy objectives in the hierarchy of Figure 9.5. The method involves the pairwise comparison of the elements at each level of the hierarchy using the scale in Table 9.1. An eigenvalue technique is then used to calculate priority weights for each element, maintaining consistency with priorities at higher levels.

As an experiment in the use of the technique, the project team themselves conducted a trial run of the exercise. The results are in Table 9.2, and indicate that the group considered short-term (peacetime materiel readiness) objectives of significantly more importance than long-term (sustainability) objectives. This could indicate a perception that the Air Force is not adequately prepared for an unexpected emergency. It could also indicate a perception that there are not enough adequately trained pilots, for aircraft must be "ready" in order to be flown in peacetime as well as in wartime.

Table 9.1   Scale of Relative Importance

Scaling Factor	Explanation
1	Equal Importance; Indifference
3	Weak Importance of One over Another
5	Essential or Strong Importance
7	Demonstrated Importance
9	Absolute Importance
2,4,6,8	Intermediate Values between the Two Adjacent Factors;Used for Compromise
Reciprocals	If Element i has One of the Above Numbers Assigned When Compared to j, Then j Has the Reciprocal Value When Compared to i.

227

Table 9.2   Strategic Priorities for Air Force
Aircraft Logistics Policy[36]

	Weights
Level I: Policy Criteria	
Peacetime Material Readiness	.9
Sustainability	.1
Level II: Logistics Activities	
Base Maintenance	.425
Depot Maintenance	.045
Base Supply	.287
Central Supply	.109
Transportation	.061
Industrial Base	.065
Level III: Policy Objectives	
Base Maintenance:	
Reduce NORM Rate	.13
Improve Maintenance Skills	.27
Increase Personnel Utilization	.03
Depot Maintenance:	
Increase Aircraft Modifications	.03
Reduce Reparable Backlog	.01
Increase Personnel Utilization	.004
Base Supply:	
Increase Fill Rate	.05
Achieve WRM Levels	.02
Reduce NORS Incidents	.21
Central Supply:	
Increase Fill Rate	.03
Improve Supply Responsiveness	.01
Improve Inventory Management	.07
Transportation:	
Reduce Transportation Delays	.03
Increase Surge Capability	.03
Industrial Base:	
Reduce Procurement Lead Time	.004
Improve Materiel Reliability	.04
Improve Materiel Maintainability	.02

Table 9.2 also suggests a strong priority on decentralization of logistics as indicated by the weights on base-level activities. There is also a slightly greater emphasis on the labor-oriented activities (maintenance). The two strategic thrusts that received highest priority were the needs to improve base level maintenance skills and to reduce the number of NORS incidents occurring as the result of base supply inventory levels. The selection of policy domains could be based on variables that reflect these priorities.

We conducted the exercise as a group process, requiring consensus on the pairwise comparisons made. Debate and discussion continued until a consensus was reached. The exercise could have also been conducted on an individual basis, and a measure of amount of disagreement calculated from the individual responses. This was the procedure followed with MFS Finance, although the hierarchical prioritization technique was not employed. An unexpected benefit of the group approach was that the participants felt they had learned something about the Air Force logistics system as a whole as a result of the exercise. Prior to this point, each project team member had concentrated their efforts on a specific logistics function. The debate and discussion served to clarify assumptions about relationships among the functions.

9.3.3 Policy Domain Selection

The variables defining policy domains could be measures representing stocks and flows, resource funding levels, or other variables. With respect to the base maintenance skills issue, the selection of an appropriate policy domain is not easy. Many factors are relevant, including the quality of recruits, the design of their training program, personnel morale, and retention of trained technicians. Many of these factors are difficult to quantify. Personnel policies were also the primary concern of the MFS Finance study. The approach used there might also be applied to DoD logistics personnel policies.

With respect to the NORS incidents issue, resource variables could be used to define a policy domain. Two variables, in particular, are relevant: spare parts procurement funding and depot component repair funding. The Air Force spare parts inventory model (referred to as the Aircraft Availability Model) provides some

229

insights on this issue, and in fact became a part of the issue in the PPBS process for Fiscal Year 1981. That model calculated the funding levels for the two resource variables that would maximize aircraft availability. The Air Force programmed more funds for spare parts procurement than was specified by the model. One reason for this divergence was that certain Air Force officials desired to divert these funds in order to increase WRM levels. However, OSD policy guidance had clearly stated that priority should be given to short-term considerations, i.e., peacetime materiel readiness. Hence, an area of conflict was surfaced, one that challenged some of the assumptions of the inventory model. In addition, the optimizing criterion of the model, aircraft availability, does not permit an adequate assessment of certain facets of the labor/capital issue, namely that humans consist of more than simply their productive capability.

9.3.4 Issue Analysis

To analyze the conflicting values and perceptions in an issue in greater depth, an instrument for extracting quantitative data from their reservoir of institutional knowledge in an organization must be selected. We recommended some form of structured group process for this purpose, although we used a questionnaire in the MFS study. The participants in the process should be genuinely interested in the outcome of policy formulation, and hence should be able to perceive that the information they provide will be used, i.e., that the process is not just an academic exercise.

A structured group process would consist of submitting responses on the minimum and maximum feasible and acceptable levels of the variables defining a policy domain. The results would be tabulated, displayed, and fed back to the group. Discussion would follow, and the exercise repeated. The purpose of the process would not be to arrive at a consensus on specific policies, but rather to challenge assumptions and generate creative alternatives. The process would be monitored with measures of disagreement and robustness. When these measures stabilize, the group would move on to another policy domain.

230

9.4 CONCEPT FOR A POLICY SUPPORT SYSTEM

Figure 9.14 is the schematic diagram of our concept of a policy support system that was submitted to OSD. The diagram depicts two types of information. First, there is the more formal type of information consisting of data extracted from reporting systems and models. Second, there is institutional knowledge. The formal data can be processed into management indicators and subjected to trend analysis and structural analysis. The indicators can serve to raise questions and identify potential policy issues.

The interpretive structural framework consists of flow analysis (flow graphs), resource analysis (bipartite graphs), and hierarchical analysis. Hierarchical analysis provides the basis for strategic prioritization, while flow and resource analysis provide the basis for issue analysis (although variables other than those in the flow graphs and bipartite graphs may also be used in issue analysis). From the entire analytical process emerges a better mutual understanding of conflicts in priorities, values, and perceptions of relationships. The subsequent formulation of policy constrains the behavior of logistics operations, changes in which should be reflected in the formal data feedback and/or the perceptions and values of policy actors.

In subsequent DoD research, we have focused attention specifically on formal sources of information and how they can be used as an aid in policy-level resource allocation. The result is depicted in Figure 9.15, which is essentially equivalent to Figure 9.14 but with greater emphasis on data collection and reporting systems, models, and other formal processing of information. In addition, the focus of Figure 9.15 is broadened to consider the readiness of all DoD forces. A primary conclusion of this research is that the application of the interpretive structural framework to formal information must rely to a great extent on qualitative evaluation. That qualitative evaluation requires subjective assessments of the quantitative data provided by the various formal sources. Of course, those formal sources themselves involve quantitative analysis, but in a form restricted by the structure and assumptions used. It is the evaluation of these structures and assumptions that is a primary role of policy-level management.

231

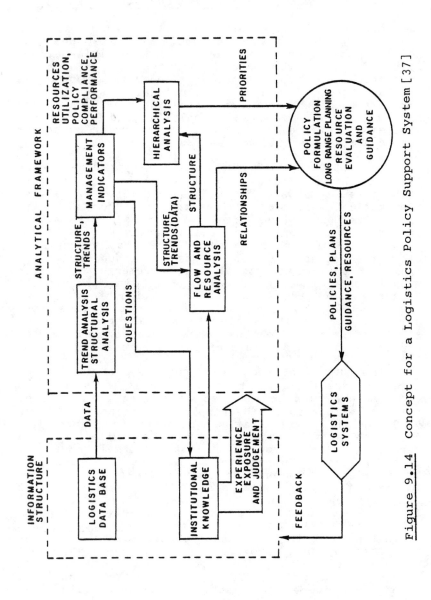

Figure 9.14 Concept for a Logistics Policy Support System [37]

232

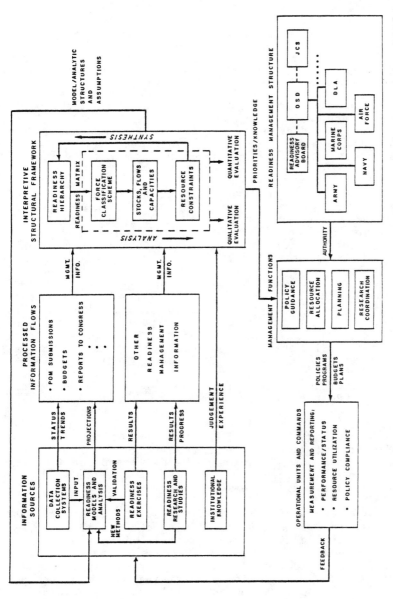

Figure 9.15 Concept for a Readiness Policy Support System [38]

233

NOTES

1. John N. Warfield, Societal Systems: Planning, Policy, and Complexity (New York: John Wiley and Sons, 1976).

2. Murray A. Geisler, Mary J. Hutzler, Robert D. Kaiser, Myron G. Myers, and Laurence D. Richards, A Macro Analysis of DoD Logistics Systems, vol. I: Logistics Systems in the Department of Defense (Washington, D.C.: Logistics Management Institute, December 1976).

3. Murray A. Geisler, Mary J. Hutzler, Robert D. Kaiser, Myron G. Myers, and Laurence D. Richards, A Macro Analysis of DoD Logistics Systems, vol. II: Structure and Analysis of the Air Force Logistics System (Washington, D.C.: Logistics Management Institute, September 1977).

4. A cruise missile is an unmanned, warhead carrying, vehicle powered by an air-breathing engine. The air-breathing engine makes ᴗhe missile capable of sustained flight and gives it maneuverability similar to that of a jet aircraft. Henry D. Levine, "Some Things to All Men: The Politics of Cruise Missile Development," Public Policy 25(Winter 1977): 117-168.

5. John D. Steinbruner, The Cybernetic Theory of Decision (Princeton, N.J.: Princeton University Press, 1974).

6. Levine, pp. 121-122. See also Coulam's discussion of the F-111 fighter-bomber: Robert F. Coulam, Illusions of Choice: The F-111 and the Problem of Weapons Acquisition Reform (Princeton, N.J.: Princeton University Press, 1977).

7. A General Accounting Office study of management practices in OSD made the following observations: "Concerning OSD's involvement in micromanagement, the Deputy Secretary of Defense stated that (1) OSD should devote its time to formulating and evaluating policy and supervising policy execution and (2) the size and complexity of OSD suggested that greater emphasis was being given to the form and process of management than to the substance of the policy issues that OSD should be treating...We

234

found, however, a trend of increasing OSD involve-
ment in the day-to-day management of the military
departments. It is especially noticeable in
installations and logistics, manpower, personnel,
and research and development." [General
Accounting Office, Highlights of a Report on
Staffing and Organization of Top-Management
Headquarters in the Department of Defense
(Washington,D.C.: Office of the Comptroller
General, July 6, 1976), pp. 24-25.]

8. For example, OSD has been the primary advocate
of the Defense Logistics Agency (DLA). DLA is the
centralized manager of consumable supply inventories
for all military services. There is also support in
OSD for making DLA a centralized organization for the
repair of certain spare parts and equipments.

9. This problem is not limited to OSD, but in fact
pervades the entire logistics establishment. Consider,
for example:
"The failure to understand modern Military
Logistics--what it is, what it does, and what its
objectives are--has led to the evolution of a
logistics system which, by its own design, cannot
be effective or efficient. It lacks control, has
split responsibilities, dual channels of
communication, is managed piece-meal, and fails to
focus on the total objective." [Fred Gluck,
"Military Logistics--A Multitude of Sins," SOLE
Spectrum, Fall 1979, p. 23.]

10. Our experience with management indicators is
also described in Murray A. Geisler and Laurence D.
Richards, "The Use of Management Indicators in a Large
Public System," in Studies in Operations Management,
ed. Arnoldo C. Hax (Amsterdam: North-Holland
Publishing Co., 1978), pp. 544-561.

11. Some of the indicators included Stock
Availability (a supply indicator), Percent
Containerization (a transportation indicator), and
Aircraft Engine Mean Time Between Overhaul (a
maintenance indicator).

12. The reporting system for operational readiness
was modified in 1978 and the name of the measure
changed to Mission Capability. However, we will use
the old term in this book.

13. Murray A. Geisler, Mary J. Hutzler, Robert D. Kaiser, and Laurence D. Richards, A Macro Analysis of DoD Logistics Systems, vol. III: A Framework for Policy-Level Logistics Management (Washington, D.C.: Logistics Management Institute, December 1978), p. 1-12.

14. Geisler, et. al., Macro Analysis, vol. II, p. 30.

15. John F. Rockart, "Chief Executives Define Their Own Data Needs," Harvard Business Review, March/April 1979, pp. 81-93. Using critical success factors (CSFs) to identify policy-level indicators, Rockart also concludes that "only very occasionally is there much overlap between financial accounting data and the type of data required to track CSFs," (p. 92) indicating that the desire by DoD administrators for a "Chairman of the Board Report" is perhaps misconceived.

16. Hoffenberg's remarks are specifically in response to Nestor E. Terleckyj, "Measuring Progress Towards Social Goals: Some Possibilities at National and Local Levels," Management Science 16(August 1970): B765-B778.

17. Marvin Hoffenberg, "Comments on 'Measuring Progress Towards Social Goals: Some Possibilities at National and Local Levels'," Management Science 16(August 1970): B-783.

18. This line of thought is expanded in Laurence D. Richards, Peter L. Eirich, and Murray A. Geisler, A Concept for the Management of Readiness (Washington, D. C.: Logistics Management Institute, January 1980). Sorley is even more critical of the indicator approach to readiness management, arguing that the impersonal nature of statistical evaluation actually degrades readiness.
    "The differences between personal leadership and evaluation on the one hand and impersonal manage-ment and statistical evaluation on the other have direct bearing on combat readiness...I believe it is not too much to suggest that depersonalized command and evaluation by statistics are major factors in producing a climate which now dispirits and repels so many of those who were initially willing to give the Army a try." [Lewis Sorley, "Professional Evaluation and Combat Readiness," Military Review, October 1979, pp. 50,

53.]

19. The complexity and ambiguity of the concept of readiness is recognized within OSD. In fact, the Secretary of Defense established the Readiness Management Steering Group (RMSG) in November 1977 to develop a long-range plan for improving the measurement and analysis of readiness. In a study of progress made by the RMSG, the General Accounting Office concluded:
"The Secretary of Defense's Readiness Management Steering Group has not taken adequate or timely action to ensure the effective development of the analytical tools and capabilities needed to link resources to readiness. Also, the Steering Group has not provided the services with the overall guidance and coordination they need to develop these capabilities." [General Accounting Office, DoD's Materiel Readiness Report to the Congress -- Improvement Needed to Better Show the Link Between Funding and Readiness (Washington, D.C.: Office of the Comptroller General, October 12, 1979), p. 9.]

20. Richards, et al., Readiness, p. 2-2.

21. Each term is defined in Richards, et al., Readiness, Chapter 2.

22. Geisler, et al., Macro Analysis, vol. III, p. 5-7.

23. Ibid., p. 3-6.

24. Ibid., p. 3-8.

25. Ibid., p. 3-10.

26. Ibid., p. 3-11.

27. See Geisler et al., Macro Analysis, vol. III, Chapter 3.

28. Jay W. Forrester, Principles of Systems (Cambridge, Mass.: Wright-Allen, 1968).

29. Richards, et al., Readiness, p. 6-7.

30. We were, for example, continually confronted with the rational mode of thinking in our discussions with DoD officials. The resolute separation of ends

237

from means (i.e., requirements from budgets) and the search for linear cause and effect often presented barriers to the communication of our ideas.

31. We believe, for example, that this is implicit in the task assigned by the Secretary of Defense to the RMSG to "develop the analytic tools necessary to relate resource inputs to resulting readiness." ("Readiness Measurement, Reporting, Analysis, and Management," Sec Def Memorandum, 2 November 1977.)

32. Richards, et al., Readiness, p. 6-7.

33. J. K. Friend and W. N. Jessop, Local Government and Strategic Choice, 2nd ed. (Oxford, England: Pergamon Press, 1977), p. 115.

34. The concern and disagreement over the types of technology that DoD is currently procuring is cogently expressed in James Fallows, "Muscle-Bound Superpower: The State of America's Defense," The Atlantic, October 1979, pp. 59-78.

35. Thomas L. Saaty, "A Scaling Method for Priorities in Hierarchical Structures," Journal of Mathematical Psychology 15(June 1977): 234-281.

36. The calculations are in Geisler, et al., Macro Analysis, vol. III, pp. 5-12, 5-13, 5-16.

37. Ibid., p. 6-6.

38. Richards, et al., Readiness, p. 7-3.

CHAPTER 10

POLICY SUPPORT: INSTITUTIONAL KNOWLEDGE

A primary conclusion of the study for the Office of the Secretary of Defense was that institutional knowledge represents a source of information of substantial relevance to policy formulation. By institutional knowledge we mean the repository of information made up of the technical backgrounds, experiences, and judgments (i.e., perceptions and values) possessed by individuals at all levels of an organization. Unfortunately, institutional knowledge is neither catalogued nor indexed. There are also significant differences in the forms in which it is packaged. We recognize it as an advanced class of information, one requiring a more generalized, yet still structured, approach if it is to be adequately exploited. The provision of an interpretive structural framework with a basis in the mathematics of constraint theory is a first step toward such an approach.

Realizing that the data collection and analysis of institutional knowledge would take a form different from that of typical questionnaires, we concluded that a demonstration of a questionnaire structure based on the constraint-theoretic language and mathematics would be a worthwhile and complementary research endeavor. While the questionnaire is not a particularly desirable medium of communications, it does provide a simple means of demonstrating the new form of data collection and analysis, a form which could readily be adapted to other media (e.g., gaming or computer conferencing). Following a period of negotiation with the President and Chairman of the Board of the MFS Finance Corporation, a research project for this purpose was mutually agreed upon.

This chapter describes the results of the MFS research project. In the first section we describe our initial investigation of the operations and policies of MFS Finance. This investigation involved interviews with managers at all levels of the organization and a review of company and industry documents. In the next section, we present and discuss the results of the first questionnaire administered to MFS personnel.

This questionnaire served the purpose of strategic prioritization in that it narrowed the focus of the second questionnaire. The results of the second questionnaire are presented in the third section. In particular, methods of nested constraint analysis --analysis of prominent points and analysis of disagreement -- are demonstrated. Difficulties experienced in the conduct of the research have implications for the successful implementation of a policy support system based on the proposed modelling approach. We discuss these implications in the fourth section.

10.1 PRELIMINARY INVESTIGATION

The MFS study began with a series of interviews conducted with MFS personnel. The purpose of the interviews was primarily to acquire sufficient knowledge of the consumer finance industry and of the MFS organization to be able to write thoughtful and meaningful questions for inclusion in the two questionnaires to be administered. If the project had been a consulting project aimed at implementing a policy support system or at making specific recommendations, more effort would have been put into interviewing personnel in the field offices. However, time and travel limitations required that the number of interviews be minimized, a requirement completely compatible with the principal objective of the research.

Interviews were accomplished with individuals from all managerial levels of the company, including both line and staff personnel. Figure 10.1 shows the titles and organizational position of the interviewees. The titles are not all precise; in fact, the organization chart was undergoing revision at the time of the research.

To place these interviews in perspective, there are over 500 employees in MFS. There are two principal Regional Directors, four Division Officers, approximately fourteen District Supervisors, and over 150 loan offices. Most loan offices are assigned a Loan Officer, an Associate Loan Officer, and a Loan Officer Trainee.

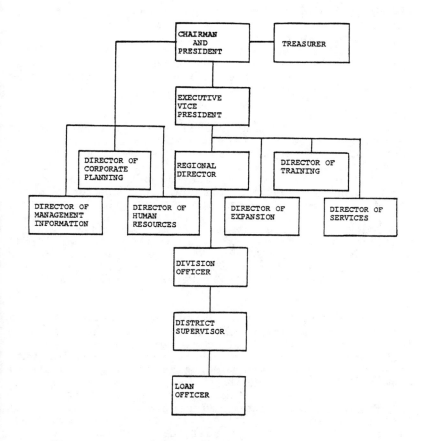

Figure 10.1   Simplified Organization Chart for
the MFS Finance Corporation

10.1.1 Description

The MFS Finance Corporation ranks in the top 50 of
over 800 consumer finance companies in the United
States.   The industry leaders are Household Finance and
Beneficial Finance, each with approximately 3000 sales
offices and $3 billion in loans outstanding.   MFS
currently has over $150 million in loans outstanding.
Total consumer finance company outstandings were $44
billion in 1977, up from $27.7 billion in 1970.

MFS has offices in ten states, but plans to eventually operate in almost every state in the country. Offices are located to serve primarily rural and suburban customers. Many city offices have been closed and further movement away from the cities appears inevitable. In one major city in which MFS at one time had twenty-five offices, for example, there are now only six offices.

The consumer finance industry is regulated by state law, and different states have different maximum loan ceilings and interest rate structures. West Virginia, for example, has a $1200 ceiling, while in Pennsylvania it is $5000 and in New Jersey, $2500. These state regulations are important factors in formulating a growth strategy in a consumer finance company. Seven states operate under the Uniform Commercial Credit Code (USCC) which sets interest rates uniformly in those states. At the time of our research, these rates were 36% for the first $300, 21% for loans up to $1000, and 15% up to $25,000, but never an overall rate less than 18%. This liberal rate structure makes these USCC states favorable locations for expansion.

While direct personal loans are the specialty of the consumer finance industry, they represent less than half of the business of consumer finance companies. Most companies complement their personal lending with services such as second mortgage lending, industrial banking, sales financing (particularly automobile sales), long-term leasing, and revolving loans. The MFS Finance Corporation currently relies on direct personal loans for three-fourths of its business, although it plans to diversify further into the above services as well as others like point-of-sale financing, thrift certificates, small business lending, and preferred customer lending.

The average MFS customer is in the 25-50 percentile (second quartile) income bracket, i.e., below the national median. In 1976, his average income was $11,000 and he was most likely to be a factory worker. Most of these customers borrow for emergencies, purchase of durables (e.g., automobiles, mobile homes, furniture), travel and vacations, education, or consolidation of existing debt. This contrasts sharply with the average customer for a second mortgage loan whose income is well above the national median (approximately the 75th percentile).

The average cash loan issued by a consumer finance company in 1977 was $1,493, as compared to the average sales loan of $5,251 for a new car and $2,787 for a used car. There are also certain market trends which should not be ignored. The average term for cash loans, for example, increased from 38.8 months in 1976 to 42.8 months in 1977. In addition, there has been a steady trend away from unsecured loans; in 1966, 35% of consumer finance industry loans were unsecured, whereas in 1976, only 20% were unsecured.

As mentioned in Chapter 1, MFS top management is concerned that loan office skills necessary for the company to achieve the growth and market strategies it has committed itself to may not be adequate. In addition, the turnover of new personnel is extremely high. In response, MFS was, at the time of this research, in the process of implementing a change in the "management style" of the organization. The program for implementing that change is called "management by planning" and is designed to increase the involvement and participation of MFS personnel in setting quarterly goals and objectives and developing plans to achieve them.

It is important to note that the management-by-planning program was not the first attempt by MFS to introduce more participation into the planning process. A few years ago a "management by objectives" program was instituted. Top management attributes failure of the program to inadequate training prior to implementing the program and, to some extent, a lack of total commitment from MFS personnel. The objectives established by Loan Officers, for example, were not consistent with the potential of the loan offices. At the quarterly planning sessions, neither Loan Officers nor District Supervisors were adequately prepared to evaluate the performance achievable by the loan offices. "Management by objectives" was replaced with "management by direction." Under management-by-direction, quarterly performance goals were established by top management and imposed on District Supervisors and Loan Officers. The management-by-panning program differs from the management-by-objectives program in that extensive training and preparation are taking place before the program is fully implemented.

10.1.2 Structural Analysis

The structure of MFS operations is not nearly as complicated as is that of DoD logistics operations. Figure 10.2 depicts the structure of loan office operations in terms of flows of cash and other communications with the customers. The two activities that make up these operations are lending activity (top of diagram) and the collecting activity (bottom of diagram). The tension between these two activities, i.e., the quantity of loans granted versus the risk of delinquency, is the essence of the consumer finance industry. The industry exists because it accepts risks that other financial institutions do not.

The role of capacity in the flow graph of Figure 10.2 is perhaps not as central as it was in the flow graphs for DoD logistics. In the private sector, the economic incentives are such that corporations attempt to operate as close to capacity as possible. The holding of excess capacity is regarded as a situation to be avoided. It could be argued that, in a highly uncertain environment, slack capacity provides a company with the ability to adapt to unanticipated circumstances. Most oligopolistic corporations, in fact, do maintain some excess capacity. In highly competitive industries, however, the survival of a company often depends on its ability to exploit its markets to the maximum extent possible with the minimum of expense. In such companies, financial statements representing flows of cash are particularly relevant as sources of management information; this is again in constrast to the lesser significance of financial information in large, bureaucratic organizations.

We were asked by MFS top management to examine, specifically, personnel processes and policies in the company. Figure 10.3 diagrams the flow of employees in MFS beginning with the recruiting process. Employees are hired, trained, and promoted. If they are satisfied, they remain with the company. Dissatisfaction with their jobs is indicated by the employee turnover rate. The inducements to stay with the company and contribute to MFS organizational objectives include the quality of the training program, salaries, job design, and prevailing patterns of communication. These, as well as recruiting and promoting practices, represent potential policy domains. A change in organizational strategy, e.g., the management-by-planning program, will undoubtedly

244

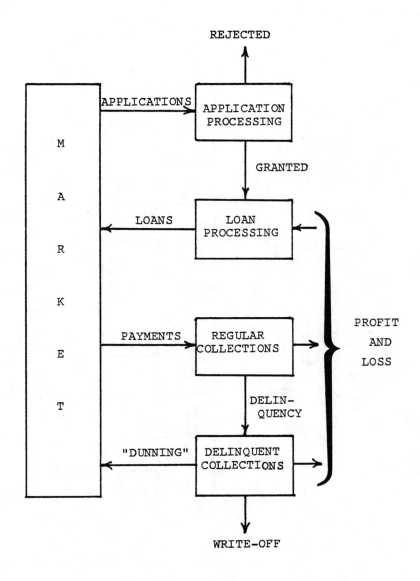

Figure 10.2   Loan Office Operations

245

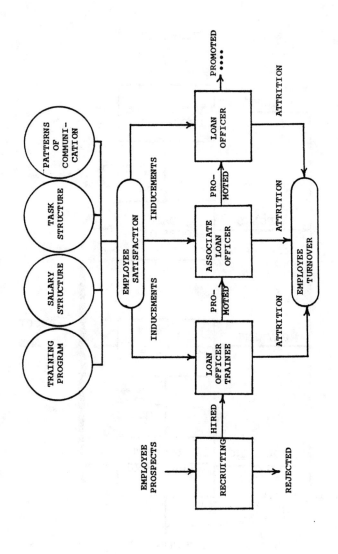

Figure 10.3 MFS Personnel Processes

246

involve some adjustments in personnel processes and policies.

10.1.3 Issue Identification

While we were asked to concentrate on policy issues related to personnel processes, the interrelationship of growth, market, and organizational strategies suggested that we investigate differences of opinion on these other aspects of strategy as well. The first questionnaire administered was aimed at pinpointing those strategic and policy issues which MFS personnel believe to be most critical, and over which there is disagreement with respect to the appropriate response. The eight broad issues selected fall into three categories as shown in Figure 10.4.

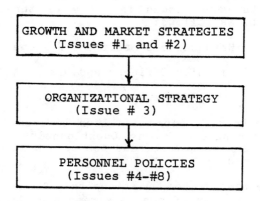

Figure 10.4 Structure of Questionnaire #1

The first two issues provide the strategic context for the issues on the remainder of the questionnaire. Issue #3 focuses on those personnel processes that are most likely to be affected by the management-by-planning program. The processes themselves represent sources of more specific policy issues. These are the subject of the last five issues of the questionnaire, and include consideration of the development of loan office skills, the loan conversion rate (i.e., percentage of applications converted to loans), the use of automated equipment in the loan offices, the employee turnover rate, and the generation of creative management and marketing ideas. The

247

selection of these issues was based primarily on the insights of, or disagreement among, interviewees.

10.2 STRATEGIC PRIORITIZATION

The research design agreed upon by MFS called for a distribution of forty questionnaires on each phase of the project. Thirty-one respondents returned Questionnaire #1. While from a statistical point of view this does not represent a large sample size, for the purpose of demonstrating the approach it was sufficient. A copy of Questionnaire #1 is enclosed in Appendix A.1, and summary data tables appear in Appendix B.1.

To analyze the results of both questionnaires, respondents were placed into one of three levels of management, as follows:

Level I -- Headquarters Staff and Regional Directors

Level II -- Division Officers and District Supervisors

Level III-- Loan Officers

Associate Loan Officers and Loan Officer Trainees did not participate. On Questionnaire #1, eleven respondents were Level I and ten each were Level II and Level III managers.

Respondents to Questionaire #1 were asked to prioritize a list of possible responses to each of the eight issues identified. The procedure was different than that proposed in the DoD project in that it involved a simple ranking of the alternatives in the order of their potential for resolving the issues. Respondents also had the opportunity to add their own responses, and a few did in fact provide some interesting alternatives.

10.2.1 Method of Analysis

The method of analysis used on the results of Questionnaire #1 involved the calculation of a mean (i.e., consensus) ranking for each of the three levels of management. The procedure involves finding the ranking that minimizes the sum of the distances between each individual ranking and the consensus ranking.[1] As an example, assume that five respondents rank four alternatives as follows:

	Respondent				
Alternative	1	2	3	4	5
1	4	3	2	1	3
2	2	4	2	2	4
3	1	1	1	3	2
4	3	2	1	2	1

The first step is to examine all pairs of alternatives for relative preference:

	Respondent					Group Preference
Alternative Pair	1	2	3	4	5	
1 > 2	-1	+1	0	+1	+1	+2
1 > 3	-1	-1	-1	+1	-1	-3
1 > 4	-1	-1	-1	+1	-1	-3
2 > 3	-1	-1	-1	+1	-1	-3
2 > 4	+1	-1	-1	0	-1	-2
3 > 4	+1	+1	0	-1	-1	0

A -1 implies that the preference does not apply; a +1 implies that it does; and a 0 implies indifference. The group preference for each pair is indicated by the sign of the sum across each row, with the exception that a row containing a majority of 0's is assigned a group preference of 0. If a unique ranking satisfies all group pairwise preferences, as it does in this case, that becomes the consensus ranking;

	Alternative			
	1	2	3	4
Rank	3rd	4th	1st	1st

Alternative 3 and 4 are tied for first.

249

However, if intransitivity occurs in the group preferences a weight (w_{ij}) must be assigned to each pair to determine which should have priority. If the group preference is <u>positive</u>, each +1 is given a weight of 1.0 and each 0 a weight of 0.5. If the group preference is <u>negative</u>, each -1 is given a weight of 1.0 and each 0 a weight of 0.5. If the group preference is <u>zero</u>, each 0 is given a weight of 1.0 and each +1 and -1 <u>pair</u> a weight of 1.0 (0.5 each).

| | Respondent | | | | | Group |
Alternative Pair	1	2	3	4	5	Weight
1 > 2	0	1.0	0.5	1.0	1.0	0.7
1 > 3	1.0	1.0	1.0	0	1.0	0.8
1 > 4	1.0	1.0	1.0	0	1.0	0.8
2 > 3	1.0	1.0	1.0	0	1.0	0.8
2 > 4	0	1.0	1.0	0.5	1.0	0.7
3 > 4	0.5	0.5	1.0	0.5	0.5	0.6
						4.6

The group weights (W_i) are the sum across each row divided by the number of respondents. If a consensus ranking violates one of the group preferences, the group weight will change for that alternative pair. The sum of the group weights divided by the number of alternative pairs represents the maximum agreement achievable in a consensus ranking, in this case $4.6 \div 6 = 0.77$. We normalize this to a scale from 0 to 1 and call it a measure of disagreement (d), a 0 indicating maximum disagreement and a 1 indicating perfect agreement. In this case d = 0.54. To calculate a consensus ranking, we minimize disagreement, i.e., maximize the measure.

Notationally, if a_{ij} is the preference of individual j with respect to alternative pair i, (-1,0,+1):

$$w_{ij} = \begin{cases} 1.0 & \text{if } \sum_j a_{ij} > 0 \text{ and } a_{ij} > 0, \\ & \quad \sum_j a_{ij} < 0 \text{ and } a_{ij} < 0, \\ & \text{or } \sum_j a_{ij} = 0 \text{ and } a_{ij} = 0 \\ 0.5 & \text{if } \sum_j a_{ij} \neq 0 \text{ and } a_{ij} = 0, \\ & \text{or } \sum_j a_{ij} = 0 \text{ and } a_{ij} \neq 0 \text{ for each} \\ & \hspace{3cm} (+1,-1)\text{ pair} \\ 0 & \text{otherwise} \end{cases} \qquad (10\text{-}1)$$

$$W_{ij} = \frac{\sum_{j=1}^{r} w_{ij}}{r} \qquad (10\text{-}2)$$

$$d = \frac{2 \sum_{i=1}^{n} W_i}{n} - 1 \qquad (10\text{-}3)$$

where r = number of respondents
m = number of alternatives
$$n = \frac{m!}{(m-2)!\,2!}$$

A comparison of the consensus rankings highlighted differences of opinion between levels of management. A comparison of measures of disagreement indicated the relative confidence of each level with respect to the appropriateness of their responses. The identification of controversial issues provided a focus for subsequent

251

analysis. Our interpretation and discussion of the results, however, should be viewed as our own subjective assessment, but one that might throw some light on these difficult issues.

10.2.2 Growth and Market Strategies

MFS is a wholly owned subsidiary of a large financial corporation, which we will refer to as Industrial Banking, Inc. (IBI). IBI has already negotiated with MFS a long-term growth and market strategy. The intent of Issues #1 and #2 was not so much to generate new insights into these strategies, but rather to put the respondents into a strategic frame of mind prior to the subsequent issues of organizational strategy. The point is that MFS had grown at an annual rate of 25 to 30 percent prior to 1978, nearly twice the average for the consumer finance industry as a whole. While their growth strategy still calls for MFS to grow at better than the industry average, the planned rate is closer to 18 percent. This aggressive growth strategy has significant implications for appropriate organizational strategies and policies.

Table 10.1 lists the four strategic alternatives that received top ranking for Issue #1 by all three levels of management. Below the table are the disagreement measures for the respective levels. There was substantial agreement on this issue among the three levels of management. This was to be expected given that MFS growth strategy is fairly well formulated and determined to a great extent by policies of the parent

Table 10.1 Average Rankings on Growth Strategy

Strategic Alternative	Overall Ranking	Level I	Level II	Level III
Open Offices in New States	1	2	1	1
Grow Through Acquisitions	2	1	2	2
Open More Offices in Current States	3	3	3	3
Slow the Growth Rate	4	4	4	4
Disagreement Measure:	.60	.74	.66	.48

company. The primary difference in the rankings was the emphasis by Level I on acquiring companies which already have established offices and clientele, as opposed to Levels II and III who placed greater emphasis on opening new offices in states where MFS does not now operate. A possible explanation for this difference is that Levels II and III are in a position to feel more threatened by acquisitions. Acquisitions will bring in new and experienced personnel who will be competing with MFS personnel already in good standing for promotions to higher level positions.

The amount of disagreement within each level was also significant. The fact that Level I had the least amount of disagreement is indicative of the role of top management in establishing the company's growth strategy. The greater disagreement within Levels II and III indicates less confidence, as a group, in the appropriate direction to take.

A couple of respondents commented that the problem with MFS growth strategy is the lack of a creative marketing strategy to accompany it. The market area mentioned most often as providing the greatest opportunity for diversification was second mortgage lending. One respondent felt that a highly trained and specialized "sales force" with responsibility only for seeking out potential customers should be considered. Such a change, however, would have to be handled very delicately to ensure no adverse effects on the MFS image. In addition, major changes in the current credit rating system might have to be instituted.

Issue #2 asked for opinions on the customers and services which offer the greatest opportunities for market penetration. Table 10.2 shows the results for the alternatives ranked first through third overall. As with growth strategy, there was substantial agreement among the three levels on the direction market strategy should proceed. While the acquisition of companies which already have a demonstrated expertise in various forms of lending, and that already have an established customer base, is a very attractive strategy, there were more respondents who felt that significant opportunities were available for the MFS organization to diversify its own line of services and to attract new customers. Again, the Loan Officers (Level III) expressed more concern about the strategy of acquisition than did middle and top management.

Table 10.2 Average Rankings on Market Strategy

Strategic Alternative	Overall Ranking	Level I	Level II	Level III
Provide New Services to New Customers	1	1	1	1
Diversify Through Acquisitions	2	2	2	3
Provide New Services to Present Customers	2	3	3	2
Disagreement Measure:	.58	.54	.60	.62

Differences in the amount of disagreement within each level are not particularly significant. It is interesting to note, however, that unlike Issue #1 the greatest amount of disagreement occurred within Level I and the least in Level III. A possible explanation of this is that those who have the closest contact with customers are the most confident with respect to what will work.

Additional comments submitted by respondents further support the contention that market opportunities exist in both new and current services, and that new services can attract both new and current customers. One District Supervisor went a step further by suggesting that diversification into new services must be accompanied by an expansion of the customer base for current services in order to take advantage of the primary form of advertising used by MFS, the referral. At present, MFS estimates that 40% of their new business comes from customer referrals and another 40% from merchant referrals. As a result, 80% of the advertising budget goes into the Very Important Merchant (VIM) and Very Important Person (VIP) programs. Virtually all solicitations are made through the people and businesses participating in these programs. It is estimated that 8-10% of solicitations result in a loan. The other 20% of the advertising budget goes into newspaper ads and yellow page ads, with some radio spots and direct mail advertising, particularly in areas where new offices have been opened. These forms of advertising are considered justifiable for providing greater name recognition, but are difficult to trace to an impact on new accounts.

10.2.3 Organizational Strategy

Whereas the first two issues addressed strategies for dealing with opportunities and uncertainties external to MFS, this issue addressed opportunities for change internal to MFS. The alternative "thrusts" selected for the question were based on concerns expressed during interviews. The remaining five issues of Questionnaire #1 address these thrusts individually. Table 10.3 shows the results for the four thrusts ranked highest. Top management (Level I) ranked the need for creative marketing and management ideas first in importance, while Levels II and III gave the need for loan office skills and lower employee turnover higher priority. This again probably reflects the responsibilities and perceived roles of the different levels of management. Top management is more concerned with the need to remain competitive in the industry as a whole, while middle and lower management are more concerned with acquiring and retaining the qualified personnel needed to achieve the results expected of them.

Table 10.3 Average Rankings on Organizational Strategy

Strategic Thrusts	Overall Ranking	Level I	Level II	Level III
Increase Loan Office Skills	1	2	1	2
Reduce Employee Turnover	1	3	2	1
Generate Creative Ideas	3	1	3	3
Improve Loan Conversion	4	4	4	4
Disagreement Measure:	.58	.58	.68	.60

While improving loan conversion was not in the same class with respect to importance as the first three thrusts, it was ranked above the thrusts dealing with automated technologies. Furthermore, because the loan conversion policies affect collections, delinquency, and loan quality and quantity, it is intrinsically related to the top three thrusts.

Again, the differences in amount of disagreement within levels is not particularly significant. However, it is interesting that on this issue it is Level II that expressed the greatest confidence in its ranking. A possible explanation might be that being situated in the middle makes Level II more aware of organizational conflicts.

The most interesting comments submitted by respondents on this issue dealt with accounts per employee. One Loan Officer argued that the increased accounts per employee made possible by automated processing of accounts was reducing time available for training. He felt that accounts per employee could actually be increased without the use of a computer, and that as a side benefit additional on-the-job training would be realized. He felt so strongly that the computers were not performing as expected that he made "using less automated technologies and procedures" the top priority issue.

Another Loan Officer expressed the opinion that these organizational issues form a "vicious circle." A high employee turnover rate results in faster promotions; faster promotions result in insufficient training in the required skills; inadequate skills result in a greater emphasis on collections and delinquency than on quality lending; and the pressure resulting from emphasis on collections and delinquency increases the employee turnover rate. This, in our opinion, is a very important observation, for it implies that a strategy is required to arrest the vicious circle by simultaneously addressing all four issues. MFS believes that the management-by-planning program is such a strategy.

10.2.4 Personnel Policies

Loan Office Skills. Deficiencies in the skills possessed by loan office personnel is an issue that was mentioned repeatedly in interviews. These skills include, first, the technical skills involved in making a loan, monitoring payments, and collecting on delinquent accounts, i.e., "learning the business." These skills can, with time and supervision, be learned by almost anyone.

More difficult are the skills involved in dealing with customers on a personal basis. These "people" skills lead to quality lending and lower rates of delinquency. There is general agreement that these skills can only be learned through on-the-job training, practice, and close supervision; and different individuals have different affinities for learning

256

these skills. Some seem to possess an inate "street sense" while others may never become proficient.

Finally, there are the administrative skills required to keep a loan office running smoothly. These include skills in organizing, planning, and time management. A major thrust of the current MFS training program is to develop these skills in Loan Officers. Running an office, of course, also involves people skills, i.e., keeping loan office personnel reasonably happy and motivated.

The explanations for current loan office skills not being adequate include hiring less than qualified personnel, promoting personnel before they have had enough experience, and training personnel insufficiently. At present, almost all hiring of loan office personnel is the responsibility of the District Supervisors and their Loan Officers. One factor believed to be contributing to the lower than desired quality hiring is the pressure felt by District Supervisors and Loan Officers to fill vacancies as soon as possible. The high turnover among new employees complicates the hiring problem further. A few years ago MFS experimented with a group of college graduates. These carefully selected individuals were given special attention and recognition. The experiment was a failure, most of the group leaving MFS within a year. At present, the typical employee has a high school diploma, with 44% owning some form of college education.

Promotion rate is also affected by turnover, as well as by the corporate growth rate. The logical place to acquire new District Supervisors and Loan Officers to manage newly opened offices is from the current crop of MFS Loan Officers and Associate Loan Officers. Furthermore, promoting Loan Officers or Associate Loan Officers opens other positions which need to be filled. While this can be an important motivating step in the career of an employee, if he/she has not had the time to learn the requisite skills it could have the opposite effect.

District Supervisors have primary responsibility for carrying out the MFS training program. Top management, however, who has responsibility for designing and directing the program, expressed the opinion that either District Supervisors are not following the program or they are not adequately

257

trained to train others. Again, part of the problem is the pressure on District Supervisors to achieve certain performance goals in his/her district. A District Supervisor would often rather spend his/her time in the Loan Offices reviewing new accounts and collecions than training. Furthermore, the larger offices, (i.e., more accounts) tend to be extremely busy, and finding time to train is difficult. It is interesting that the larger offices also apparently have a higher turnover rate than others (according to interviewees).

Table 10.4 shows the results for the six top ranked alternatives for Issue # 4. The primary difference of opinion on this issue was that Level III placed greatest importance on receiving better training in organizing, planning, and time management. Levels I and II, on the other hand, felt that training District Supervisors in how to train was most important. In fact eight out of ten Level II respondents gave this alternative top priority. Of course, these two alternatives are overlapping and improvement in one could require or lead to improvement in the other.

Table 10.4   Average Rankings for Policies on
Loan Office Skills

Alternative Policies	Overall Ranking	Level I	Level II	Level III
Train Supervisors Better	1	1	1	2
Train Loan Office Personnel in Administrative Skills	2	2	2	1
Recruit More Selectively	3	3	4	5
Train New Employees More	4	5	3	2
Train More After First Year	5	6	5	2
Use Personnel Specialists to Hire	5	4	6	6
Disagreement Measure:	.52	.60	.66	.36

Comments accompanying this issue included the opinion of a Loan Officer that too rapid promotions was the principal cause of inadequate loan office skills. A Division Officer predicted that the loan office of

258

the future would have 2000 to 5000 accounts, compared to approximately 1000 at present. To achieve this, he proposes a high degree of specialization among loan office personnel; that is, new employees should be trained in a specialized area, e.g., lending, collecting, marketing, etc. He added that specialization would become essential as the services offered by MFS become more diversified. A District Supervisor felt that company specialists should be used to train and to develop marketing programs.

Loan Conversion. The ratio of loans granted to loan applications made has dropped in recent years from 33% to approximately 25%, according to an informed source in MFS. This compares with a conversion rate for banks of 40-50%. A number of people complained about the wording of this issue, claiming that MFS cannot be compared to the banks. This is, of course, true. However, during the interviews a few MFS managers mentioned the trend as one deserving close scutiny; but no one could articulate clear-cut criteria for determining what an acceptable conversion rate ought to be.

The consumer finance industry differs from banks in that it assumes risks which a bank, sales finance company, credit union, or retailer will not. This justifies the higher interest rates charged by consumer finance companies. In 1977, the average interest rate for cash loans was 20.5%, compared with 17% for retail revolving credit. Despite the higher interest rates, however, the average return on invested capital in 1976 was 10.7% for consumer finance companies, compared with 10.8% for sales finance companies and 10.9% for commercial banks.

Collections are still generally regarded as the most undesirable aspect of the business, although collection methods have changed significantly over the last two decades. However, less than 3% of MFS personal cash loans are charged off as uncollectible. Furthermore, these loans are transferred to a collection agency or an attorney for disposition, and some recovery is usually made.

The procedure for assessing a loan applicant involves a point scoring system which assigns a credit rating to the applicant. An application with a score of 200 or less must, by company policy, be turned down. Approximately 35% of applicants fall into this category. To score over 235, an applicant must have excessive credit; as a result he is also usually turned down. The most critical range is 200-215, where experience and judgment become extremely important in reaching a decision. The types of information used to assign a score include applicant stability as reflected by employment record, marital status, and character references; and ability to pay as reflected by salary, financial obligations, and previous credit record. An applicant who has substantial financial obligations, however, may be accepted if those obligations can be consolidated into a single loan. The point scoring system only provides an indication of credit risk; it does not offer guidance with respect to how much to loan.

The trend toward a lower conversion rate coincides with the trend toward fewer unsecured loans. The explanations for this apparent reduction in willingness to accept a credit risk are not at all clear. Federal and state discrimination laws have required a more careful consideration of turndowns, but there are other economic forces at work also. Some MFS interviewees expressed the opinion that lack of experience, resulting from too rapid promotions and inadequate supervision, was a key factor. Loans processed by a new employee are reviewed by a Loan Officer and occasionally a District Supervisor. After a reasonable period of time, the employee is granted limited authority to make his/her own decisions. A typical procedure is to have the employee write up his/her reasons for making a decision and then critically discuss the decision with the Loan Officer or District Supervisor. While the intent is to build confidence in the trainee, it is questionable how well this procedure is being followed.

Another factor thought to influence the conversion rate is the emphasis placed on "delinquency" as a measure of loan office performance. Some think that loan offices may not be as aggressively converting applicants as they could be in order to avoid delinquency and the hassle required to collect on delinquent accounts. Performance measurement is discussed further under Issue #7, Employee Turnover.

Table 10.5 shows the results for the five responses to Issue #5 ranked highest. The most significant difference here is that Levels II and III apparently believe that the conversion rate can be

Table 10.5 Average Ranking for Policies on
Loan Conversion

Alternative Policies	Overall Ranking	Level I	Level II	Level III
Provide More Training	1	2	1	1
Solicit Higher Socioeconomic Class of Customer	2	1	2	2
Revise Point Scoring System	3	3	3	2
Increase Emphasis on # Accounts as Performance Measure	4	6	3	5
Maintain Current Policy	5	4	7	2
Disagreement Measure:	.46	.54	.56	.40

increased with current applicants simply by providing
personnel with better training. Top management,
however, feels that a change in the customer profile
offers the most potential for improvement, although
there is no reason why both alternatives cannot be
pursued. Changing the customer profile implies
offering a more diversified line of services, a course
of action which will require even more training. There
is some question about the skills required to market a
new line of services, and whether placing emphasis on
acquiring these skills will complicate the current loan
conversion situation even further.

Loan Officers (Level III) expressed a stronger
opinion that the current conversion rate was acceptable
than did the other two levels. They also indicated a
stronger opinion that loan office performance should be
based less on delinquency than is currently the case,
ranking that response tied for fifth, out of the ten
provided. Top management ranked "reducing emphasis on
delinquency" last, with Level II ranking it sixth. Top
management felt that District Supervisors could assume
more of the burden of loan approval, ranking that
alternative tied for fourth. Level II ranked it
seventh and Level III, tied for last.

One Loan Officer suggested changing current
comaker policies as an alternative. The same person
also suggested that the minimum credit rating (200)
could be reduced on an office-by-office basis,

depending on lending performance demonstrated by the office and the payback characteristics of the customers in the particular area.

Automation. MFS began computerizing its operations in 1974. The hope was that quicker service would be provided to the customer and that information on the status and performance of individual offices would be available to top management on a more timely basis. As a result, the average accounts per employee have increased from 260 to 325. Top management now receives information on ten areas of loan office operation (e.g., good to bad loan ratio, waiver of interest or late charges, charge off to profit and loss, and delinquency measured in two ways). The ten offices scoring lowest in each of the ten areas are given closer scrutiny; if an office scores among the lower ten in a number of the areas, it is immediately called to the attention of the appropriate District Supervisor.

It is not clear how the quality of services provided to the customer has changed as a result of automation, however. During interviews with MFS personnel, there were numerous complaints expressed with respect to the quality and reliability of the computer services provided by the current vendor. The problem is known to all levels of management, but the attitude of top management is that the problem will be solved in time and the result will reduce the clerical work performed by the loan office personnel. Loan officers seem much more skeptical of computerization in general, complaining about the extra time required to close the books at the end of the month and the lack of experience in performing this task when the computer is not operating properly. As an illustration of the complications that can occur, it took a month to institute changes into the current computer programs when a new state law changed the interest rate structure in that state.

The automation issue was not as important as the others in Questionnaire #1, but it is related to the others. Policy with respect to computerization will have an effect on the ability of MFS to diversify and grow and on the requirements for specialized skills and training. Furthermore, it changes the relationships between MFS personnel and their customers and between MFS personnel themselves in a fundamental way. After discussions with individuals both within MFS and elsewhere, the general consensus is that, despite the complications and problems, the movement toward more automated processing of information is necessary if any finance company is to remain competitive in the industry. A major challenge in the development and implementation of computerized information systems is to discover better ways to integrate people and technology into a total "socio-technical" system.

After carefully considering the responses to this issue, it was decided to analyze only the first six alternatives. Table 10.6 shows the results. The fact that the overall measure of disagreement was significantly less than the disagreement measure within each level indicates that there was substantial disagreement between levels. Level I placed top priority on pressuring the current vendor to increase reliability, while Levels II and III placed their top priority on investing in a computer of their own. Level I ranked investment in a computer tied for last among the six alternatives considered, placing greater emphasis on better training, more skilled personnel, and changing vendors if necessary.

Table 10.6 Average Rankings for Policies on Automation

Alternative Policies	Overall Ranking	Level I	Level II	Level III
Put More Pressure on Vendor	1	1	2	2
Invest in Own Computer	2	5	1	1
Train in Use of Computer	3	2	4	3
Hire Skilled Personnel	4	3	4	5
Change Vendor	5	4	3	6
Train in Manual Tasks	6	5	4	4
Disagreement Measure:	.30	.44	.50	.42

The rankings also support the observation that Loan Officers are more skeptical of computerization in general. They apparently believe that changing vendors would not solve the problem, ranking that alternative last. They even put more emphasis on training personnel to perform manually the tasks which the computer is responsible for than on hiring personnel

263

skilled in the use of automated technology.

A District Supervisor and Division Officer (Level II) both commented that the current problem is not with the use of computer terminals by loan office personnel. The problem is with programming and day-to-day dependability. Both individuals placed top priority on MFS acquiring a computer of its own, apparently feeling that only limited success could be achieved by putting pressure on the current vendor or changing vendors.

With respect to automated collection procedures, another District Supervisor expressed the opinion that they would not work. He commented that the consumer finance business requires personal contact with the customer. He went on to state that "our big problem with delinquency now is a lack of one-to-one dealing with the customer."

Employee Turnover. The turnover among new employees in the consumer finance industry is high, approximately 30%. In MFS, the turnover has averaged about 33%. While MFS is in line with the industry in general, there is concern that the turnover rate is higher than it ought or needs to be. There is also a belief that, as MFS diversifies and more skilled personnel become necessary, retaining qualified employees must become a priority issue.

Almost all the turnover occurs during the first year of employment. In the first nine months of 1978, approximately 145 people left MFS; 40-50 of those left during the first 30 days of employment. When an employee leaves MFS, he/she is asked to fill out a form which, among other things, asks the individual why he/she is leaving. Typical answers include "poor communication," "insufficient compensation," "lack of opportunities for advancement," and "harassment of customers." There is no question that consumer finance is a pressure business and that collecting can be a disagreeable and demanding task. But there seem to be other forces at work as well, namely (1) inadequate fit between the employee and the job, (2) insufficient compensation, and (3) poor perception of career opportunities.

Achieving a good fit between the employee and the job is accomplished through the hiring process. MFS tries to attract lower-middle class recruits, 19-22 years of age. It purports to offer the prospect a chance to get into management, to move up to the middle class, and to become a respected and influential citizen in the community. There is some indication, however, that in the haste to fill a position some recruits are not adequately screened. Some employee applicants are simply looking for any form of employment; others are trying to acquire enough business experience to move on to a larger company, and possibly a more lucrative salary arrangement. There is also some indication that recruits are not being told the "whole story" about what they will be doing in their first year as a Loan Officer Trainee. During interviews, top management expressed the opinion that the screening process must be improved, possibly through the use of personnel specialists. Division Officers tended to agree, but were doubtful about the feasibility of a large personnel office in MFS. District Supervisors and Loan Officers definitely wanted to keep responsibility for hiring, but felt that more training and advice in recruiting techniques would be useful. One procedure which has been implemented in MFS is the use of a formal interview guide, as the interview is regarded as the most important tool in hiring.

A new employee hired as a Loan Officer Trainee in January 1979 received a salary of $605-$675 per month. A Loan Officer Trainee is promoted to Associate Loan Officer within 12-18 months, where the salary is $950-$1000 per month. These salaries are considered to be close to the average for the consumer finance industry, and current plans are to increase them even more to be competitive with other companies. An Associate Loan Officer may be promoted to Loan Officer within 4-6 months of the previous promotion. Loan Officers generally remain in that position for a minimum of four years. As previously mentioned, there is some concern that many promotions occur too soon to provide employees with adequate experience.

The promotion policy seems to indicate that the opportunities for advancement are wide open; individuals interviewed at all levels of management agreed. However, some expressed the opinion that a new employee may not perceive these opportunities nor his/her own personal development during the first months on the job. If this is so, responsibility must be placed on existing "patterns of communication" in MFS and on the characteristics of the tasks assigned to the employee. Perception of personal development is cultivated through slowly increasing (1) responsibilities, (2) variety of activities performed, (3) participation in company affairs, (4) involvement in training programs, and (5) "supportive" communications. Supportive communications refers to close supervision oriented toward learning, discussions with respect to career development, and continual encouragement as opposed to harsh criticism. The management-by-planning program is designed to improve this form of communication.

One of the problems with supportive communications is in finding the correct balance between performance measurement and employee satisfaction and motivation. Performance goals set too high can have a negative effect on morale, while goals set too low can lead to complacency. The performance measures regarded as most important include number of accounts, loans outstanding, the delinquency cut (loans delinquent more than 30 days, 60 days, and 90 days), and charge off to profit and loss. District Supervisors generally visit their loan offices at least once a month to review progress toward goals and discuss any problem areas. They will, of course, spend more time in offices having difficulty. Likewise, District Supervisors meet with their Division Officers about once a month.

Table 10.7 shows the results for the five responses to Issue #7 ranked highest. The last alternative listed under Issue #7, maintaining current

Table 10.7   Average Rankings for Policies on
Employee Turnover

Alternative Policies	Overall Ranking	Level I	Level II	Level III
Inform Job Applicants Better	1	1	1	1
Provide Better Motivational Training	2	2	2	2
Increase Participation in Planning	3	5	2	8
Emphasize Career Planning	3	7	4	5
Improve Hiring Techniques	5	3	7	3
Disagreement Measure:	.52	.56	.62	.56

policies, was regarded as totally inappropriate by an overwhelming number of respondents. All levels felt that employee applicants ought to be better informed about their job and that better motivational training is essential, if turnover is to be reduced.

Noteworthy among the top five alternatives was (1) that Level III ranked participation in planning eighth out of fourteen with respect to reducing employee turnover, but ranked it first on Issue #8 with respect to improving creativity; (2) that Level II ranked the need for better hiring methods seventh, while the other two levels ranked it tied for third; and (3) that better compensation was not in the top five. Level III ranked "reducing emphasis on delinquency" and "increasing compensation" higher than participative planning. Level II ranked "using personnel specialists" and "increasing compensation after the first year of employment" higher than "improving hiring techniques." The point is that while better compensation was not ranked in the top five overall, it was still an important alternative in the minds of individuals at all levels and should not be ignored. While quality hiring and training are directly relevant to perception of personal development in a new employee, compensation is a "symbol" or company recognition of an employee's personal development.

Table 10.8 Controversial Alternatives for Policies on Employee Turnover

1. Use of Personnel Specialists to Hire

Level	Rank
I	3
II	4
III	last
Overall	6

2. Decrease Emphasis on Delinquency as a Performance Measure

Level	Rank
I	11
II	10
III	3
Overall	9

267

Two alternatives which were particularly controversial are shown in Table 10.8. On these two alternatives, Level III (Loan Officers) indicated opinions which differed significantly from those of the other two levels. The patterns that are manifest in the responses to Issue #7 are very complicated. However, one possible scenario might go like this:

Loan Officers feel that they, and their District Supervisors, are rushing the hiring process in order to fill empty positions. The emphasis on delinquency as a performance measure is an important incentive for filling these positions as rapidly as possible, in order to have more personnel to perform the collecting activity. Once new employees are hired, they are quickly assigned the collecting task, and little time is put aside for motivational training or for training in other activities. Unless emphasis on delinquency is reduced, there will not be sufficient time to recruit more selectively or to train more adequately. Relying on personnel specialists to recruit more selectively would simply complicate the problems of the Loan Officer by introducing additional delay into the hiring process.

District Supervisors and Division Officers agree that Loan Officers feel pressured to achieve certain delinquency goals; but they think that the answer is not to reduce emphasis on delinquency but rather to allow greater participation by Loan Officers and District Supervisors in setting the goals. They feel that they are performing the hiring function as well as is possible, but that they do not have the time to investigate job applicants as thoroughly as they should. Hence, they could use some help from personnel specialists.

Top management feels strongly that emphasis on delinquency as a performance measure cannot be reduced. As one individual from Level I put it, delinquency "is the guts of our business." They believe that using personnel specialists and better investigative methods are the most important backup alternatives to informing applicants better about the job and providing better motivational training. Top management is implicitly placing the hiring responsibility on the District Supervisor, while offering some alternatives which

268

might <u>assist</u> him/her in that task. To address the problems of the Loan Officers, top management is putting their emphasis on the change in management style, which is intended to increase participation in the goal setting process.

One of the suppositions of the second questionnaire is that management by planning, to be successful, will require a change in the task structure of loan office personnel. Again, specialization was mentioned by a respondent as a possible solution to the turnover problem; but, whether tasks become more specialized or not, more time must be made available for hiring, training, and planning.

<u>Generating Creative Ideas</u>. How to generate innovative management and marketing ideas is perhaps the most complicated issue that can face an organization. One Loan Officer, for example, stated that he did not feel qualified to respond to the issue. Yet, innovation is an essential ingredient to the growth and market strategy of any organization that intends to remain competitive in a rapidly changing and uncertain economic and social environment. Top management placed highest priority on this issue (see Table 10.3).

The results for Issue #8 are shown in Table 10.9. The surprise here is that Level III, based on the

Table 10.9 Average Rankings for Policies on
Creative Ideas

Alternative Policies	Overall Ranking	Level I	Level II	Level III
Increase Participation in Planning	1	2	2	1
Improve Training in Creativity	2	2	3	2
Hire Consultants	3	1	4	4
Increase Visibility in Incentives	3	4	1	3
Bring in Outsiders	5	5	5	4
Disagreement Measure:	.36	.38	.40	.64

269

disagreement measure, expressed the highest amount of confidence in their responses. They placed top priority on participative planning, and expressed the strongest opinion against bringing a cross section of outsiders into middle and top management or hiring professional marketing or management consultants to advise top management. Level I, on the other hand placed highest priority on using consultants. It is understandable that lower and middle management would feel threatened by the introduction of outsiders directly into middle and top management. The "promotion from within" policy is a key to their perception of career opportunities. They also perhaps feel that, if given a chance, they could themselves generate some creative ideas. Level II, in fact, placed top priority on providing better incentives for engaging in creative thinking.

One Division Officer suggested that some people should be given two or three days, twice a year, to go away alone and just think. He supports such a policy by arguing that MFS personnel are so task-minded and so involved in producing results that they do not have time to think, nor do they have the inclination to do so. An important point here is that middle management tends to get caught between the needs to produce short-term results at the loan offices on the one hand and to be responsive to the long-term interests of top management on the other. If the tension between these needs becomes too great, one response is to "play it safe," i.e., avoid being controversial. Since creative ideas tend to be controversial by their very nature, the outcome is obvious. When this situation occurs it is unfortunate, for some of the most original ideas are likely to come from those close to the market, the customer, and the operations of the field offices.

10.3 ISSUE ANALYSIS

The issues receiving the greatest attention in Questionnaire #1 were those associated with loan office skills, employee turnover, and the generation of creative ideas. The strategic response to these organizational issues has been the institution of a change in management style, "management by planning." This management style has implications for MFS personnel processes and policies of which policy-level management may not be completely aware. It represents a fundamental change in the "culture" of the MFS organization, and hence in the values and behavior of its personnel. To be successful it requires, first, a total commitment from top management, which it apparently has in MFS; but it also requires a proper perspective on what can be expected of the rest of the organization. The explicit and implicit changes in personnel processes and organizational policies are likely to be met with some resistance and will require a period of adjustment; there are likely also to be consequences which were not anticipated.

The intent of Questionnaire #2 was to make a more detailed and quantitative examination of the values and perceptions of MFS personnel in order to identify conflicts, generate insights and hypotheses, and stimulate creative thinking with respect to alternative approaches to personnel policies. To design this questionnaire required, first, the selection of a policy domain. Six candidate policy domains emerged from the results of Questionnaire #1:

- hiring policies (in terms of quantifiable characteristics of new employees, i.e., age, education, etc.);

- training policies (in terms of quantity and timing of training programs);

- promotion policies;

- job design (i.e., task structure);

- patterns of compensation; and

- patterns of communication.

A proper balance among these policies leads to enhanced employee skills as well as employee perception of personal development--hence lower turnover and greater contribution to organizational objectives, including higher quality and quantity lending and generation of the creative ideas needed for corporate adaptation and growth.

The selection of task structure as policy domain was based on two considerations. First, we hypothesized that, more than any of the other candidates, imminent shifts in policy would be reflected in shifts in task structure. We felt that

271

the success of the MFS organizational strategy would depend on the priorities given to certain activities, e.g., planning, hiring, and training. Second, task structure is more easily quantified in terms of concrete variables than it is for some of the other candidates, in particular, patterns of communication. Hence, the task structures of five key managerial positions--Loan Officer Trainee, Associate Loan Officer, Loan Officer, District Supervisor, and Division Officer--were examined.

The policy variables selected were the percentages of time devoted to each of six task-related activities: lending, collecting, hiring/training, planning/creative thinking, auditing/accounting/security, and monitoring performance/other administrative. The selection of these six categories of activity was the most difficult aspect of the questionnaire design. It was important, for example, to define activities in such a way that they did not overlap. This presents a problem when an individual is actually performing two activities at the same time, e.g., training and lending. The definitions eventually formulated appear in Questionnaire #2, a copy of which is provided in Appendix A.2. Summary data tables appear in Appendix B.2.

10.3.1 Method of Analysis

As with Questionnaire #1, we were permitted to distribute forty copies of Questionnaire #2. We received twenty-one returns, seven from each of the three levels of management. Again, the sample was sufficient for the purposes of our demonstration.

The large quantity of data produced by the second questionnaire made it necessary to be selective in performing the analysis. This required the exercise of judgment on our part, and the interpretations offered do not by any means exhaust the possibilities. We cannot divorce our own values and perceptions from our interpretations. We emphasized this point in both our presentation to the MFS Executive Planning Committee and our final report. The interpretations should be treated as hypotheses with respect to alternative "directions" in which organizational policy might or could proceed in realizing the specified strategic posture.

An analysis of each position was performed separately. While the respondents were asked to express, for each position, the percentage of time that should be devoted to each activity, the absolute numbers are not as important as the degree of change from the present task structure represented by those numbers. Our assumption is that, with a knowledge of the expectations of MFS personnel, policy-level management is in a better position to develop an appropriate training program and to elucidate rough guidelines for time management. The broad results of the first questionnaire provided a strategic context for interpreting the specific shifts indicated in the responses to the second questionnaire.

Of the twelve questions on Questionnaire #2, we concentrated most of our analysis effort on Questions #1 through #4. Question #1 asked for perceptions of how time was currently spent, on the average, in the six task-related activities. Questions #2 and #3 asked for opinions about what minimum and maximum amount of time will have to be spent in the six activities if the management-by-planning program is to be successful. specifically, respondents were to put themselves in the position of policy-level management with the task of developing company-wide guidelines for the management of time. Question #4 asked for opinions on the task structure that respondents felt would be ideal, i.e., how they would redesign organizational roles if given the opportunity. The interesting result of Question #4 was that very seldom did a respondent give an ideal that was outside the limits specified in Questions #2 and #3.

Questions #5 through #9 asked for opinions on how activities should be adjusted if certain conditions were imposed on the task. The intent of these questions was to identify where individuals placed priorities and in which activities they perceived the most flexibility to adjust. Question #10 asked for opinions on what a realistic turnover rate could be. Question #11 asked for opinions on salary increases. Question #12 asked how long the respondent had been employed by MFS. The intent was to examine if there were differences of opinions between those who had been with MFS a few years and those who had been there many years. We will briefly discuss the result of Question #10 and #11. However, we were unable to extract any significant insights from Questions #5-#9 or #12 and will not discuss them further here.

273

Questions #2 and #3 were the keys to the demonstration of constraint analysis. Because they solicited responses on the acceptable <u>variation</u> in task structure, these questions are, we contend, fundamentally different than typical questions that ask for a mean or median. Furthermore, the analysis of a set of data on variation is not as straightforward as the analysis of a set of data on means. The method of constraint analysis is, at present, heuristic in nature, requiring the identification of <u>patterns</u> in the data.

The method of nested constraint analysis suggests that data be analyzed first in one dimension, then two, etc., until sufficient information is acquired to develop some hypotheses about constraint on the variables and on the relationships among the variables. Hence, the analysis performed first involved an examination of each variable independently. An average variation was calculated for each level of managment (Question #2 and #3), and compared to the average perception of time currently spent in each activity (Question #1) and to the average ideal (Question #4). Of particular interest were those cases were the average current time specified in Question #1 was outside the acceptable range specified in Questions #2 and #3. In this chapter one-dimensional analysis is presented in table form, although selected graphical displays are provided in Appendix C.1.

As a result of one-dimensional analysis, we were often able to eliminate certain variables from further consideration. Analysis in two dimensions involved the development of two-dimensional graphs, with each dimension corresponding to a relevant variable; individual responses for the two variables are superimposed on the graph. Two observations are immediately possible with these graphs. First, regions of strong response (i.e., regions that a large number of respondents included within their acceptable range) represent <u>potential</u> coalitions. In a structured group exercise, the dynamic behavior of these regions would be particularly interesting to monitor. Second, responses that are totally out of line with all other responses could be identified. These "outliers" <u>may</u> possess unique insights into possible arrangements of the variables.

While each respondent was not required to provide information on the relationships among variables, the individual responses do <u>bound</u> the perception of

274

relationships. By superimposing these bounded regions, shape begins to emerge in the graph. We contend that one can take advantage of the different perspectives that individual participants bring to an exercise in order to hypothesize the nature of a relationship. We did this through an analysis of prominent points.

The analysis of prominent points as described in Chapters 7 and 8 begins with the transformation of the two-dimensional graph from an interval representation to a discrete representation. (The same procedure is followed for n-dimensional analysis.) In our analysis five percentage point increments were used to discretize the state space. The use of five percent increments also diluted some of the bias toward five and ten percent responses. The set of all ordered pairs (n-tuples) of five percent increments defines the state space. Prominent points are those ordered pairs that a large number of respondents included within their acceptable range of variation. An examination of prominent points often resulted in the identification of some pattern from which we hypothesized a relationship.

In this chapter, two dimensional graphs are presented for all positions except that of Loan Officer. The Loan Officer's task proved sufficiently complex to require a higher dimensional analysis. Two-dimensional graphs are, however, provided in Appendix C.2. Multi-dimensional evaluation of the Loan Officer's task structure also involved analysis of prominent points. The interesting result here is that prominent points in one or two dimensions do not necessarily remain the prominent points in higher dimensions.

If this questionnaire structure were to be adapted to a structured group exercise, analysis of disagreement and robustness, as described in Chapter 7, would be useful in monitoring the exercise or in studying the dynamics of the group process. We demonstrate the analysis of disagreement for the case of the Loan Officer. Analysis of robustness would be very similar.

10.3.2 Loan Office Personnel

Loan Officer Trainee. The task structure of the Loan Officer Trainee is relatively simple. He spends over 85 percent of his time in either the lending or

Table 10.10 Loan Officer Trainee Task Structure

	Current(#1)	Minimum Acceptable(#2)	Maximum Acceptable(#3)	Ideal(#4)
Level I				
Lending	29.3%	24.3%	33.6%	35.0%
	(Range:10-50)	(Range:0-40)	(Range:20-50)	(Range:20-60)
Collecting	56.9%	38.6%	48.6%	45.0%
	(Range:50-85)	(Range:20-60)	(Range:30-70)	(Range:30-65)
Level II				
Lending	31.3%	38.6%	49.3%	45.0%
	(Range:20-45)	(Range:20-70)	(Range:35-70)	(Range:25-70)
Collecting	59.3%	28.9%	40.0%	32.1%
	(Range:35-75)	(Range:25-40)	(Range:25-50)	(Range:25-45)
Level III				
Lending	27.5%	33.3%	41.7%	40.0%
	(Range:15-40)	(Range:25-50)	(Range:35-50)	(Range:30-50)
Collecting	53.5%	32.5%	40.8%	36.7%
	(Range:40-80)	(Range:20-45)	(Range:25-60)	(Range:25-50)
Overall				
Lending	29.5%	32.0%	41.5%	40.0%
	(SD:10.5)	(SD:13.9)	(SD:11.5)	(SD:13.9)
Collecting	56.7%	35.4%	43.3%	38.0%
	(SD:13.2)	(SD:10.2)	(SD:12.1)	(SD:11.5)

collecting activities. Table 10.10 presents the one-dimensional results for these two variables. The columns of the table correspond to the first four questions of Questionnaire #2. The average percentages for each of the three levels of management are provided for each question. Below each percentage is the range of the responses submitted. The overall percentages are averages for all respondents; a standard deviation is provided below those percentages.

The obvious observation is that perceptions of the amount of time spent by Loan Officer Trainees on the collecting activity is well outside the limits deemed acceptable if the management-by-planning program is to be successful. In fact, of the twenty-one respondents only two placed the current situation within the maximum limit, with two others placing it right on the limit. It is also noteworthy that while Levels II and III completely reversed the emphases placed on lending and collecting, Level I maintained higher emphasis on collecting than on lending. This is evident from the responses to Question #4, in particular, where the ideal is outside the limits perceived as permissible. Level II perceived the amount of change needed to be greater than the other two levels, indicating strong concern with the current situation. This could also be interpreted as indicating that middle management perceives the management-by-planning program as representing a major shift in policy with ramifications which top management does not perceive.

Of the other task-related activities, the time spent by Loan Officer Trainees in the auditing/accounting/security activity was perceived to be greater by Level III respondents than by the other two levels. Level III also felt that this was too much time to spend in this activity. All levels indicated that Loan Officer Trainees should spend slightly more time than they currently do in the planning activity. Since the lending and collecting activities dominate the task structure of the Loan Officer Trainee, these variables were selected for two-dimensional analysis. Figure 10.5 is a superposition of all responses to Questions #2 and #3. The numbers within the rectangles represent the number of respondents who included that region within their acceptable limits. The pronounced lines and points represent the responses of individuals who gave the same percentage to both the minimum and maximum limits, i.e., no variation allowable. The circles indicate prominent points. The numbers within

277

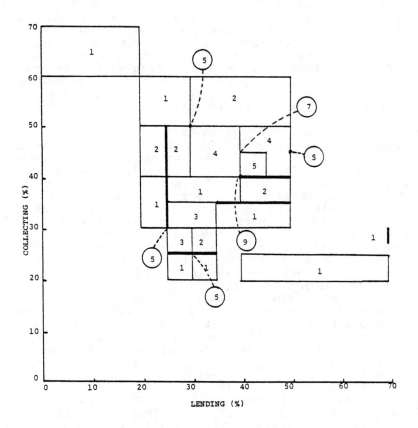

Figure 10.5   Variation in Task Structure for
the Loan Officer Trainee

the circles corresponding to the number of respondents
who included that prominent point within their
acceptable limits.

Two regions stand out as potential coalitions,
although this can only be hypothetical since there was
no interaction among the participants.   The prominent
point that dominates in Figure 10.5 is   40%-lending/
45%-collecting, with 40%-lending/40%-collecting being
second strongest.   The other region that represents a
potential   coalition   is   that   between   30%-lending/

278

25%-collecting and 25%-lending/30%-collecting. These individuals felt that more of the Loan Officer Trainee's time should be spent in training and planning than did other respondents. The pattern exhibited by the prominent points is as expected, namely that if more time is spent in one of the activities less time is available to spend in the other. This relation, of course, results from the overall constraint on available time.

The outliers in Figure 10.5 contributed some interesting comments. The individual in the upper lefthand corner felt that Loan Officer Trainees should be put through a period of trial by experience, primarily in the unpleasant collecting activity. In this way, those Trainees with adequate motivation and career potential with MFS can be screened. While one might expect that this respondent would also be willing to accept a higher turnover rate than the other respondents, this was not the case. The two respondents in the lower righthand corner, on the other hand, felt that alternatives to the collecting activity should be pursued, e.g., greater use of collection agencies.

Associate Loan Officer. The position of Associate Loan Officer is very similar to that of Loan Officer Trainee with respect to task structure. The primary difference is that the Associate Loan Officer spends slightly less time in the collecting activity and slightly more in the other activities. Table 10.11 presents the one-dimensional results of Questionnaire #2 for the lending and collecting activities of the Associate Loan Officer, where approximately 80% of his or her time is spent. There was not as much disagreement between levels of management on the minimum (Question #2) and maximum (Question #3) acceptable amount of time spent in the lending and collecting activities or on the ideal amount of time (Question #4) as there was for the Loan Officer Trainee. All levels, on the average, agreed that the Associate Loan Officer should spend more time in the lending activity than in the collecting activity (the overall average being about 40%-lending and 33%-collecting).

With respect to perceptions of the current situation, all levels agreed that the Associate Loan Officer spends substantially more time collecting than lending. All but three of the respondents placed the

Table 10.11 Associate Loan Officer Task Structure

	Current(#1)	Minimum Acceptable(#2)	Maximum Acceptable(#3)	Ideal(#4)
Level I				
Lending	32.1% (Range:15-45)	27.4% (Range:10-40)	40.0% (Range:25-50)	37.1% (Range:25-50)
Collecting	45.0% (Range:35-70)	30.7% (Range:20-50)	40.3% (Range:22-60)	34.3% (Range:20-50)
Level II				
Lending	27.1% (Range:20-40)	36.4% (Range:25-45)	45.0% (Range:40-50)	39.7% (Range:25-53)
Collecting	60.7% (Range:40-70)	31.4% (Range:20-40)	37.9% (Range:30-50)	30.3% (Range:20-40)
Level III				
Lending	30.5% (Range:20-50)	32.5% (Range:15-45)	43.3% (Range:25-60)	41.8% (Range:30-50)
Collecting	43.8% (Range:25-60)	30.0% (Range:15-40)	40.0% (Range:20-50)	34.5% (Range:20-40)
Overall				
Lending	29.9% (SD:9.3)	32.1% (SD:9.8)	42.8% (SD:8.8)	39.5% (SD:8.1)
Collecting	50.2% (SD:14.0)	30.8% (SD:8.8)	39.4% (SD:10.0)	33.0% (SD:7.9)

average time currently spent in the collecting activity at or outside the maximum acceptable limit. Again, Level II perceived the time spent collecting to be much higher than did the other two levels. Level II also indicated that the degree of change desired was much greater than what the other two levels indicated, expressing the opinion that the ideal amount of time spent in the collecting activity would by one-half of what is currently the case. They did realize, however, that their ideal was at present slightly outside the minimum acceptable limit.

In addition, all levels indicated that the current time devoted by an Associate Loan Officer to training and planning was slightly below the minimum acceptable limit. Level II felt that the time currently spent in monitoring performance and other administrative activities was below acceptable limits. Level III's responses indicate that they believe Associate Loan Officers are spending too much time in auditing/accounting/security activities.

The Associate Loan Officer two-dimensional graph for the lending and collecting activities is presented in Figure 10.6. The dominating prominent point for these two variables was the same for both the Loan Officer Trainee and the Associate Loan Officer, 40%-lending and 40%-collecting. However, there was still a significant difference in the prescribed task structure as indicated by the different patterns in the two diagrams.

Table 10.12 shows a comparison of the ranges in which the most significant prominent points occurred for the Loan Officer Trainee and the Associate Loan Officer. Hence, there is definitley more emphasis on lending and less on collecting for the Associate Loan Officer than for the Loan Officer Trainee. For the planning activity, the dominating prominent point is again the same for the two positions, 5%. However,

Table 10.12   Comparison of Task Structure for the Loan Officer Trainee and the Associate Loan Officer

	Lending	Collecting	Planning
Loan Officer Trainee	30%-40%	40%-50%	2-5%
Associate Loan Officer	35%-45%	30%-40%	5-10%

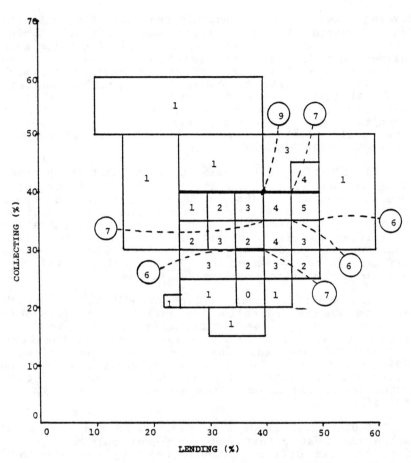

Figure 10.6 Variation in Task Structure for the Associate Loan Officer

there is greater emphasis on planning for the Associate Loan Officer than for the Loan Officer Trainee. In fact, a general statement that can be made for all positions is that as emphasis on the lending activity is increased, emphasis on the planning activity tends also to increase. Correspondingly, emphasis on collecting must decrease.

When asked how they would reallocate their time if the collecting activity was somehow eliminated (Question #6), Level II respondents indicated that they

282

would put substantially more time into the training and planning activities than did the respondents of the other two levels. Level I (top management) would absorb the extra time by having Associate Loan Officers put most of it into lending activities. Level III (Loan Officers) were about half way between Levels I and II on the lending and planning activities.

Loan Officer. The results of Questionnaire #2 indicate that the Loan Officer has the most complex task structure of the five positions studied. That is, the Loan Officer is more intensely involved in a wider variety of activities that are the other positions. This essentially means that the Loan Officer has very little flexibility in how much time he spends in the six activities. In fact, the Loan Officer probably has difficulty in finding the time to perform all the tasks expected of him. The management of time, then, is of particular concern to the Loan Officer. The District Supervisor position, while involving more responsibility than that of the Loan Officer, was deemed to be slightly less complex. The consequence of this conclusion about the Loan Officer and District Supervisor positions is that even small changes in the allocation of time, as may be required by the management-by-planning program, could present difficulties.

The Loan Officer gets involved in all six of the task-related activities; however, for the purposes of analysis only the top five time consumers were considered. There was substantial agreement among the respondents that 5-9 percent of the Loan Officer's time is and must be devoted to auditing/accounting/security activities. Table 10.13 presents the one-dimensional results for the other five activities. Because there was, with a couple of exceptions, only slight differences of opinion between the levels of management, Table 10.13 includes only the overall averages. One of the exceptions was that Level I perceived the time spent by Loan Officers in the collecting activity as being about one-half of that perceived by Level II, with Level III in between. The other exception was that Level III (Loan Officers) indicated that the Loan Officer should spend more time in the lending activity and less in the hiring/training activity than did the other two levels. This difference, however, may be a result of different interpretations of what is included in the hiring/training category.

Table 10.13   Loan Officer Task Structure

	Current(#1)	Minimum Acceptable(#2)	Maximum Acceptable(#3)	Ideal(#4)
Lending	42.1% (SD:11.1)	33.0% (SD:10.6)	45.8% (SD:14.4)	41.6% (SD:10.3)
Collecting	22.8% (SD:11.6)	14.1% (SD:7.5)	22.3% (SD:8.5)	15.8% (SD:8.6)
Hiring/Training	10.8% (SD:5.7)	14.1% (SD:5.7)	19.7% (SD:7.1)	16.4% (SD:7.7)
Planning/Creative Thinking	6.3% (SD:3.6)	10.6% (SD:6.3)	15.9% (SD:8.2)	9.5% (SD:5.1)
Monitoring Performance/ Other Administrative	10.5% (SD:5.6)	6.9% (SD:4.1)	13.9% (SD:7.5)	10.0% (SD:5.8)

The primary observation of Table 10.13 is that the respondents believe that the management-by-planning program will require the Loan Officer to spend more time in the hiring/training-and planning activities and less in the collecting activity than is currently the case. The average perception of time currently spent in these activities is outside the average acceptable limits specified in responses to Questions #2 and #3. However, there were some reservations expressed about the possibility of successfully changing the current situation. A Loan Officer submitted the following comment, expressing his opinion on this topic:

> It appears to me that increasing our workload will cut down on productivity. I can't see that I could set aside, say 20% of my working hours for thought; which means it would have to be done after hours. I may be willing to do it, but what about newer Loan Officers? Would they be willing to give up their free time hours for MFS?

This comment raises a crucial issue with respect to the role of the Loan Officer in the success of the management-by-planning program.

On Question #6, where the collecting activity was eliminated, Level I placed almost all the excess time into the lending activity, while the other two levels spread it out over the hiring/training and planning activities as well. Level I also diverged from the other two levels on Question #7, where the time devoted to the lending activity was arbitrarily increased. Level I absorbed a large amount of that increase by decreasing the time spent in monitoring performance/other administrative activities. The other two levels absorbed the increase by substantially reducing the time spent collecting. Apparently top management believes that the monitoring performance/other administrative category is less important or more easily adjusted that do the other two levels.

The complexity of the Loan Officer's task structure suggests that higher dimensional analysis might provide insights not possible in one dimension. Our analysis in two dimensions, however, provided little additional information. The two-dimensional graphs for the ten combinations of the five variables selected for analysis are presented in Appendix C.2. The only interesting observations are, first, that the

285

planning element of the dominating prominent point in
both one dimension and all two-dimensional combinations
is 10%, which is outside the average acceptable limits
for that variable (see Table 10.13). Second, one of
the prominent points for the hiring/training activity,
20%, is outside its average acceptable limits, as is
one of those for the collecting activity, 10%. This
suggests that these activities might be worth
monitoring closely in higher dimensional analysis.

Table 10.14 provides data on dominating prominent
points and measures of disagreement for selected sets
of variables of varying dimensionality. Our selection
of sets for display is based on hypotheses of possible
relationships. Each entry in Table 10.14' should be
read as in the following example:

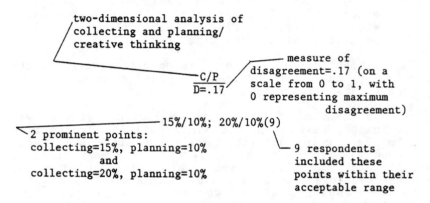

The measures of disagreement can be of assistance
in monitoring the higher dimensional analysis. For
example, analysis of the monitoring performance/other
administrative activity in one dimension yields a
relatively high measure of agreement (i.e., less
disagreement than for other variables). Not
surprisingly, this element of the dominating prominent
point remains at the same state (10%) throughout the
multi-dimensional analysis. Of more interest are those
variables and sets of variables over which there is
substantial disagreement. The most disagreement in one
dimension, for example, was on the lending activity.
In three dimensions, three new states of this variable
(30%, 45%, and 50%) enter into the dominating prominent
points. One new state for the hiring/training activity
(10%) enters in three dimensions.

286

Table 10.14 Prominent Points for Loan Officer Task Structure

5 Dimensions

L/C/H/P/M
D=.01
40%/10%/10%/15%/10%; 45%/10%/10%/15%/10%; 40%/20%/20%/10%/10%(4)

4 Dimensions

L/C/H/P
D=.02
40%/10%/10%/15%; 45%/10%/10%/15%;
40%/20%/20%/10%(4)

L/C/P/M
D=.03
45%/10%/15%/10%; 50%/10%/10%/10%;
40%/20%/20%/10%(5)

3 Dimensions

L/C/H
D=.03
30%/20%/20%; 30%/20%/15%; 40%/20%/20%;
40%/10%/10%; 45%/10%/10%(4)

L/C/P
D=.06
50%/10%/10%(6)

L/P/M
D=.08
40%/10%/10%(8)

2 Dimensions

L/H	C/H	L/C	C/P	L/P	P/M	L/M
D=.10	D=.12	D=.11	D=.17	D=.15	D=.22	D=.16
40%/10%(7)	20%/20%(8)	40%/10%(8)	15%/10%; 20%/10%(9)	40%/10%(10)	10%/10%(11)	40%/10%(11)

1 Dimension

L	C	H	P	M
D=.21	D=.33	D=.30	D=.36	D=.46
40%(11)	10%; 15%; 20%(11)	15%;20% (10)	10%(14)	10%(16)

L=Lending   C=Collecting   H=Hiring/Training   P=Planning/Creative Thinking
M=Monitoring Performance/Other Administrative

While we would expect that disagreement would increase as variables are added to the analysis, the disagreement is so high at three dimensions and above that any interpretation can only be conjectural. This is one case where a larger number of respondents would have been desirable. However, we did observe that whenever the dominating prominent point in three dimensions or above contained 20%-collecting as one element, 20%-hiring/training usually accompanied it. Likewise, when 10%-collecting was one of the elements, it was always accompanied by 10%-hiring/training. We can explain this if we postulate that a reduction in the collecting activity, in general, will reduce the employee turnover rate and hence reduce the need for hiring and training new employees.

A new state for the planning activity (15%) does not enter the dominating prominent point until four dimensions. We also observed that 45%-lending is always accompanied by 15%-planning, although 15%-planning also accompanies 40%-lending in some prominent points. While the evidence is not strong, we conjecture that an increase in emphasis on the lending activity requires additional planning and thinking, particularly with respect to market strategy.

In the case of the Loan Officer, no new information is added when we go to five dimensions. Four dimensional analysis of lending, collecting, hiring/training, and planning yields the same prominent points as in five dimensions. Synthesis of all six variables provides an indication of the necessary shift in task structure perceived by the participants in the exercise. If we permit 8% for auditing/accounting/security and 10% for monitoring performance/other administrative, the remaining 82%, according to the prominent points, could be allocated in a number of ways. The three prominent points for the remaining activities (see Table 10.14, 4-Dimensions) provide a narrow range of variation within which the actual average would probably fall. However, if the collecting activity <u>cannot</u> be reduced, the hiring/training activity <u>must</u> be increased, and the planning activity could not be increased substantially. However, if the collecting activity <u>can</u> be reduced, the hiring/training activity would not have to be increased as much and more time could be allocated to planning and also possibly to lending. In this case, the average might approximate 40%-lending, 15%-collecting, 15%-hiring/training, and 12%-planning, for a total of

82%. A further increase in lending and planning would require a further decrease in collecting and hiring/training. These insights were not evident in the one, two, or even three dimensional analyses.

The point is that the Loan Officer's task structure is complex, and he may have difficulty in adjusting his allocation of time. Yet, the Loan Officer is a key to the success of the management-by-planning program, and even small changes in his task structure could have significant implications.

10.3.3 Middle Management

District Supervisor. The position of District Supervisor is almost as complex as that of the Loan Officer, and is very critical to the success of the management-by-planning program. The District Supervisor gets involved in all six activities, as does the Loan Officer, but the activities do not appear to be as highly interrelated as they were for the Loan Officer. The District Supervisor spends some time in lending and collecting, allocating about equal time to each. District Supervisors (Level II) indicated that they were spending more time in these activities than was perceived by the other two levels. However, all levels felt that the time currently spent in lending and collecting (about 15% each) was about what it should be. The time spent in monitoring performance and other administrative activities is significant, i.e., over 20%. However, this was also deemed by all levels to be a satisfactory allocation of time.

Table 10.15 shows the overall one-dimensional results for the hiring/training, planning, and auditing/accounting/security activities as performed by the District Supervisor. In these activities, the only significant difference of opinion between levels occurred in the planning activity. Levels I and III perceived the District Supervisor as spending more time planning than the District Supervisors themselves did. All agreed, however, that substantially more time in this activity was required.

The primary conclusion of Table 10.15 is that the time devoted to planning and hiring/training activities must increase. To accommodate these increases, the auditing/accounting/security activities must decrease. The average time currently spent in all three of these

289

Table 10.15 District Supervisor Task Structure

	Current(#1)	Minimum Acceptable(#2)	Maximum Acceptable(#3)	Ideal(#4)
Hiring/Training	18.2% (SD:8.0)	20.3% (SD:9.8)	30.0% (SD:10.6)	25.2% (SD:10.2)
Planning/Creative Thinking	14.3% (SD:9.7)	15.8% (SD:10.8)	23.8% (SD:11.1)	17.8% (SD:7.9)
Auditing/Accounting/ Security	20.0% (SD:10.4)	11.1% (SD:9.0)	15.7% (SD:10.6)	12.8% (SD:9.4)

categories was perceived to be outside the average acceptable range as specified by the respondents. The questions this raises are: Why is so much of the District Supervisor's time currently spent in the auditing/accounting/security activities? And, how can it be reduced? A further examination of the District Supervisor's task might throw some light on these questions. One District Supervisor commented that additional training in organizing, planning, and time management skills was definitely needed.

Figures 10.7, 10.8, and 10.9 show the two-dimensional variation in task structure as specified in the responses to Questions #2 and #3 for the hiring/training, planning, and auditing/accounting/security activities of the District Supervisor. Each figure represents two of the three activity categories. The first observation is that the prominent points in Figure 10.7 and 10.8 are in a vertical line. This indicates relatively little flexibility in the average percentage of a District Supervisor's time that should be devoted to hiring/training but considerable uncertainty with respect to how much time should or must be devoted to planning and auditing/accounting/security.

Figure 10.9 provides some additional insight. Here, we see that for planning vs. auditing/accounting/security the prominent points are spread out, 10-15% for planning and 5-10% for auditing/accounting/security. But notice that each of these four prominent points represents only five of the twenty-one respondents. Again, this indicates uncertainty on the part of the respondents, as a group, with respect to the acceptable and reasonable amount of time that can be spent in these activities. However, Figure 10.9 also indicates that if the time devoted to planning is to be increased, the time spent in auditing/accounting/security activities will probably have to be decreased. The problem facing MFS is to discover means to reduce the auditing/ accounting/ security demands placed on the District Supervisor.

Division Officer. The position of Division Officer is one over which interviewees from Level I expressed considerable concern. The concern was that Division Officers are not placing adequate emphasis on planning and providing guidance to their District Supervisors. If the management-by-planning program is to be successful, this is an issue that should be

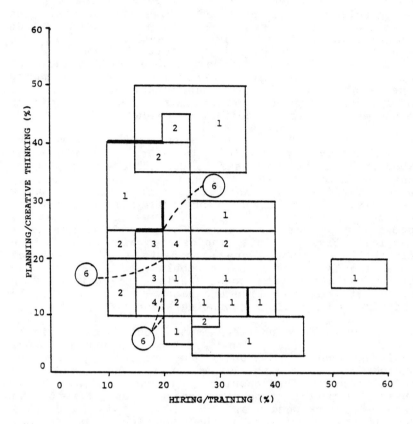

Figure 10.7   Variation in Task Structure for the
               District Supervisor: Hiring/
               Training and Planning

addressed. It was for this reason that the Division
Officer task structure was included in Questionnaire
#2.

    Table 10.16 shows the overall one-dimensional
results for the three categories that respondents
indicated were most important to the Division Officer's
task: hiring/training, planning, and monitoring
performance and other administrative activities. The
significant finding of the table is that the time

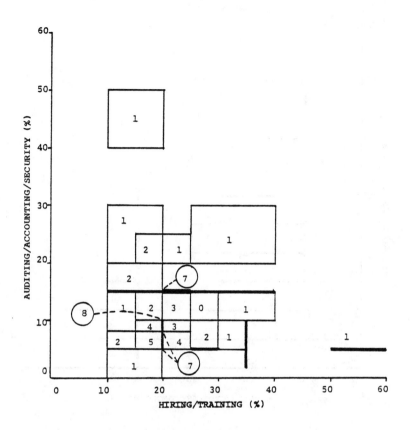

Figure 10.8   Variation in Task Structure for the District Supervisor: Hiring/Training and Auditing/Accounting/Security

currently allocated to planning and monitoring performance and other administrative activities is outside the <u>average</u> acceptable limits specified in Questions #2 and #3, with time spent in the hiring/training activity at the lower limit. The opinion expressed by the respondents, then, is that more time needs to be devoted to the planning and hiring/training activities; to permit this, time spent in monitoring performance and other administrative activities must be reduced.

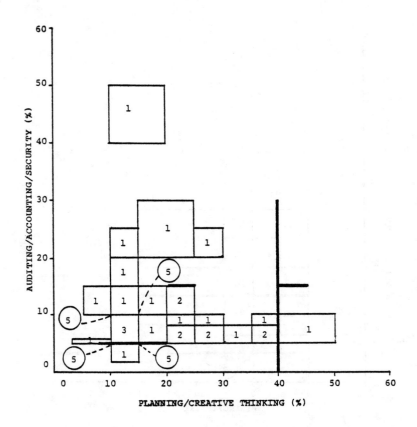

Figure 10.9   Variation in Task Structure for the
District Supervisor: Planning and
Auditing/Accounting/Security

The perception of time currently devoted to the hiring/training activity as indicated in Table 10.16 is somewhat misleading. There was significant disagreement between levels on this, with Level II indicating that Division Officers are putting more than twice as much time into the hiring/training activity than was perceived by the other two levels. Levels I and II indicated that the time currently devoted to hiring/training is well below the acceptable limit as expressed in Question #2. Table 10.17 presents the primary differences which occurred between levels.

294

Table 10.16 Division Officer Task Structure

	Current(#1)	Minimum Acceptable(#2)	Maximum Acceptable(#3)	Ideal(#4)
Hiring/Training	15.1% (SD:11.2)	14.8% (SD:10.8)	22.6% (SD:13.3)	19.5% (SD:11.8)
Planning/Creative Thinking	30.0% (SD:16.3)	32.2% (SD:15.0)	41.1% (SD:15.9)	34.6% (SD:14.6)
Monitoring Performance/ Other Administrative	35.0% (SD:12.6)	22.1% (SD:8.4)	33.9% (SD:14.4)	26.1% (SD:10.8)

295

Table 10.17 Disagreement Over the Allocation of
            Division Officer Time

		Current(#1)	Ideal(#4)
Hiring/Training			
	Level I	10.9%	14.6%
	Level II	22.9%	26.4%
	Level III	10.0%	16.6%
Planning/Creative Thinking			
	Level I	28.6%	33.6%
	Level II	22.9%	33.6%
	Level III	42.0%	37.4%

In addition to the hiring/training category, there was
disagreement over time devoted by Division Officers to
planning. Level III perceived Division Officers as
spending much more time in performing this activity
than did the other two levels. We received some
comments to the effect that the Loan Officer's (Level
III) perception of the Division Officer's task
structure is a result of inadequate communication
between the two positions. However, whether more
communication between the two positions is desirable or
not is another question, one which would seem relevant
to the management-by-planning program.

Figure 10.10 presents the two-dimensional results
of Questions #2 and #3 for the planning and monitoring
performance/other administrative tasks of the Division
Officer. One observation is that the prominent points
are in a horizontal line, perhaps indicating less
flexibility in the amount of time required for
monitoring performance and conducting other
administrative activities than in the planning
activity. This could be significant; if many
administrative demands are placed on the Division
Officer, it may indicate that he will absorb them by
cutting back on his planning activities. To
shortchange these activities, of course, is not in the
spirit of the management-by-planning program.

10.3.4 Turnover Rate and Salary

Personnel turnover is one of the symptoms of
organizational instability, and hence one of the
justifications for implementing a change in management
style. Question #10 asked for opinions on the minimum

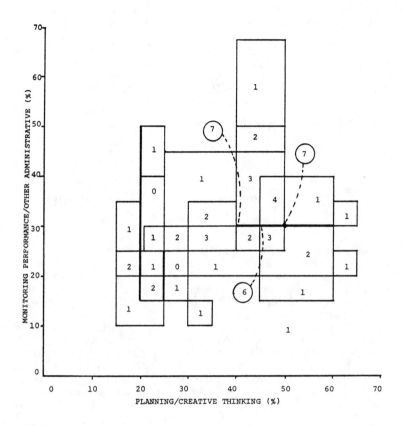

Figure 10.10   Variation in Task Structure for the
Division Officer: Planning and
Monitoring Performance/Other
Administrative

turnover rate achievable and the maximum turnover rate
acceptable among managerial personnel once the change
to   management-by-planning   is   made.   Table   10.18
summarizes the average results for each of the three
levels.   Level II is apparently more optimistic about

the possibility of reducing the turnover rate than the other two levels, with Level III more pessimistic. All levels, however, indicated that some reduction from the current rate of 33% was needed and possible.

Table 10.18   Opinions on Turnover Rate

	Minimum Possible	Maximum Acceptable
Level I	19.2% (Range:10-25)	27.5% (Range:20-35)
Level II	17.1% (Range:10-25)	23.6% (Range:15-35)
Level III	20.0% (Range:20-25)	30.7% (Range:25-40)
Overall	17.9%	26.0%

The reason for the difference between Level II and Level III is not clear. A reduction in turnover would certainly facilitate the job of the District Supervisor by requiring less hiring and training of new personnel; but the Loan Officer would also benefit. As has been noted before, Loan Officers do tend to be more conservative and skeptical than do middle managers. Perhaps one of the roles of middle management in MFS is to be optimistic and to set high goals for themselves and their subordinates. It may also be that they perceive this "can do" role as one rewarded by their superiors and, hence, as necessary to their career ambitions.

Question #11 asked respondents to indicate whether a 20%-25% turnover rate is possible without changes in salaries. As discussed under the results of Questionnaire #1, salary was not at the top of the list of organizational policies that need revision. However, it was perceived to be a significant factor. Table 10.19 presents the results of Question #11 for each of the three levels. Again, Level II was much more optimistic than the other two levels. One District Supervisor, however, qualified his "yes" by commenting that, while salaries have recently been increased to competitive levels, MFS should consider ongoing bonus programs as well.

298

Table 10.19 Opinions on Salary Structure

Question: In your opinion, do you think it is possible
to achieve a 20-25% turnover rate among
managerial personnel without increases in
salaries?

	Yes	No
Level I	2	4
Level II	4	3
Level III	1	6
Overall	7	13

10.3.5 Summary of Hypotheses

Questionnaire #2 produced a tremendous amount of
data and many methods could be used to analyze it.
Hence, there are also many possible interpretations of
the responses to each question. Since the primary role
of the modelling approach is to facilitate
participation and stimulate thinking on policy issues,
the development of hypotheses from the analysis can
provide substance for further interaction in the policy
formulation process. In this subsection, we summarize
some of the hypotheses generated from the analyses of
both questionnaires in the context of the change in
organizational strategy represented by the
management-by-planning program.

We separate these hypotheses into six categories
of personnel policies. Recruiting, training, and
promoting are processes that all MFS personnel go
through in their career; satisfactory task structure,
compensation, and patterns of communication should
result from adequate personnel processes and should
represent both the individual's contribution to MFS
strategic objectives as well as the individual's
psychological and social needs. Questionnaire #1
addressed all six of these policy areas, while
Questionnaire #2 focused on task structure.

1. Recruiting.

Hypothesis 1: If MFS is to grow and diversify as
planned, new employees must be more selectively
recruited.

Hypothesis 2: The use of personnel specialists to
train District Supervisors and Loan Officers in the
application of investigative methods could improve

299

the quality of new recruits.

2. Training.

Hypothesis 3: District Supervisors and Loan
Officers are the keys to the success of an intense
training program.

Hypothesis 4: District Supervisors and Loan
Officers need training in how to train their subordinates, as well as in planning, organizing, and
time management skills, if the quality and quantity
of training expected by the management-by-planning
program is to be achieved.

3. Promoting.

Hypothesis 5: Although it may be unavoidable,
promotions are currently granted too quickly for the
skills required of Loan Officers and District
Supervisors to mature.

Hypothesis 6: If MFS growth strategy and the
current turnover rate make rapid promotions unavoidable, high priority should be given to
recruiting and retaining high quality personnel.

Hypothesis 7: If a rapid promotion rate is unavoidable, loan officer personnel should perhaps
be allowed to make mistakes (i.e., given responsibility for loan approval) earlier than is currently
the practice, and in general to have their training
accelerated.

4. Task Structure.

Hypothesis 8: A reduction in the time devoted by
loan office personnel to the collecting activity is
suggested by the management-by-planning program, in
order that more time can be devoted to lending and
planning tasks.

Hypothesis 9: Reduction in the emphasis on
collecting could be accomplished by placing greater
reliance on collection agencies, shifting the
socioeconomic market for MFS services through diversification, or revising the point scoring system.
While the latter two actions could result in both a
higher loan conversion rate and enhanced loan
quality, greater reliance on collection agencies

300

could result in diminished loan quality.

Hypothesis 10: A reduction in the time devoted by District Supervisors to auditing/accounting/ security activities is suggested by the management-by-planning program, in order that more time can be devoted to hiring/training and planning activities.

Hypothesis 11: A reduction in the time devoted by Division Officers to monitoring performance/other administrative activities is suggested by the management-by-planning program, in order that more time can be devoted to planning and creative thinking.

Hypothesis 12: The task structure of the Loan Officer is the most complex, and hence the most critical to the success of the management-by-planning program in that there is little flexibility to adjust the time devoted to each activity.

Hypothesis 13: While greater diversification of services and markets may make a trend toward task specialization inevitable, a task structure that involves a variety of activities and skills has the advantage of developing in employees the broad knowledge of the consumer finance industry and of MFS business operations essential for effective performance in higher managerial positions.

5. Compensation.

Hypothesis 14: A significant reduction in personnel turnover is possible, but will be difficult without further increases in loan office salaries.

Hypothesis 15: A bonus program represents a viable altenative to salary increases and should be considered for both loan office personnel and middle management.

6. Patterns of Communication.

Hypothesis 16: The training and planning activities provide a forum for the type of supportive communications implied by the management-by-planning program. These are the activities, however, that tend to get shortchanged when other demands are made on a manager's time.

301

These hypotheses, of course, do not all represent new insights. However, the very fact that they emerged in the interview and questionnaire process indicates that they are worthy of further dialogue and investigation.

10.4 IMPLEMENTATION OF A POLICY SUPPORT SYSTEM

Our experience in extracting institutional knowledge from the MFS Finance Corporation presented difficulties that have implications for the implementation of a policy support system. If a questionnaire or a group exercise with a structure similar to that of Questionnaire #2 is used, we suggest the following alterations:

1. Participants in the process should be briefed on the design and content of the questionnaires and questions prior to responding to them. This may require, in some circumstances, that the management scientist personally administer the questions.

2. On Questionnaire #2, only Questions #1 through #3 or #4, #10, and #11 should be used. This would reduce the time required to answer questions considerably, and possibly increase participation.

3. Ideally, all individuals in the organization should be given the opportunity to participate, not only to increase the sample size but also to identify as many outliers as possible.

4. Following the dissemination of the results of the exercise, follow-up interviews and questions should be administered. Of particular interest would be the dynamics of the process resulting from the feedback of institutional knowledge.

Of most importance to successful implementation, however, is an organizational climate in which individuals are regarded as valuable resources in strategy and policy formulation and encouraged to share their ideas and opinions. These individuals must be willing to participate and to experiment with methods for faciliating participation. This cooperative attitude exists to some extent in MFS Finance, but

302

there is little evidence of it in the Department of Defense except in isolated instances. DoD policy formulation processes tend to reward rational advocacy and "objective" data and analyses, rather than human insight and ingenuity.

NOTES

1. For additional discussion of the distance technique, see Fred S. Roberts, Discrete Mathematical Models (Englewood Cliffs, N.J.: Prentice-Hall, 1976), pp. 455-472.

CHAPTER 11

CONSTRAINT THEORY REVISITED

We have, throughout this book, argued that the language used to describe, and the mathematics used to structure, complex phenomena are embedded in certain philosophical and logical assumptions. Furthermore, the enculturation of these assumptions produces conceptual barriers to the development of new methodological approaches for researching such phenomena. We have found the language of rational decisionmaking and the mathematics of cause and effect, probability, and optimization, for example, to be too restrictive to permit an adequate assessment of complex policy issues.

The value conflicts, structural uncertainty, and inherent dilemmas that characterize policy issues require a divergence from rational dichotomies like "objective/subjective," "cause/effect," "means/ends," "observed/observer," and "art/science." However, in proposing an alternative we run the risk of creating a dichotomy of our own. To circumvent this tendency we have advanced our theoretical framework and modelling approach as a complement to current operations research and organizational development methods, not as a mutually exclusive alternative. The policy formulation concepts and philosophical perspectives presented in Chapters 2 and 3 should also be regarded as complementary, the more generalized concepts transcending the earlier, more narrow concepts.

Constraint theory represents a pattern of thought (i.e., "negative reasoning") that stands in sharp contrast to the "rational" pattern of thought that dominates management science modelling practice. Yet, our own organization of these existential concepts in this book is quite rational, a choice made for very pragmatic reasons. It is in this context that we now take stock of where the book has brought us. In this chapter, we evaluate the potential of the modelling approach as a whole based on our demonstration of certain aspects of it; we appraise the contibution that constraint theory makes to management science; and we discuss the directions in which further research should proceed.

11.1 EVALUATION OF APPROACH

The modelling approach described in Chapter 8 emphasizes structural change and institutional knowledge. This emphasis is based on a view of policy formulation as a political process where the more informal, subjective forms of information play a major role in the resolution of conflicts in values and perceptions. We assume that an appropriate criterion in the search for conflict resolution is robustness, although it is not an absolute criterion. There is always a dialectical tension between the criteria of robustness and flexibility on the one hand, and efficiency and achievement on the other.

We have argued that robustness leads to value-rich policy and is supportive of the variety amplification mode of control. This assumption represents our own values and is a frame of reference which may itself conflict with those of the organizational participants to whom we would like to apply the modelling approach. This leads to a problem in self-reference for the management scientist and suggests a process-oriented, participant-observer approach for research on policy issues.

The intent of this book has been to demonstrate that <u>quantitative</u> analysis of some form can serve a significant role in the policy formulation process. We regard the research reported in Chapters 9 and 10 as successfully demonstrating that constraint theory provides a new mathematical perspective on policy issues. In particular, we emphasize the importance of a structural framework with a <u>mathematical</u> basis and information on perceptions and values with respect to permissible <u>variation</u> in policy variables. Disagreement over either an appropriate macrostructure or an acceptable range of variability within that structure provides substance for interaction among policy actors.

In the Department of Defense study, it became apparent that there did not exist any commonly accepted macrostructure, particularly with respect to logistics policy criteria (i.e., readiness), that could provide a context for constructive communications and dialogue on broad policy issues. Whether the provision of such a

306

structure can be agreed upon or, if agreed upon, whether it will be used for the purpose intended is yet to be seen. We suspect that the culture of DoD is such that a major change in management style and patterns of thought will be necessary before the analysis of second-order (structural) change and the structured use of institutional knowledge can become accepted policy practices.

In the MFS Finance study, a change in management style had already been initiated and a major commitment to its success made by policy-level management. While we received many encouraging remarks from MFS on the results of our analysis, the primary purpose of the research was not to produce the richness that we think represents the potential of constraint theory. Rather, our purpose was to demonstrate the constraint-theoretic approach to soliciting subjective responses and analyzing them in as simple a format as possible. The realization of its full potential will require considerably more sophistication. In particular, we recognize a need for (1) alternative media of communication that allow rapid feedback of results; (2) intervention methods that ensure greater participation in the exercise; and (3) innovative displays of multi-dimensional results.

One of the most interesting results of the MFS study was the degree to which multiple perspectives on task structure, i.e., the policy domain, could be used to develop shape in the relationships among variables. We postulate that these different perspectives are in large part due to different frames of reference. That is, some individuals view certain aspects of task structure as more important, or in relation to a different policy domain, than do others. We analyzed some of these differences by comparing the responses of different levels of management; other differences are manifest in the responses of "outliers."

Watzlawick, et al., contend that the examination of frames of reference provides the key to second-order change.[1] In our approach, the management scientist selects the policy domain and defines its variables; but this represents his frame of reference and should itself be open for discussion. It is worth noting that the "universal set," taken for granted in Aristotelian logic, represents a frame of reference in constraint theory. In Spencer Brown's logic, the frame of reference is embedded in the act of observation. Our

307

state space representation of mental models, then, should be regarded as a closed frame of reference, but one subject to meta-evaluation.

The complexity of a policy domain, e.g., employee task structure, is often not well understood by those who formulate strategy and policy. Yet, the success of a strategy can be intrinsically linked to such a policy domain. The complexity of an employee's task, for example, is not simply the result of the degree of skill required to perform it; it is also a consequence of the perceptions and attitudes of the employee and of others in the organization. Hence, what might appear as a simple technical problem of allocating an individual's time in accordance with his skills and the needs of the company, is in fact a complex social process. That process is characterized by conflict and coalition formation. The intent of the proposed modelling approach is to explore the complexity of these aspects of policy issues, and in the process to facilitate communications and stimulate creative thinking.

11.2 CONTRIBUTION OF CONSTRAINT THEORY

We regard the contribution of constraint theory as primarily threefold. First, it is a paradigm, a different and complementary way of describing, structuring, and thinking about so-called "ill-structured" problems. The negative form of reasoning reverses the focus of the logic and mathematics of decision theory from those states most likely to occur to those totally excluded from consideration. This reversal permits a treatment of frames of reference and is, we argue, more reflective of the intuitive, heuristic process of human cognition than is the paradigm of rationality.[2]

Second, constraint theory provides an integrating framework for interpreting information generated by diverse sources. Aggregate performance data, computerized model outputs, case studies, etc. are all types of information representing different perspectives on a situation and, hence, are potentially useful in policy formulation. The constraint-theoretic framework assists a policy actor in identifying patterns of constraint in the available information. The methods of constraint theory are, at present, primarily heuristic, as are pattern recognition techniques in general, requiring discretion and judgment in their use. The integrating power of the framework is realized through the superposition of multiple perspectives, most importantly the perspectives of individuals with conflicting mental models. We regard the collection of mental models in an organization, i.e., its institutional knowledge, as its most valuable (yet often most underutilized) resource for coping with complexity. As such, institutional knowledge is central to our concept of a policy support system.

Third, constraint theory represents a potential bridge between science and art. Citing Snow's The Two Cultures,[3] Hirshfeld calls on the management science community to initiate such a bridge between the "scientific/technical culture" and the "literary/ humanistic culture."[4] Because constraint theory emphasizes the multi-dimensional patterns in a set of data, there is a need for innovative and artistic displays for communicating those patterns. In the MFS study, any information greater than two dimensions was presented to MFS management in expository form. We see wide-open opportunities for exploiting the richness of artistic media as radical as poetry and music for communicating multi-dimensional insights. It is through such vehicles of communication that new constraints are woven into the social fabric, emerging as restructured values, patterns of culture, and paradigms of thought and action. Consider the following as an example of the potential of the fictional art form:

> ...scholars ought to explore fiction for experi-
> ence and data not obtainable in the real world of
> megabureaucracy. It is possible using developing
> techniques from simulation, role-playing, and
> closed circuit television to create fiction in the
> laboratory. Herein one discovers the economical
> advantages of fiction over current administrative
> research methods. Fiction collapses the time
> frame, heightens conflict where necessary, omits
> periods of rest and routine, creates stress, and
> allows repetition of the same events to test
> certain variables.[5]

Computer graphics and computerized music, as well as other cybernetic art forms, are particularly exciting developments that may eventually be built into policy support systems.[6]

11.3 RESEARCH DIRECTIONS

A number of avenues for further research are suggested by this book. First, media other than questionnaires need to be experimented with. In particular, we think gaming simulations, computerized conferencing, and other structured group exercises can be adapted to the constraint-theoretic framework. These offer the advantage of rapid feedback, and hence the opportunity to study and contribute to a more dynamic process than is possible with questionnaires. However, although we advance our modelling approach as a means of facilitating communications, this should not be interpreted as advocacy of the philosophy that more communication is better. To the contrary, it is the nature of the communications process that is important, what we referred to in the MFS study as "supportive" communications. The introduction of structured exercises into the policy formulation process runs the risk of increasing the amount of communication to a point where existing supportive communications get muffled. Developing criteria for determining the extent to which structured exercises should be used in a policy support system represents another research topic.

There is also a need for exploring methods of pattern recognition that go beyond those developed and used in this book. Again, developments in computer graphics show significant potential. In an exposé on the future of logistics research, for example, Wagner states that:

> Much progress is needed in techniques that help
> human analysis comprehend large sets of data.
> (Recent developments in computer graphics are
> good examples of what can be done to let a
> human literally see multidimensional phenomena.)
> A related problem is the development of methods
> for testing model assumptions and data error
> sensitivity...A higher level of computer-assisted
> thinking is needed to alert the model builder to
> the weak points of the model.[7]

In this context, the development and application of concepts in artificial intelligence may provide some relief. Experimentation with rule-oriented systems involving nested rules and questions is one example.[8]

These concepts may also be applied to the design of the structured exercises themselves.

While we have justified the exclusion of time as a variable in policy domains by arguing that fields of behavior (topological concepts) rather than lines of behavior (vector concepts) are more appropriate concepts for policy formulation, we think that conflicting perceptions of time may be relevant to policy issues. Another research topic, then, would be the development of rigorous representations of different perceptions of time. One approach to this method might be to explore in depth the implications of Spencer Brown's logic as discussed in Chapter 5.

Finally, if the business office of the future is to be in one's home with the computer as the primary means of communication to the outside world, as suggested by some,[9] computerized conferencing will play a more central role in policy support than it does now. There is a tremendous amount of research to be done, however, on the nature of the man-machine interface and on the social, psychological, and cultural consequences of such a dramatic change in the conduct of business. While computerized conferencing accommodates the type of policy support system we are proposing, we doubt that it can ever replace intense face-to-face interaction.

In summary, we believe that there are many opportunities for further research on the methods and applications of constraint theory, and that this research could make a significant contribution to both the understanding of the policy formulation process and the robust resolution of complex policy issues. The extent of that contribution, however, will depend on our willingness, as both scientists and managers, to accept innovative forms of organization, to adventure into uncharted regions of the human mind and human culture, and to recognize that limitations on individual rationality make these actions essential if we are to adapt to an increasingly turbulent world.

> Once a British seer named Ashby
> Viewed the world with equanimity.
>   "I have no complaints
>   For I know the constraints
> Are what tell us what can and cannot be."[10]

NOTES

1. Paul Watzlawick, John Weakland, and Richard Fisch, Change: Principles of Problem Formation and Problem Resolution (New York: W.W. Norton & Company, 1974), p. 101.

2. The constraint-theoretic paradigm is discussed further in Laurence D. Richards, "Beyond Planning: Controllability vs. Predictability," The Proceedings of the XXIst Annual North American Meeting of the Society for General Systems Research, 1977, pp. 314-323.

3. C. P. Snow, The Two Cultures and the Scientific Revolution (New York: Cambridge University Press, 1960).

4. David S. Hirshfeld, "Management Science and the Two Cultures," OR/MS Today 7(March/April 1980): 10.

5. Howard E. McCurdy, "Fiction, Phenomenology, and Public Administration," Public Administration Review, Jaunuary/February 1973, pp. 54-55.

6. See, for example, Jean-Paul Jacob, "Potential of Graphics to Enhance Decision Analysis," IBM Research Report, IBM Research Laboratory, San Jose, Calif., 1979.

7. Harvey M. Wagner, "The Next Decade of Logistics Research," in Science, Technology, and the Modern Navy, ed. Edward I. Salkovitz, ONR-37 (Arlington, Virginia: Office of Naval Research, 1976), p. 101.

8. D. A. Waterman, R. H. Anderson, Frederick Hayes-Roth, Philip Klahr, Gary Martins, and Stanley J. Rosenschein, "Design of a Rule-Oriented System for Implementing Expertise," RAND Note N-1158-1-ARPA (Santa Monica, Calif.: The RAND Corporation, May 1979).

9. See Hollis Vail, "The Automated Office," The Futurist (April 1978), pp. 73-78.

10. Stuart A. Umpleby, quoted in Laurence D. Richards, "Cybernetics and the Management Science Process," OMEGA 8(1980):

APPENDICES

APPENDIX A

QUESTIONNAIRES

A.1   QUESTIONNAIRE #1

This is the first of a series of two questionaires designed to collect information and opinions on strategic issues facing the M.F.S. Finance Corporation. The results will be subjected to formal analysis and presented to M.F.S. top management. In addition, the analysis will become a significant part of a Ph.D. thesis in management science at the Wharton School, University of Pennsylvania. In responding to questions, please be as candid and precise as possible; all responses will be kept completely confidential. The questionaire is designed to take 15-30 minutes to complete. It is recommended that you fill it out away from your usual work location, i.e., a place where you will not be interrupted. Your cooperation is greatly appreciated.

Laurence D. Richards

Laurence D. Richards

*   *   *   *   *   *   *   *   *   *   *   *   *

Please check the most appropriated box below:

☐ Loan Officer   ☐ District Supervisor   ☐ Division Officer
        ☐ Headquarters Staff

Eight issues which may or may not be critical in developing long-term strategies for the M.F.S. Finance Corporation are identified below. Following a statement of each issue is a list of several possible responses to it. You are asked to rank the responses to each issue in the order of their potential for resolving the issue, and, hence of their importance in establishing a strategic "posture" for M.F.S. That is, give a "1" to the most important, a "2" to the second most important, etc. If you judge two items to be exactly equal in importance, give them both the same rank. Give a "0" to any response you judge to be infeasible, unacceptable, or irrelevant. Give an "X" to any response that you do not feel sufficiently knowledgeable to evaluate; however, do <u>not</u> use an "X" unless you have absolutely no opinion at all. Place your rankings in the blanks immediately preceding each response.

In evaluating your choices, consider both M.F.S.'s current situation and the possible <u>long-term</u> effects of making current commitments in the directions indicated. Include consideration for costs, legal complications, impacts on M.F.S. personnel and customers, or any other factors as you see fit. The ranking should be based on <u>your</u> perceptions of potential problems and opportunities, not on how you think <u>others</u> might respond. Some blank spaces are provided at the end of each list for you to add other responses which you feel are important, but which have not been included. Also, it may be useful to read through the <u>entire</u> questionaire before performing the rankings.

ISSUE #1: M.F.S. has grown in size substantially in the past few years. What direction should further growth and development take?

    ____ increasing the number of branch offices in those states where M.F.S. is currently operating

    ____ opening branch offices in new states

    ____ increasing the number of employees per branch office

    ____ increasing the productivity(#of accounts per office) through more automated record keeping and procedures

    ____ strengthening the current customer base through higher quality service and efficient operations(that is, slowing the growth rate)

    ____ acquiring other companies

    ____ other_____

ISSUE #2: If M.F.S. is to continue to grow, a market penetration strategy will be necessary. On which services and customers should market emphasis be placed?

    ____ increasing the variety of services offered to M.F.S.'s present customers

    ____ increasing the socioeconomic distribution of customers using M.F.S.'s current services

    ____ shifting the average socioeconomic status of the customers using current services

    ____ maintaining M.F.S.'s present customers, but adding new services which will appeal to new customers

    ____ increasing the variety of services offered through acquisition of companies with an established customer base(and expertise) for these services

    ____ maintaining the present customer base and current services(keeping the current market penetration strategy)

    ____ other_____

ISSUE #3: Given a growth and market strategy(issues #1 and #2),
shifts in organizational policy may be called for.
Which of the following policy areas are most critical?

_____ increasing the qualifications and skills of branch
office employees(issue #4)

_____ more aggressively converting loan applicants into
M.F.S. customers(issue #5)

_____ using more automated technologies and procedures
(issue #6)

_____ using less automated technologies and procedures
(issue #6)

_____ reducing first year employee turnover and/or improving
overall job satisfaction of new employees(issue #7)

_____ generating fresh marketing and management ideas
(issue #8)

_____ other_____
_____

ISSUE #4: Branch office personnel qualifications and skills can be
improved in a number of ways. Which offer the most
potential?

_____ providing more training to new employees before they
start on their job

_____ providing more training sessions _after_ the first
year of employment

_____ providing more training in organizing, planning, and
time management skills

_____ providing supervisors with more training in how to
train and motivate new employees

_____ recruiting new employees more selectively(by _district_
supervisors)

_____ recruiting new employees more selectively(by
personnel _specialists_)

_____ recruiting more college graduates

_____ transferring employees more frequently to broaden
their experience and responsibilities

_____ other_____
_____

317

ISSUE #5: Consumer finance companies have a lower rate of conversion than do the banks. Furthermore, M.F.S.'s conversion rate has decreased in recent years. What is an appropriate response to this trend?

_____ maintaining current policies(the conversion rate is and will continue to be acceptable)

_____ aggressively pursuing a higher socioeconomic class of customer

_____ reducing the minimum acceptable credit rating

_____ revising present point scoring system for determining credit risks

_____ providing more formal training in assessing credit risks

_____ giving less experienced or new loan officers more leeway in making credit decisions

_____ referring more loan applications to district supervisors for making credit decisions

_____ increasing current emphasis on "number of accounts" as a measure of branch office performance

_____ decreasing current emphasis on "deliquency" as a measure of branch office performance

_____ implementing more automated collection procedures

_____ other_____

ISSUE #6: Increased use and reliance on automation and computerization appear inevitable in the banking and finance industries. Implementation of more sophisticated technologies, however, can create problems. In what direction should M.F.S. policy move to help alleviate potential problems?

_____ training more personnel to be prepared to perform automated tasks manually if necessary

_____ providing more training in the effective use of automated technology

_____ recruiting more personnel skilled in the use of automated technology

_____ investing in _own_ computer services(rather than relying on time-sharing services)

_____ putting more pressure on current vendor to increase reliability of services

(continued)

318

_____ changing vendors until a sufficiently reliable one is
found

_____ using automated procedures less for bookkeeping
and more for loan processing

_____ using automated procedures less for loan processing
and more for bookkeeping

_____ using automated procedures less at the branch office
level and more at the higher levels of management

_____ using automated procedures more at the branch office
level and less at the higher levels of management

exploiting innovative uses of automated technology,
such as:

_____ automated collection procedures

_____ electronic funds transfer systems(EFTS)

_____ cathode ray tube(CRT) displays

_____ other_____

ISSUE #7: The turnover rate for first year M.F.S. employees is
relatively high. It is not clear what an acceptable turnover rate ought to be. On the one hand, the turnover rate
reflects the suitability of the particular individual to
his/her task. On the other hand, the turnover rate can
reflect the individual's perception of career opportunities
in M.F.S. In what direction should M.F.S. policy move to
better match new employees with their jobs and to improve
their perception of career opportunities?

_____ better acquainting new employees with their job before
they start

_____ providing more "motivational" training to new
employees during their first year of employment

_____ improving investigative methods used prior to
hiring new employees

_____ recruiting new employees more selectively(by
personnel specialists)

_____ recruiting through professional personnel research
centers

_____ increasing average starting salaries

(continued)

319

_____ granting more rapid promotions to the positions of
loan officer and district supervisor

_____ granting more substantial salary increases <u>after</u>
the first year of employment

_____ transferring employees more frequently to broaden
their experience and responsibilities

_____ increasing the use of automated collection procedures

_____ requiring new employees to have more frequent
communications with supervisors concerning career
plans and opportunities

_____ increasing the planning responsibilities of loan
officers and district supervisors(for example, in
establishing quarterly performance goals)

_____ decreasing the current emphasis on deliquency as a
performance measure

_____ maintaining current policies(a high turnover rate
is inevitable)

_____ other_____
_____

ISSUE #8: In the highly competitive consumer finance industry, those
companies that can generate and implement fresh marketing
and management ideas will gain a distinct competitive
advantage. Which of the following offer the most potential
for stimulating creative thinking in M.F.S.?

_____ bringing a cross section of outsiders into
middle and top management

_____ hiring professional marketing and management specialists
or consultants to advise top management

_____ training middle and top management in creative
marketing and management strategies

_____ increasing visibility of incentives(bonuses,
promotions, etc.) for creative thinking

_____ encouraging lower level management contributions
through more participative planning

_____ other_____
_____

320

If you have any comments on the questionaire or explanations of the responses you made, please enter them here. Any insights would be most useful.

If you would have no objections to discussing the questionaire or related topics with me, please write your name in the space below. Again, all responses will be kept strictly confidential.

Please return the completed questionaire in the enclosed envelope as soon as possible. If you have any questions about the use to be made of the questionaire, please contact Mr. Roger L. Brown, Senior Vice President, M.F.S. Finance Corporation(999-555-1111). If you have any questions about instructions or items on the questionaire, please call me collect: Larry Richards, LaSalle College (215 951-1089). Thank you.

A.2 QUESTIONNAIRE #2

This is the second in a series of two questionaires designed
**to collect information and opinions on strategic issues facing
the M.F.S. Finance-** Corporation. The results will be subjected
to formal analysis and presented to M.F.S. top management. In
addition, the analysis will become a significant part of a
Ph.D. thesis in management science at the Wharton School,
University of Pennsylvania. In responding to questions, please
be as candid and precise as possible; all responses will be kept
completely confidential. The questionaire is designed to take
approximately 40 minutes to complete. It is recommended that
you fill it out away from your usual work location, i. e., a
place where you will not be interrupted. Your cooperation is
greatly appreciated.

Laurence D. Richards
Laurence D. Richards

****

Please check the most appropriate box below:

☐ Loan Officer   ☐ District Supervisor

☐ Division Officer   ☐ Regional Director

☐ Headquarters Staff   ☐ _____

In terms of loans outstanding, the M.F.S. Finance   Corporation,
prior to 1978, grew at an annual rate of approximately 25-35%,
nearly twice the average for the consumer finance industry.
M.F.S.'s strategy is to continue to grow, although at a slightly
lower rate of about 18%. To achieve this growth, M.F.S. top
management and its parent company, Industrial Banking, Inc., have
decided to expand the variety of services it offers to take better
advantage of markets such as: second mortgage lending, industrial
banking, point-of-sale financing, thrift certificates, small
business lending, revolving loans, and preferred customer lending.
New offices will be opened, not only in the ten states where
M.F.S. currently operates, but also in new states. The expectation
is to eventually be nationwide. A major thrust is to identify
and acquire finance companies which already have a demonstrated
expertise in these services, and that already have offices with
an established customer base in regions where M.F.S. does not
now operate.

An aggressive strategy such as this is obviously going to have certain consequences for the functioning of the M.F.S. organization. The increase in variety of services offered by M.F.S. may require a higher level of lending expertise at the loan office level. Planning and time management skills will be increasingly important in assuring the productivity of a much larger number of offices. There will also be a need for more creative marketing and management ideas at the middle and top management levels. Because the investment required to acquire and train personnel in these skills will be substantial, organizational policies designed to retain them are a critical concern.

The managerial turnover rate in 1978 was approximately 33%. Most of this turnover was among short-term employees. While it is not clear what an acceptable turnover rate ought to be, many believe that it can and should be reduced(perhaps to 15-25%), not only to retain skilled personnel but also to minimize the impact that a high turnover rate can have on office efficiency and morale, and on customer loyalty and goodwill. The reasons why an individual chooses to resign vary. Some individuals simply cannot handle the pressure of the job and choose to leave the consumer finance business altogether. For those motivated primarily by compensation, a better monetary arrangement may have been found with another company. Still others may perceive the career opportunities with M.F.S. as not meeting their expectations. This may occur despite what the real opportunities are. For most individuals, a combination of these and other considerations influence their decision to leave.

To help ensure the success of their long-term strategy, M.F.S. Finance has initiated a program that is intended to change the prevailing management style of the corporation. The program is called "management by planning" and is designed to increase the involvement and participation of M.F.S. personnel in setting goals and objectives and developing plans to attain them. If this program is to achieve the results intended, certain changes will have to occur in the allocation of managerial time and in the amount and nature of communications between managerial levels. The degree of change will depend on the extent to which the planning activity is given priority over other managerial activities. Likewise, the success of the program in reducing personnel turnover, developing managerial skills, and stimulating creative thinking will depend on these priorities.

In this questionaire, you are asked to consider the allocation of time to various task-related activities—namely, the per cent of time that managerial, supervisory, and division officer personnel spend in performing the following activities:

1. Lending - all time spent soliciting customers, processing applications, assessing credit risk, and performing follow-up on customer satisfaction and referrals. This includes all time in direct contact with a customer or potential customer, and his/her loan application. It also includes marketing efforts such as visitations to local businesses or other promotional activities designed to create new business.

323

2. Collecting - all time spent monitoring individual accounts, reminding customers of payments due or overdue, and taking other action as necessary to collect on a loan.

3. Hiring/Training - all time spent recruiting, screening, hiring, and orienting employee applicants plus all time spent training subordinates and being trained by superiors that would not have occurred except for the purpose of training. This includes all formal training or individualized instruction, but does not include on-the-job training which deals directly with customers, loan applications, and collections. Training serves the purpose of developing technical lending and collecting skills, managerial skills, creative skills, and career motivation.

4. Planning and Creative Thinking - all time spent developing goals and objectives and plans of action for achieving them. It also includes time spent developing creative marketing and management ideas and communicating these ideas to others in M.F.S.

5. Auditing/Accounting/Security - all time spent auditing and updating required reports and records, including legal documents, financial books, and any other reports required for security reasons.

6. Monitoring Performance and Other Administrative Activities - all time spent reviewing the performance of subordinates and advising them of their progress and deficiencies. This activity is for purposes of maintaining control and increasing productivity and efficiency, not for training. Performance evaluation is also used to make decisions on employee promotions and salaries, whereas training is for developing skills only. Also included in this category are other administrative activities not included in any other category.

While the following questions require serious thought, your first reactions should provide fairly accurate estimates. Do not read through the entire questionaire before answering. It is suggested, however, that you use a pencil so that mistakes can be erased if necessary. In each question you will be asked to provide estimates of (or opinions about) the per cent of time spent in the six task-related activities. Use the following table to help convert amount of hours to a percent. Some of the activities are performed every week, while others may be performed only once or twice a month, or once a quarter (three months). The table assumes that there are approximately 40 working hours in a week, 170 working hours in a month, and 500 working hours in a quarter. If 2 hours a week are spent on a particular activity, for example, that would correspond to 5% of the time. If 10 hours per quarter were spent on an activity, that would correspond to 2% of the time.

Per Cent	0%	1%	2%	3%	4%	5%	10%	15%	20%	25%	30%	35%	40%	45%	50%
Hours per Week	0 hr	½ hr	3/4 hr	1¼ hr	1½ hr	2 hr	4 hr	6 hr	8 hr	10 hr	12 hr	14 hr	16 hr	18 hr	20 hr
Hours per Month	0 hr	1½ hr	3½ hr	5 hr	6½ hr	8½ hr	17 hr	25½ hr	34 hr	42½ hr	51 hr	60 hr	68 hr	77 hr	85 hr
Hours per Quarter	0 hr	1-5 hr	10 hr	15 hr	20 hr	25 hr	50 hr	75 hr	100 hr	125 hr	150 hr	175 hr	200 hr	225 hr	250 hr

Of the following questions, #2 and #3 are the most important; they are also the most difficult. Please put more time into answering these two questions than the rest. Questions #2 and #3 ask you to indicate what you think should be the least amount of time(#2) and the most time(#3) that should be devoted to each activity, irrespective of how good an individual may be in performing the activity. Put yourself in the position of top management; your job is to establish some rough guidelines for managing time. There are some examples at the end of this questionaire to assist you in following the instructions.

QUESTION #1: Fill in the table below, indicating what you estimate to be the average per cent of time currently spent by loan officer trainees, associate loan officers, loan officers, district supervisors, and division officers in the six task-related activities. Base your estimates on your own perception of these five positions, and round your estimates to the nearest percentage point(for example, 23%). There will probably be zeros in some of the categories for certain positions, indicating that position does not have responsibility for that activity. If you have absolutely no idea at all about what a particular position does, place an "X" in the box at the left of the table. However, you should be able to provide some estimates for, at least, all your subordinates and your immediate supervisor. In the last column, on the right side of the table, add up the per cents in each row. The totals should be approximately EQUAL TO 100%.

Task-related Activities

Positions	Absolutely No Idea	Lending	Collecting	Hiring/ Training	Planning and Creative Thinking	Auditing/ Accounting/ Security	Monitoring Performance and other Administrative	Total
Loan Officer Trainee								
Associate Loan Officer								
Loan Officer								
District Supervisor								
Division Officer								

325

QUESTION #2: The "management by planning" program will undoubtedly require M.F.S. personnel to adjust, to some extent, the management of their time. In this question follow the same instructions given for Question #1, except this time indicate what you think would be a <u>minimum acceptable</u> per cent of time that should be devoted to each activity for the "management by planning" program to be successful in achieving the desired results. The total for each row should be <u>LESS THAN</u> 100%.

Task-related Activities

Positions	Absolutely No Idea	Lending	Collecting	Hiring/ Training	Planning and Creative Thinking	Auditing/ Accounting/ Security	Monitoring Performance and other Administrative	Total
Loan Officer Trainee								
Associate Loan Officer								
Loan Officer								
District Supervisor								
Division Officer								

QUESTION #3: Again in this question, follow the same instructions given in Question #1, except this time indicate what you think would be a <u>maximum feasible</u> per cent of time that could be devoted to each activity for the "management by planning" program to be successful in achieving the desired results. That is, what is the most time that can be spent in any one activity and still have time to adequately perform other activities. The totals should be <u>GREATER THAN</u> 100%.

Task-related Activities

Positions	Absolutely No Idea	Lending	Collecting	Hiring/ Training	Planning and Creative Thinking	Auditing/ Accounting/ Security	Monitoring Performance and other Administrative	Total
Loan Officer Trainee								
Associate Loan Officer								
Loan Officer								
District Supervisor								
Division Officer								

326

QUESTION #4: In this question indicate what, in your opinion, would
be the ideal assignment of time for the five positions. That is,
if you were given the authority to determine the amount of time each
person spends in the s i x activities, how would you do it so as to
best achieve your own goals? Follow the same instructions given in
Question #1. The totals should be approximately EQUAL TO 100%.

Task-related Activities

Positions	Absolutely No Idea	Lending	Collecting	Hiring/ Training	Planning and Creative Thinking	Auditing/ Accounting/ Security	Monitoring Performance and other Administrative	Total
Loan Officer Trainee								
Associate Loan Officer								
Loan Officer								
District Supervisor								
Division Officer								

QUESTION #5: If the "management by planning" program requires that all
positions spend 5% more of their time in planning and creative
thinking than what you indicated in Question #4, how would you adjust
the time devoted to the other activities? First, add 5% to your
answers for Planning and Creative Thinking in Question #4; then,
adjust the other categories. The totals should be approximately
EQUAL TO 100%.

Task-related Activities

Positions	Absolutely No Idea	Lending	Collecting	Hiring/ Training	Planning and Creative Thinking	Auditing/ Accounting/ Security	Monitoring Performance and other Administrative	Total
Loan Officer Trainee					+5			
Associate Loan Officer					+5			
Loan Officer					+5			
District Supervisor					+5			
Division Officer					+5			

327

QUESTION #6: If collection agencies were used to handle all deliquent loans, reducing the time spent by Loan Office personnel to zero, how would you adjust the time devoted to other activities? First, put zeros for the Collecting activity; then, adjust the answers you gave in Question #4 for the other activities. The totals should be approximately EQUAL TO 100%.

Task-related Activities

	Absolutely No Idea	Lending	Collecting	Hiring/ Training	Planning and Creative Thinking	Auditing/ Accounting/ Security	Monitoring Performance and other Administrative	Total
Loan Officer Trainee			0%					
Associate Loan Officer			0%					
Loan Officer			0%					

QUESTION #7: If, in order to more thoroughly investigate loan applications, all Loan Office personnel were required to spend 10% more of their time in the lending activity than what you indicated in Question #4, how would you adjust the time devoted to the other activities? First, add 10% to your answers for Lending in Question #4; then, adjust the other categories. The totals should be approximately EQUAL TO 100%.

Task-related Activities

	Absolutely No Idea	Lending	Collecting	Hiring/ Training	Planning and Creative Thinking	Auditing/ Accounting/ Security	Monitoring Performance and other Administrative	Total
Loan Officer Trainee		+10						
Associate Loan Officer		+10						
Loan Officer		+10						

QUESTION #8: If, in order to more thoroughly screen potential employees and train/motivate new employees, all positions were required to spend 10% more time in the Hiring/Training activity than what you indicated in Question #4, how would you adjust the time devoted to the other activities? First, add 10% to the answer you gave for the Hiring/Training category in Question #4; then adjust the other categories. The totals should be approximately EQUAL TO 100%.

Task-related Activities

Positions	Absolutely No Idea	Lending	Collecting	Hiring/ Training	Planning and Creative Thinking	Auditing/ Accounting/ Security	Monitoring Performance and other Administrative	Total
Loan Officer Trainee				+10				
Associate Loan Officer				+10				
Loan Officer				+10				
District Supervisor				+10				
Division Officer				+10				

QUESTION #9: If all positions were required to spend 10% more time in hiring/training and 5% more time in planning activities than what you indicated in Question #4, how would you adjust the time devoted to other activities? First, add 10% to the answers you gave in Question #4 for Hiring/Training and 5% to your answers for Planning and Creative Thinking; then adjust the other categories. The totals should be approximately EQUAL TO 100%.

Task-related Activities

Positions	Absolutely No Idea	Lending	Collecting	Hiring/ Training	Planning and Creative Thinking	Auditing/ Accounting/ Security	Monitoring Performance and other Administrative	Total
Loan Officer Trainee				+10	+5			
Associate Loan Officer				+10	+5			
Loan Officer				+10	+5			
District Supervisor				+10	+5			
Division Officer				+10	+5			

329

QUESTION #10: Having now completed this questionaire, how low do you think the turnover rate can be realistically reduced through more participative planning, more selective recruiting, and better training? What is the <u>minimum</u> possible turnover rate consistent with M.F.S.'s strategic objectives?

Check one:

0%   5%   10% 15% 20% 25% 30% 35% 40%

What should be considered a <u>maximum</u> acceptable rate if M.F.S. is to achieve its objectives?

Check one:

5%   10% 15% 20% 25% 30% 35% 40% 45%

QUESTION #11: In your opinion, do you think it is possible to achieve a 20-25% turnover rate among managerial personnel without increases in salaries? Check one:

yes   no

QUESTION #12: How many years have you been employed by M.F.S. Finance? Check one:

0-1yr   1-2yrs   3-4yrs   5-10yrs   more than
                                        10 years

If you have any comments on the questionaire or explanations of the responses you made, please enter them here. Any insights would be most useful.

If you would have <u>no</u> objections to discussing the questionaire or related topics with me, please write your name in the space below. Again, all responses will be kept <u>strictly</u> confidential.

Please return the completed questionaire in the enclosed envelope as soon as possible. If you have any questions about the use to be made of the questionaire, please contact Mr.Roger L. Brown, Senior Vice President, M.F.S. Finance Corporation(999-555-1111). If you have any questions about instructions or items on the questionaire, please call me collect: Larry Richards, LaSalle College (215 951-1089). Thank you.

For Questions #1, #4, #5, #6, #7, #8, #9; your answers should look something like this:

Task-related Activities

Positions	Absolutely No Idea	Lending	Collecting	Hiring/Training	Planning and Creative Thinking	Auditing/Accounting/Security	Monitoring Performance and other Administrative	Total
Loan Officer Trainee		38%	23%	12%	10%	16%	3%	102%
Associate Loan Officer		42%	24%	10%	10%	14%	2%	102%
Loan Officer		40%	24%	14%	8%	10%	4%	100%
District Supervisor		30%	5%	20%	12%	14%	14%	98%
Division Officer		25%	0%	16%	22%	20%	18%	101%

Notice that the totals are <u>approximately</u> 100%.

For Question #2, your answers should look something like this:

Positions	Absolutely No Idea	Lending	Collecting	Hiring/Training	Planning and Creative Thinking	Auditing/Accounting/Security	Monitoring Performance and other Administrative	Total
Loan Officer Trainee		20%	12%	10%	12%	15%	3%	72%
Associate Loan Officer		25%	20%	10%	12%	12%	2%	81%
Loan Officer		25%	20%	12%	15%	10%	3%	85%
District Supervisor		15%	5%	20%	15%	12%	8%	75%
Division Officer		10%	0%	15%	20%	20%	10%	75%

Notice that the totals are <u>less than</u> 100%.

For Question #3, the totals should be <u>greater than</u> 100%.

331

APPENDIX B

SUMMARY DATA TABLES

B.1   QUESTIONNAIRE #1

The following data summarize the results for each issue of Questionnaire #1. The average rankings for each issue are provided first, followed by the number of individuals who ranked the responses to that issue first. The response numbers across the top correspond to the list of responses provided for each issue in the questionnaire (see Appendix A.1). The results are provided for Level I, II, and III respondents and for all respondents together. Of the thirty-one total respondents, eleven were Level I, and ten each were Level II and III. Some respondents gave top ranking to more than one response. On Issue #6, only the first six responses were analyzed; on Issue #7, the last response was dropped from consideration.

ISSUE #1

Average Ranking:		Response Number				
	1	2	3	4	5	6
Level I	3	2	6	5	4	1
Level II	3	1	6	5	4	2
Level III	3	1	6	5	4	2
Overall	3	1	6	5	4	2

First's:	1	2	3	4	5	6
Level I	2	5	0	0	0	6
Level II	1	7	1	0	0	4
Level III	1	7	0	1	3	4
Total	4	19	1	1	3	14

ISSUE #2

Average Ranking:		Response Number				
	1	2	3	4	5	6
Level I	3	4	5	1	2	6
Level II	3	4	5	1	2	6
Level III	2	4	5	1	3	6
Overall	2	4	5	1	2	6

First's:	1	2	3	4	5	6
Level I	3	1	2	8	5	0
Level II	5	1	0	7	3	0
Level III	7	0	0	8	4	0
Total	15	2	2	23	12	0

ISSUE #3

	Response Number					
	1	2	3	4	5	6
Average Ranking:						
Level I	2	4	5	6	3	1
Level II	1	4	5	6	2	3
Level III	2	4	5	5	1	3
Overall	1	4	5	6	1	3
First's:						
Level I	6	0	0	0	2	5
Level II	7	0	0	0	5	4
Level III	5	2	0	1	7	1
Total	18	2	0	1	14	10

ISSUE #4

	Response Number							
	1	2	3	4	5	6	7	8
Average Ranking:								
Level I	5	6	2	1	3	4	7	8
Level II	3	5	2	1	4	6	7	7
Level III	2	2	1	2	5	6	6	6
Overall	4	5	2	1	3	5	7	7
First's:								
Level I	0	0	3	4	4	2	0	0
Level II	2	1	5	8	1	1	0	0
Level III	3	3	3	3	2	1	0	1
Total	5	4	11	15	7	4	0	1

ISSUE #5

			Response Number							
	1	2	3	4	5	6	7	8	9	10
Average Ranking:										
Level I	4	1	8	3	2	8	4	6	8	6
Level II	7	2	9	3	1	9	7	3	6	5
Level III	4	2	7	2	1	7	7	5	5	7
Overall	5	2	9	3	1	9	5	4	8	5
First's:										
Level I	0	7	0	3	3	0	0	0	0	0
Level II	0	4	0	1	8	0	0	1	0	0
Level III	2	2	1	2	4	0	0	1	1	0
Total	2	13	1	6	15	0	0	2	1	0

ISSUE #6

			Response Number			
	1	2	3	4	5	6
Average Ranking:						
Level I	5	2	3	5	1	4
Level II	4	4	4	1	2	3
Level III	4	3	5	1	2	6
Overall	6	3	4	2	1	5
First's:						
Level I	2	3	1	1	5	0
Level II	2	2	2	6	4	0
Level III	2	2	1	5	3	1
Total	6	7	4	12	12	1

ISSUE #7

	Response Number												
	1	2	3	4	5	6	7	8	9	10	11	12	13
Average Ranking:													
Level I	1	2	3	3	9	6	12	7	12	9	7	5	11
Level II	1	2	7	4	11	8	11	6	11	9	4	2	10
Level III	1	2	3	11	11	5	9	5	9	11	5	8	3
Overall	1	2	5	6	11	6	11	8	11	9	3	3	9
First's:													
Level I	5	4	3	6	0	2	0	0	0	1	3	2	0
Level II	7	3	2	3	0	1	0	1	0	1	2	4	0
Level III	7	4	0	0	0	1	0	1	1	0	3	4	2
Total	19	11	5	9	0	4	0	2	1	2	8	10	2

ISSUE #8

	Response Number				
	1	2	3	4	5
Average Ranking:					
Level I	5	1	2	4	2
Level II	5	4	3	1	2
Level III	4	4	2	3	1
Overall	5	3	2	3	1
First's:					
Level I	2	3	2	0	3
Level II	0	5	4	4	4
Level III	0	1	5	3	6
Total	2	9	11	7	13

336

B.2 QUESTIONNAIRE #2

The data below are the average responses (i.e., average percentages of time) of Level I, Level II, and Level III respondents to Questions #1 through #4 of Questionnaire #2 (see Appendix A.2). Of the twenty-one respondents to Questionnaire #2, there were seven from each of the three levels. An overall average is also provided.

LOAN OFFICER TRAINEE

	Lend	Collect	Hire/Train	Planning	Aud/Acc/Sec	Mon Perf/Admin
Question #1:						
Level I	29.3	56.9	5.7	1.1	5.7	1.3
Level II	31.3	59.3	4.7	0.4	2.9	0.9
Level III	27.5	53.5	6.7	2.8	9.3	0.3
Overall	29.5	56.7	5.7	1.4	5.8	0.9
Question #2:						
Level I	24.3	38.6	2.1	4.3	5.0	1.9
Level II	38.6	28.9	7.0	3.6	3.9	1.9
Level III	33.3	32.5	3.3	4.7	4.5	1.5
Overall	32.0	35.4	4.2	4.2	4.5	1.8
Question #3:						
Level I	33.6	48.6	7.1	6.4	11.0	4.7
Level II	49.3	40.0	10.1	6.9	5.3	2.6
Level III	41.7	40.8	6.8	10.0	7.8	3.2
Overall	41.5	43.3	8.1	7.7	8.1	3.5
Question #4:						
Level I	35.0	45.0	5.7	3.0	9.0	2.4
Level II	45.0	32.1	10.1	5.1	5.0	2.3
Level III	40.0	36.7	4.8	6.7	7.0	4.7
Overall	40.0	38.0	7.0	4.9	7.0	3.1

ASSOCIATE LOAN OFFICER

	Lend	Collect	Hire/Train	Plan-ning	Aud/Acc/Sec	Mon Perf/Admin
Question #1:						
Level I	32.1	45.0	5.7	3.1	8.9	5.4
Level II	27.1	60.7	5.9	2.0	3.0	1.6
Level III	30.5	43.8	6.8	5.7	8.5	4.8
Overall	29.9	50.2	6.1	3.5	6.7	3.9
Question #2:						
Level I	27.4	30.7	6.9	8.0	5.4	5.1
Level II	36.4	31.4	10.3	5.4	4.0	4.1
Level III	32.5	30.0	5.7	6.0	4.8	3.7
Overall	32.1	30.8	7.7	6.5	4.8	4.4
Question #3:						
Level I	40.0	40.3	13.6	12.1	8.1	8.3
Level II	45.0	37.9	13.6	8.4	6.1	6.6
Level III	43.3	40.0	9.8	11.2	7.0	6.7
Overall	42.8	39.4	12.5	10.6	7.1	7.2
Question #4:						
Level I	37.1	34.3	8.1	5.7	9.0	5.7
Level II	39.7	30.3	12.9	5.1	5.1	6.6
Level III	41.8	34.5	7.3	8.0	4.5	4.8
Overall	39.5	33.0	9.6	6.2	6.3	5.8

LOAN OFFICER

	Lend	Collect	Hire/Train	Planning	Aud/Acc/Sec	Mon Perf/Admin
Question #1:						
Level I	42.9	16.4	12.1	5.7	10.7	12.9
Level II	43.6	30.0	11.6	4.6	6.3	6.7
Level III	39.3	21.7	8.3	9.0	9.7	12.0
Overall	42.1	22.8	10.8	6.3	8.9	10.5
Question #2:						
Level I	29.3	10.7	15.0	11.9	6.9	6.9
Level II	32.1	18.6	17.1	9.6	4.7	6.7
Level III	38.3	12.8	9.3	10.3	5.5	7.0
Overall	33.0	14.1	14.1	10.6	5.7	6.9
Question #3:						
Level I	40.0	20.0	23.1	16.4	10.3	13.3
Level II	43.6	25.0	22.1	14.7	7.9	14.3
Level III	55.0	21.7	12.8	16.7	9.7	14.2
Overall	45.8	22.3	19.7	15.9	9.3	13.9
Question #4:						
Level I	42.1	14.0	15.3	8.6	9.3	10.6
Level II	39.3	15.9	22.4	8.9	4.4	9.3
Level III	43.5	17.7	10.7	11.3	6.8	10.0
Overall	41.6	15.8	16.4	9.5	6.9	10.0

DISTRICT SUPERVISOR

	Lend	Collect	Hire/Train	Plan-ning	Aud/Acc/Sec	Mon Perf/Admin
Question #1:						
Level I	12.1	13.1	15.4	14.3	23.6	21.7
Level II	18.6	18.6	20.7	9.3	13.6	20.1
Level III	12.5	6.0	18.3	20.0	23.3	21.2
Overall	14.5	12.9	18.2	14.3	20.0	21.0
Question #2:						
Level I	7.9	7.1	21.4	19.3	12.1	16.1
Level II	17.4	12.9	22.9	12.3	6.7	17.9
Level III	8.2	4.5	15.8	15.8	15.0	20.0
Overall	11.3	8.4	20.3	15.8	11.1	17.9
Question #3:						
Level I	12.9	9.3	30.0	27.1	17.1	25.0
Level II	24.3	17.0	33.6	17.9	10.1	23.6
Level III	15.5	8.2	25.8	26.7	20.5	30.0
Overall	17.7	11.7	30.0	23.8	15.7	26.0
Question #4:						
Level I	12.9	10.7	21.3	18.6	15.9	20.7
Level II	18.6	10.7	29.3	15.0	7.6	19.3
Level III	9.8	6.5	24.6	20.0	15.2	23.7
Overall	14.0	9.5	25.2	17.8	12.8	21.1

DIVISION OFFICER

	Lend	Collect	Hire/Train	Plan-ning	Aud/Acc Sec	Mon Perf/Admin
Question #1:						
Level I	7.9	4.9	10.9	28.6	12.1	36.4
Level II	9.4	3.9	22.9	22.9	10.7	31.4
Level III	1.2	1.0	10.0	42.0	8.0	38.0
Overall	6.7	3.5	15.1	30.0	10.5	35.0
Question #2:						
Level I	6.4	5.7	14.3	31.4	6.3	21.4
Level II	6.7	2.4	18.9	33.0	7.3	20.0
Level III	0.6	0.8	10.0	32.0	9.0	26.0
Overall	5.0	3.2	14.8	32.2	7.4	22.1
Question #3:						
Level I	10.7	7.1	22.9	39.3	11.7	30.0
Level II	10.0	4.1	27.1	39.3	10.4	35.0
Level III	5.0	3.0	16.0	46.0	12.2	38.0
Overall	8.9	4.9	22.6	41.1	11.4	33.9
Question #4:						
Level I	11.0	6.9	14.6	33.6	8.9	24.4
Level II	6.7	2.4	26.4	33.6	6.7	24.0
Level III	5.0	3.0	16.6	37.4	7.2	31.2
Overall	7.8	4.2	19.5	34.6	7.6	26.1

APPENDIX C

SELECTED GRAPHICAL DISPLAYS

C.1 ONE-DIMENSIONAL DISTRIBUTIONS

The graphs on the next few pages display individually the distribution of responses to Questions #2 and #3 of Questionnaire #2 for each of the six task-related activities. The height of each line represents the number of respondents who placed that particular percentage within their <u>acceptable range</u>. The overall perception of the <u>current</u> percentage of time spent in each activity (Question #1) and of the <u>ideal</u> percentage of time to spend in each activity (Question #4) are indicated beneath each graph. While these graphs are useful for showing tendencies within each task-related activity, they cannot be used to analyze relationships among activities. Higher dimensional analysis is needed for that purpose. Of course, if no relationships exist between categories of activity, then the one-dimensional graphs are sufficient. But, the very fact that the total amount of time available to an employee is limited, inevitably results in some form of relationship among activities.

LOAN OFFICER TRAINEE

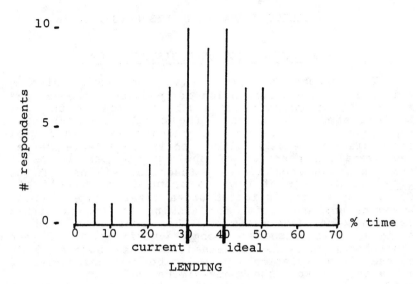

LENDING

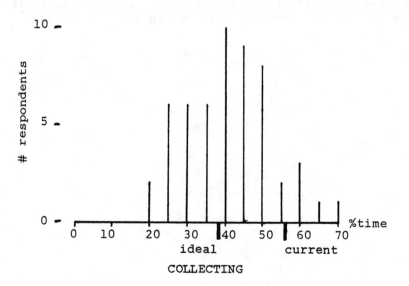

COLLECTING

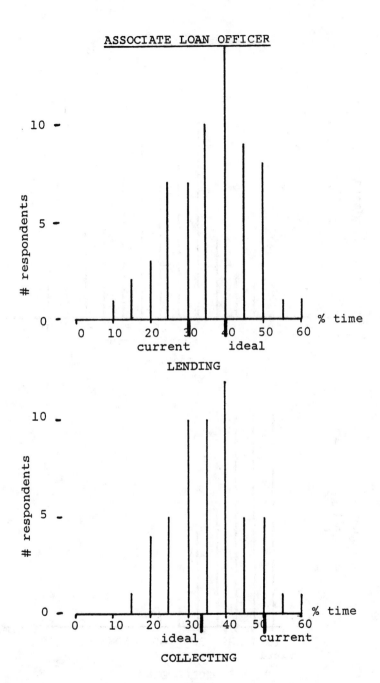

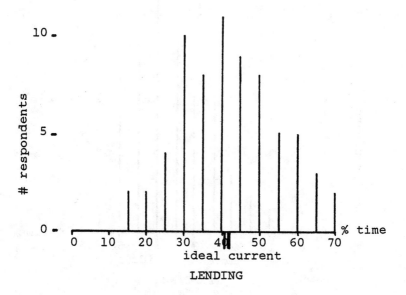

LENDING

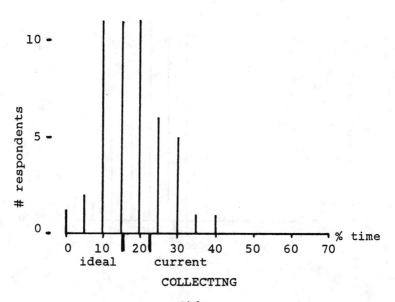

COLLECTING

LOAN OFFICER

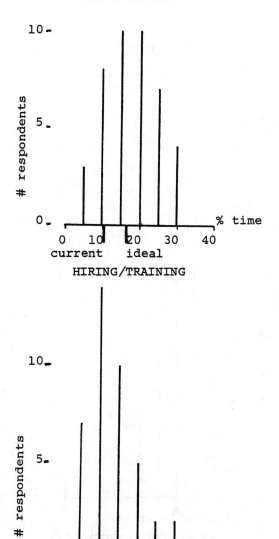

LOAN OFFICER

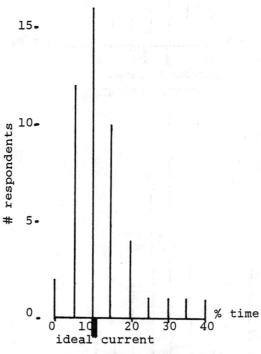

MONITORING PERFORMANCE/
OTHER ADMINISTRATIVE

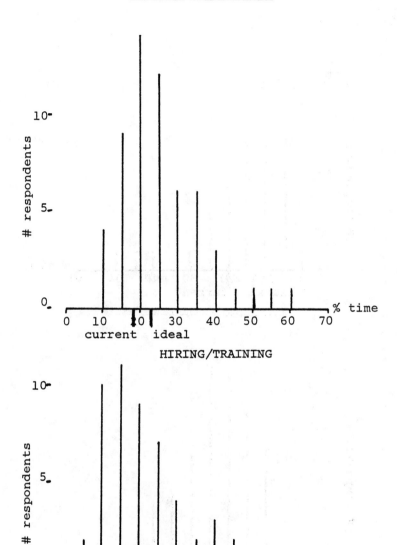

DISTRICT SUPERVISOR

HIRING/TRAINING

PLANNING/CREATIVE THINKING

DISTRICT SUPERVISOR

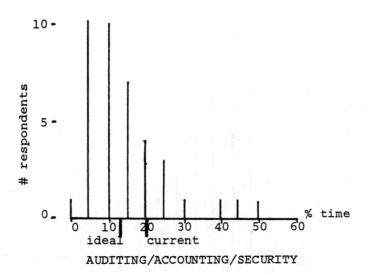

AUDITING/ACCOUNTING/SECURITY

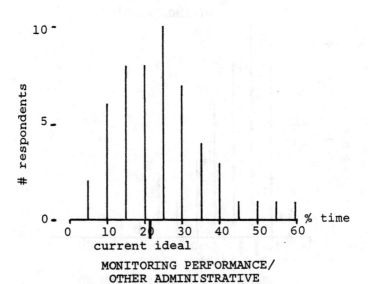

MONITORING PERFORMANCE/
OTHER ADMINISTRATIVE

DIVISION OFFICER

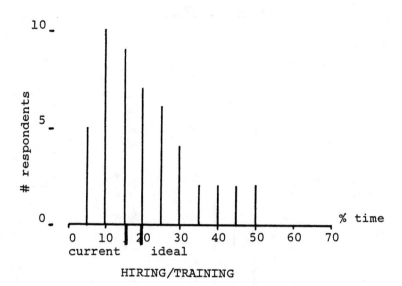

HIRING/TRAINING

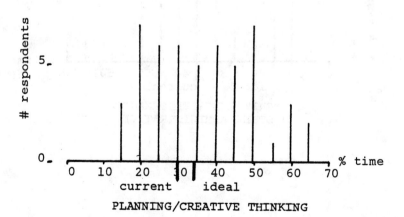

PLANNING/CREATIVE THINKING

351

DIVISION OFFICER

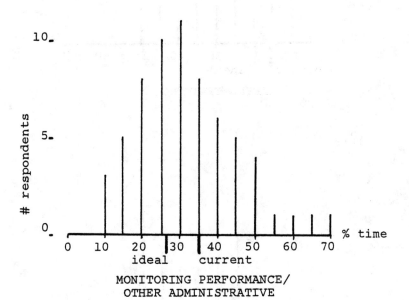

MONITORING PERFORMANCE/
OTHER ADMINISTRATIVE

C.2 TWO-DIMENSIONAL DISTRIBUTIONS

The following graphs display the distribution of responses to Questions #2 and #3 of Questionnaire #2 for pairs of task-related activities. They are presented here for the Loan Officer, rather than in the main body of the book, because it was difficult to extract any significant insights from them. The Loan Officer task structure is sufficiently complex to require higher than two dimensional evaluation.

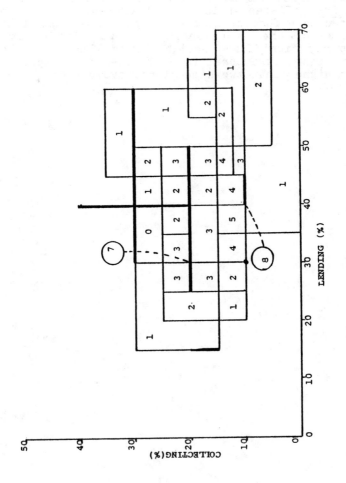

VARIATION IN LOAN OFFICER TASK STRUCTURE

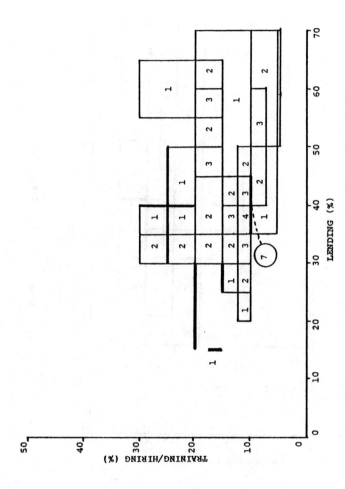

VARIATION IN LOAN OFFICER TASK STRUCTURE

355

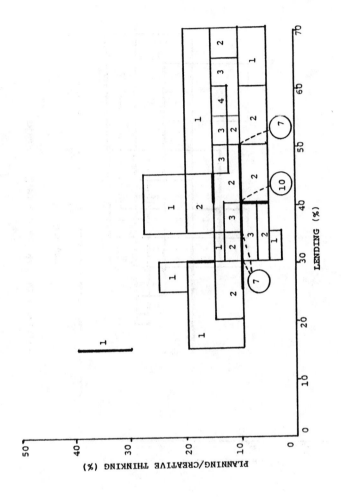

VARIATION IN LOAN OFFICER TASK STRUCTURE

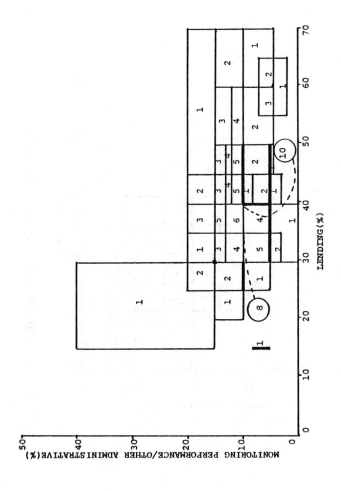

VARIATION IN LOAN OFFICER TASK STRUCTURE

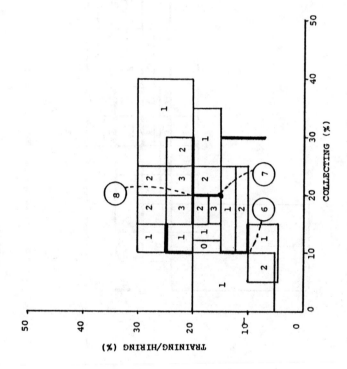

VARIATION IN LOAN OFFICER TASK STRUCTURE

358

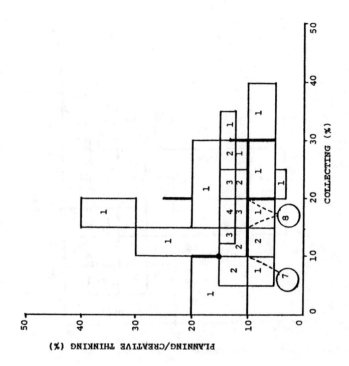

PLANNING/CREATIVE THINKING (%)

VARIATION IN LOAN OFFICER TASK STRUCTURE

COLLECTING (%)

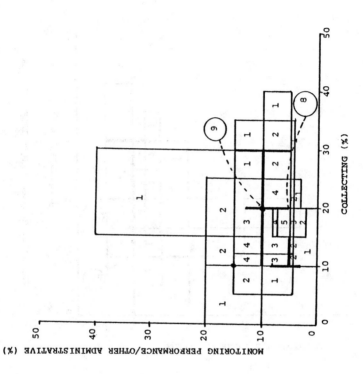

VARIATION IN LOAN OFFICER TASK STRUCTURE

360

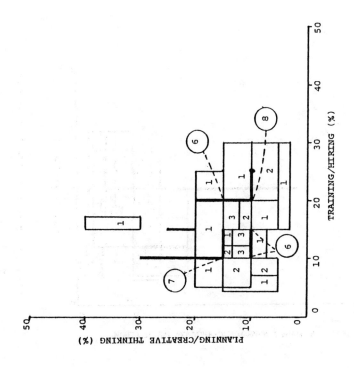

VARIATION IN LOAN OFFICER TASK STRUCTURE

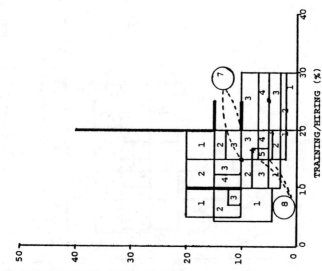

VARIATION IN LOAN OFFICER TASK STRUCTURE

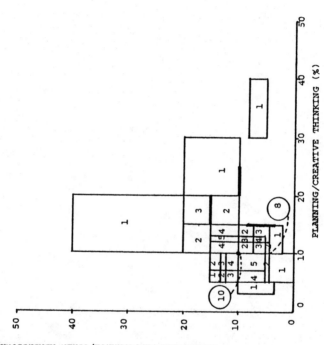

VARIATION IN LOAN OFFICER TASK STRUCTURE

363

BIBLIOGRAPHY

Ackoff, Russell L. "Management MISinformation Systems."
     Management Science 14 (December 1967):

_____. A Concept of Corporate Planning. New York:
     John Wiley & Sons, 1970.

_____. "Beyond Problem Solving." General Systems XIX
     (1974): 237-239.

_____. Creating the Corporate Future. New York:
     John Wiley & Sons, 1981.

Adam, Everett E., Jr. and Ebert, Ronald J. Production
     and Operations Management. Englewood Cliffs, N .
     J.: Prentice-Hall, 1978.

Alexander, Christopher. Notes on the Synthesis of
     Form. Cambridge, Mass.: Harvard University
     Press, 1964.

Allison, Graham T. Essence of Decision. Boston:
     Little, Brown, and Company, 1971.

Ansoff, H. Igor. Corporate Strategy. New York:
     McGraw-Hill, 1965.

_____. "The State of Practice in Planning Systems."
     Sloan Management Review, Winter 1977, pp. 1-24.

Ansoff, H. Igor and Slevin, Dennis P. "An Appreciation
     of Industrial Dynamics." Management Science 14
     (March 1968): 383-397.

Anthony, Robert N. Planning and Control Systems: A
     Framework for Analysis. Boston: Division of
     Research, Graduate School of Business, Harvard
     University, 1965.

Arbib, Michael A. Brains, Machines, and Mathematics.
     New York: McGraw-Hill, 1964.

_____. The Metaphorical Brain. New York: John Wiley
     & Sons, 1972.

Archibald, K. A. "Three Views of the Expert's Role in

Policymaking: Systems Analysis, Incrementalism,
and the Clinical Approach." Policy Science 1
(1970):   73-86.

Argenti, John. Corporate Collapse: The Causes and
Symptoms. New York: John Wiley & Sons, 1976.

Argyris, Chris. "Management Information Systems: The
Challenge to Rationality and Emotionality."
Management Science 17 (February 1971): B275-B292.

_____. The Applicability of Organizational Sociology.
London: Cambridge University Press, 1972.

_____. "Some Limits of Rational Man Organization
Theory." Public Administration Review. May/June
1973, pp. 253-267.

Argyris, Chris and Schön, Donald A. Theory in
Practice: Increasing Professional Effectiveness.
San Francisco: Jossey-Bass, 1974.

Arrow, Kenneth J. Social Choice and Individual Values.
2nd ed. New York: John Wiley & Sons, 1963.

Ashby, W. Ross. An Introduction to Cybernetics.
London: Chapman & Hall, 1956.

_____. Design for a Brain. London: Chapman & Hall,
1960.

_____. "The Set Theory of Mechanism and Homeostasis."
General Systems IX (1964):   83-97. Also in
Automaton Theory and Learning Systems. Ed. D. J.
Stewart. London: Academic Press, 1967, pp. 23-
51.

_____. "Constraint Analysis of Many-Dimensional
Relations." General Systems IX (1964):   99-105.

_____. "Principles of the Self-Organizing System."
In Modern Systems Research for the Behavioral
Scientist. Ed. Walter Buckley. Chicago: Aldine
Publishing Company, 1968, pp. 108-118.

_____. "Systems and Their Informational Measures."
In Trends in General Systems Theory, Ed. George J.
Klir. New York: John Wiley & Sons, 1972, pp.
78-97.

Bacharach, Michael. "Group Decisions in the Face of Differences of Opinion." Management Science 22 (October 1975): 182-191.

Bariff, M. L. and Lusk, E. J. "Cognitive and Personality Tests for the Design of Management Information Systems." Management Science 23 (April 1977): 820-829.

Barnard, Chester. The Functions of the Executive. Cambridge, Mass.: Harvard University Press, 1938.

Bartee, Edwin M. "A Holistic View of Problem Solving." Management Science 20 (December, Part I, 1973): 439-448.

Bass, Mernard M. "Business Gaming for Organizational Research." Management Science 10 (April 1964): 545-556.

Bateson, Gregory. "Information and Codification: A Philosophical Approach." In Ruesch, Jurgen and Bateson, Gregory. Communication: The Social Matrix of Psychiatry. New York: W. W. Norton & Company, 1968, pp. 168-211.

_____. Steps to an Ecology of Mind. New York: Ballantine Books, 1972.

_____. Mind and Nature: A Necessary Unity. New York: E. P. Dutton, 1979.

Bauer, Raymond A. "The Study of Policy Formation: An Introduction." The Study of Policy Formation, Ed. Raymond A. Bauer and Kenneth J. Gergen. New York: The Free Press, 1968, pp. 2-26.

Bauer, Volker; Ruppert, Wolf-Reiner; and Wegener, Michael. "Simulation, Evaluation and Conflict Analysis in Urban Planning." In Portraits of Complexity. Ed. H. Baldwin. Columbus, Ohio: Battelle Memorial Institute, 1975, 179-193.

Beckhard, Richard. Organization Development: Strategies and Models. Reading, Mass.: Addison-Wesley, 1969.

Beer, Stafford. Decision and Control. London: John Wiley & Sons, 1966.

_____. Designing Freedom. London: John Wiley & Sons, 1974.

_____. Platform for Change. London: John Wiley & Sons, 1975.

_____. The Heart of Enterprise. Chichester: John Wiley & Sons, 1979.

_____. Brain of the Firm. Rev. ed. Chicester: John Wiley & Sons, 1981.

Beged-Dov, Aharon G. "An Overview of Management Science and Information Systems." Management Science 13 (August 1967): B817-B831.

Bellman, R. E. and Zadeh, L. A. "Decision-Making in a Fuzzy Environment." Management Science 17 (December 1970): B141-B164.

Bennis, Warren G. Organization Development: Its Nature, Origins and Prospects. Reading, Mass.: Addison-Wesley, 1969.

Bettman, James R. "A Graph Theory Approach to Comparing Consumer Information Processing Models." Management Science 18 (December 1970, Part II): 114-128.

Black, Duncan. The Theory of Committees and Elections. London: Cambridge University Press, 1958.

Blin, Jean-Marie, "Fuzzy Sets in Multiple Criteria Decision-Making." In Starr and Zeleny, eds., 1977, pp. 129-146.

Blin, J. M. and Whinston, A. B. "A Note on Majority Rule Under Transitivity Constraints." Management Science 20 (July 1974): 1439-1440.

Blin, J. M. and Whinston, Andrew B. "Discriminant Functions and Majority Voting," Management Science 21 (January 1975): 557-566.

Bloom, Mitchel F. "Designing a Time-Dependent Technology Assessment Model: Problems and Pitfalls." Proceedings of the XXIst Annual North American Meeting of the Society for General Systems Research, 1977, pp. 238-242.

Bogart, Kenneth P. "Preference Structures I: Distances Between Transitive Preference Relations." Journal of Mathematical Sociology 3 (1973): 49-67.

_____. "Preference Structures II: Distances Between Asymetric Relations." SIAM Journal of Applied Mathematics 29 (1975): 254-262.

Borch, Karl Henrik. The Economics of Uncertainty. Princeton, N. J.: Princeton University Press, 1968.

Botkin, J. W. "An Intuitive Computer System: A Cognitive Approach to the Management Learning Process." Ph.D. dissertation, Harvard Business School, 1973.

Bower, Joseph L. "Descriptive Decision Theory from the 'Administrative' Viewpoint." In The Study of Policy Formation. Ed. Raymond A. Bauer and Kenneth J. Gergen. New York: The Free Press, 1968.

Bowman, V. J. and Colantoni, C. S. "Majority Rule Under Transitivity Constraints." Management Science 19 (May 1973): 1029-1041.

Boyce, David E.; McDonald, Chris; and Farhi, Andre. An Interim Report on Procedures for Continuing Metropolitan Planning. Federal Highway Administration Contract FH-11-7068. Philadelphia: Regional Science Department, University of Pennsylvania, 1970.

Braybrooke, David and Lindblom, Charles E. A Strategy of Decision. New York: The Free Press, 1970.

Broekstra, G. "Constraint Analysis and Structure Identification." Annals of Systems Research 5 (1976): 67-80.

_____. "Constraint Analysis and Structure Identification II." Annals of Systems Research 6 (1977): 1-20.

_____. "Structure Modelling: A Constraint (Information) Analytic Approach." In Applied General Systems Research: Recent Developments and Trends. Ed. George J. Klir. New York: Plenum Press,

1978, pp. 117-132.

_____. "(Non)Probabilistic Constraint Analysis and a
Two-Stage Approximation Method of Structure
Identification." Proceedings of the 23rd Annual
North American Meeting of the Society for General
Systems Research, 1979, pp. 73-81.

Buckley, Walter. Sociology and Modern Systems Theory.
Englewood Cliffs, N. J.: Prentice-Hall, 1967.

Burns, Thomas and Stalker, G. M. The Management of
Innovation. London: Tavistock Publications,
1961.

Burton, Dudley J. "Methodology and Epistemology for
Second-Order Cybernetics." The Proceedings of the
XXIst Annual North American Meeting of the Society
for General Systems Research, 1977, pp. 324-333.

Carroll, Douglas J. and Wish, Myron. "Multidimensional
Scaling: Models, Methods, and Relations to
Delphi." In Linstone and Turoff, eds., 1975,
pp. 402-431.

Chandler, Alfred D., Jr. Strategy and Structure:
Chapters in the History of the American Industrial
Enterprise. Cambridge, Mass.: The M.I.T. Press,
1962.

Charnes, A. W. and Cooper, W. W. Management Models and
Industrial Applications of Linear Programming.
New York: John Wiley & Sons, 1961.

Charnes, A.; Kozmetsky, G.; and Ruefli, T. "Information Requirements for Urban Systems: A View into
the Possible Future." Management Science 19
(December, Part 2, 1972): 7-20.

Churchman, C. W. and Schainblatt, A. H. "The
Researcher and the Manager: A Dialectic of Implementation." Management Science 11 (February
1965): B69-B87.

Clark, R. H. and Pipino, L. L. "Fuzzy Sets and Utility
Theory." Working Paper #74-47, School of
Business Administration, University of Massachu-
setts, 1974.

Clarkson, Geoffrey P. E. Portfolio Selection--A

Simulation of _Trust Investment_. Englewood Cliffs, N. J.: Prentice-Hall, 1962.

Conant, Roger C. and Ashby, W. Ross. "Every Good Regulator of a System Must be a Model of that System." _International Journal_ of _Systems Science_ 1 (1970): 89-97.

Cook, Wade D. and Seiford, Lawrence M. "Priority Ranking and Consensus Formation." _Management Science_ 24 (December 1978): 1721-1732.

Cosier, Richard A.; Ruble, Thomas L.; and Aplin, John C. "An Evaluation of the Effectiveness of Dialectical Inquiry Systems." _Management Science_ 24 (October 1978): 1483-1490.

Coulam, Robert F. _Illusions_ of _Choice_: _The F-111_ and _Problem_ of _Weapons Acquisition Reform_. Princeton, N. J.: Princeton University Press, 1977.

Crozier, Michel. _The Bureaucratic Phenomenon_. Chicago: The University of Chicago Press, 1964.

Cyert, Richard M. and March, James. _A Behavioral Theory_ of _the Firm_ . Englewood Cliffs, N. J.: Prentice-Hall, 1963.

Dalkey, Norman C. "An Elementary Cross-Impact Model." In Linstone and Turoff, eds., 1975, pp. 327-337.

_____. "Toward a Theory of Group Estimation." In LInstone and Turoff, eds., 1975, pp. 236-261.

Dalkey, N. and Helmer, O. "An Experimental Application of the Delphi Method to the Use of Experts." _Management Science_ 9 (February 1964): 458-466.

Davis, O. A.; Degroot, M. H.; and Hinich, M. J. "Social Preference Orderings and Majority Rule." _Econometrica_ 40 (1972): 147-157.

Davis, Stanley M. "Two Models of Organization: Unity of Command versus Balance of Power." _Sloan Management Review_, Fall 1974, pp. 29-40.

Davis, Stanley M. and Lawrence, Paul R. _Matrix_. Reading, Mass.: Addison-Wesley, 1977.

de Brabander, Bert and Edstron, Anders. "Successful

371

Information System Development Projects."
Management Science 24 (October 1977): 191-199.

Deutsch, Karl W. The Nerves of Government. New York:
The Free Press, 1966.

Dickson, Gary W.; Senn, James A., and Chervany, Norman
L. "Research in Management Information Systems:
The Minnesota Experiments." Management Science
23 (May 1977): 913-923.

Diesing, Paul. Patterns of Discovery in the Social
Sciences. Chicago: Aldine-Atherton, 1971.

Dill, William R. and Doppelt, Neil. "The Acquisition
of Experience in a Complex Management Game."
Management Science 10 (October 1963): 30-46.

Docktor, Robert H. and Hamilton, William F. "Cognitive
Style and the Acceptance of Management Science
Recommendations." Management Science 19 (April
1973): 884-894.

Dror, Yehezhel. "Muddling Through--'Science' or
Inertia?" Public Administration Review XXIV
(September 1964): 153-157.

_____. "Prolegomena to Policy Sciences." Policy
Science 1 (1970): 135-150.

Drucker, Peter F. The Age of Discontinuity. New York:
Harper & Row, 1968.

Duncan, W. Jack. "The Researcher and the Manager: A
Comparative View of the Need for Mutual Understanding." Management Science 20 (April 1974):
1157-1163.

Dyckman, Thomas R. "Management Implementation of
Scientific Research: An Attitudinal Study."
Management Science 13 (June 1967): B612-B620.

Dyer, J. S. "Interactive Goal Programming." Management
Science 19 (September 1972): 62-70.

Eastman, Charles; Johnson, Norman J.; and Kortanek,
Kenneth. "A New Approach to an Urban Information
Process." Management Science 16 (August 1970):
B733-B748.

Eilon, Samuel. "Goals and Constraints in Decision-making." Operational Research Quarterly 23 (March 1972): 3-15.

Ein-Dor, Philip and Segev, Eli. "Organizational Context and the Success of Management Information Systems." Management Science 24 (June 1978): 1064-1077.

Ein-Dor, Philip and Segev, Eli. "Strategic Planning for Management Information Systems." Management Science 24 (November 1978): 1631-1641.

Emery, F. E. and Trist, E. L. Towards a Social Ecology. London: Plenum Press, 1972.

Emshoff, James R. Analysis of Behavioral Systems. New York: The Macmillan Company, 1971.

_____. "Planning the Process of Improving the Planning Process: A Case Study in Meta-Planning." Management Science 24 (July 1978): 1095-1108.

_____. "Experience-Generalized Decision Making: The Next Generation of Managerial Models." Interfaces 8 (August 1978): 40-48.

Emshoff, James R. and Finnel, Arthur. "Defining Corporate Strategy: A Case Study Using Strategic Assumptions Analysis." Sloan Management Review, Spring 1979, pp. 41-52.

Eoyang, Carson. "Requisite Variety in Organizations." Proceedings of the 22nd Annual North American Meeting of the Society for General Systems Research, 1978, pp. 369-378.

Fallows, James. "Muscle-Bound Superpower: The State of America's Defense." The Atlantic, October 1979, pp. 59-78.

Fayol, Henri. Industrial and General Administration. Trans. J. A. Coubrough. Geneva: International Management Institute, 1929.

Ferber, Robert C. "The Role of the Subconscious in Executive Decision-Making." Management Science 13 (April 1967): B519-B526.

Ferrence, Thomas P. "Organizational Communications

Systems and the Decision Process." <u>Management</u>
<u>Science</u> 17 (October 1970): B83-B96.

Feyerabend, Paul. <u>Against</u> <u>Method</u>. London: Verso
Editions, 1975.

Fishburn, Peter C. "Preferences, Summation, and Social
Welfare Functions." <u>Management</u> <u>Science</u> 16 (1969):
179-186.

Ford, L. R., Jr., and Fulkerson, D. R. <u>Flows</u> <u>in</u>
<u>Networks</u>. Princeton, N. J.: Princeton University
<u>Press, T</u>962.

Forrester, Jay W. <u>Industrial</u> <u>Dynamics</u>. Cambridge,
Mass.: The M.<u>I</u>.T. Press, 1961.

_____. <u>Principles</u> <u>of</u> <u>Systems</u>. Cambridge, Mass.:
The M.I.T. Press, 1968.

Friedman, George J. "Constraint Theory: An Overview."
<u>International</u> <u>Journal</u> <u>of</u> <u>Systems</u> <u>Science</u> 7 (1976)
<u>11</u>13-1151.

Friedman, George J. and Leondes, Cornelius T.
"Constriant Theory." <u>IEEE</u> <u>Transactions</u> <u>on</u> <u>Systems</u>
<u>Science</u> and <u>Cybernetics</u> SSC-5. "Part I:
<u>Fundamentals</u>" (January 1969): 48-56. "Part II:
Model Graphs and Regular Relations" (April 1969):
132-140. "Part III: Inequality and Discrete
Relations" (July 1969): 191-199.

Friedman, John. <u>Retracking</u> <u>America</u>: <u>A</u> <u>Theory</u> <u>of</u>
<u>Transactive</u> <u>Planning</u>. Garden City, N. Y.: Anchor
Press/Doubleday, 1973.

Friend, J. K. and Jessop, W. N. <u>Local</u> <u>Governement</u> <u>and</u>
<u>Strategic</u> <u>Choice</u>. 2nd ed. Oxford: Pergamon
Press, 1977.

Galbraith, Jay. <u>Designing</u> <u>Complex</u> <u>Organizations</u>.
Reading, Mass.: Addison-Wesley, 1973.

Galbraith, Jay R. and Nathanson, Daniel A. <u>Strategy</u>
<u>Implementation</u>: <u>The</u> <u>Role</u> <u>of</u> <u>Structure</u> <u>and</u>
<u>Process</u>. St. Paul, Minn.: West Publishing
<u>Company</u>, 1978.

Gardner, Martin. "On the Fabric of Inductive Logic,
and Some Probability Paradoxes." In <u>Mathematics</u>:

An <u>Introduction</u> <u>to</u> <u>its</u> <u>Spirit</u> and <u>Use</u>. Readings
from Scientific American, with introductions by
Morris Kline. San Francisco: W. H. Freeman and
Company, 1979, pp. 161-164.

Garner, Wendell R. <u>Uncertainty</u> <u>and</u> <u>Structure</u> <u>as</u>
<u>Psychological</u> <u>Concepts</u>. Huntington, N. Y.:
Robert E. Krieger Publishing Company, 1975.

Garner, W. R. and McGill, W. J. "The Relation Between
Information and Variance Analysis." <u>Pychometrika</u>
21 (1956): 219-228.

Geisler, Murray A. and Richards, Laurence D. "The Use
of Management Indicators in a Large Public
System." In <u>Studies</u> <u>in</u> <u>Operations</u> <u>Management</u>.
Ed. Arnoldo C. Hax. Amsterdam: North-Holland
Publishing Co., 1978, pp. 544-561.

Geisler, Murray A. and Richards, Laurence D. "A Macro-
Analysis Approach to Defense Management." In
<u>Applied</u> <u>Cybernetics</u> <u>and</u> <u>Planning</u>. Ed. A. Ghosal.
<u>New Delhi</u>: South Asian Publishers, 1980,
pp. 205-217.

Geisler, Murray A.; Hutzler, Mary J.; Kaiser, Robert
D.; Myers, Myron G.; and Richards, Laurence D.
<u>A</u> <u>Macro</u> <u>Analysis</u> <u>of</u> <u>DoD</u> <u>Logistics</u> <u>Systems</u>. Vol.
<u>I</u>: <u>Logistics</u> <u>Systems</u> <u>in</u> <u>the</u> <u>Department</u> <u>of</u>
<u>Defense</u>. Washington, D. C.: Logistics Management
<u>Institute</u>, December 1976.

Geisler, Murray A.; Hutzler, Mary J.; Kaiser, Robert
D.; Myers, Myron G.; and Richards, Laurence D.
<u>A</u> <u>Macro</u> <u>Analysis</u> <u>of</u> <u>DoD</u> <u>Logistics</u> <u>Systems</u>. Vol.
<u>II</u>: <u>Structure</u> <u>and</u> <u>Analysis</u> <u>of</u> <u>the</u> <u>Air</u> <u>Force</u>
<u>Logistics</u> <u>System</u>. Washington, <u>D. C.</u>: Logistics
Management <u>Institute</u>, September 1977.

Geisler, Murray A.; Hutzler, Mary J.; Kaiser, Robert D.
and Richards, Laurence D. <u>A</u> <u>Macro</u> <u>Analysis</u> <u>of</u> <u>DoD</u>
<u>Logistics</u> <u>Systems</u>. Vol. <u>III</u>: <u>A</u> <u>Framework</u> <u>for</u>
<u>Policy-Level</u> <u>Logistics</u> <u>Management</u>. Washington,
D. C.: Logistics Management Institute, December
1978.

General Accounting Office. <u>Highlights</u> <u>of</u> <u>a</u> <u>Report</u> <u>on</u>
<u>Staffing</u> <u>and</u> <u>Organization</u> <u>of</u> <u>Top-Management</u>
<u>Headquarters</u> <u>in</u> <u>the</u> <u>Department</u> <u>of</u> <u>Defense</u>.
<u>Washington, D. C.</u>: Office of the Comptroller

General, July 6, 1976.

General Accounting Office. DoD's Materiel Readiness Report to the Congress--Improvement Needed to Better Show the Link Between Funding and Readiness. Washington, D. C.: Office of the Comptroller General, October 12, 1979.

Gluck, Fred. "Military Logistics--A Multitude of Sins." SOLE Spectrum, Fall 1979, pp. 22-25.

Gödel, Kurt. "Ueber formal unentscheidbare Sätze der Principia Mathematica und verwandter Systeme I." Monatshefte fur Mathematik and Physik 38 (1931): 173-198.

Gouldner, Alvin W. Patterns of Industrial Bureaucracy. New York: The Free Press of Glencoe, 1954.

Green, Paul E. and Carmone, Frank J. Multidimensional Scaling and Related Techniques in Marketing Analysis. Boston: Allyn & Bacon, 1970.

Gupta, Shiv K. and Richards, Laurence D. "A Language for Policy-Level Modelling." Journal of the Operational Research Society 30 (1979): 297-308.

Gupta, Shiv K. and Rosenhead, Jonathan. "Robustness in Sequential Investment Decisions." Management Science 15 (October 1978): B18-B29.

Hainer, Raymond M. "Rationalism, Pragmatism, and Existentialism: Perceived but Undiscovered Multi-cultural Problems." In The Research Society. Ed. Evelyn Glatt and Maynard Shelly. New York: Gordon and Breach, Inc., 1968. pp. 7-50.

Hall, A. D. and Fagen, R. E. "Definition of System." General Systems I (1956): 18-29.

Hand, Herbert H. and Sims, Henry P., Jr. "Statistical Evaluation of Complex Gaming Performance." Management Science 21 (February 1975): 708-717.

Hanssmann, Fred. "The Case for Static Models in Strategic Planning." In Studies in Operations Management. Ed. Arnoldo C. Hax. Amsterdam: North-Holland Publishing Company, 1978, pp. 117-136.

Harary, F.; Norman, R. Z.; and Cartwright, D. Structural Models: An Introduction to the Theory of Directed Graphs. New York: John Wiley & Sons, 1965.

Havens, Harry S. "MBO and Program Evaluation, or Whatever Happened to PPBS?" Public Administration Review, January/February 1976, pp. 40-45.

Herbst, Ph. G. Alternatives to Hierarchies. Leiden, The Netherlands: Martinus Nijhoff Social Sciences Division, 1976.

Hertzberg, Frederick; Mausner, Bernard; and Snyderman, Barbara Bloch. The Motivation to Work. 2nd ed. New York: John Wiley & Sons, 1959.

Hirshfeld, David S. "Management Science and the Two Cultures." OR/MS Today 7 (March/April 1980): 10.

Hodgetts, Richard M. Management: Theory, Process and Practice. Philadelphia: W. B. Saunders Company, 1979.

Hofer, Charles W. and Schendel, Dan. Strategy Formulation: Analytical Concepts. St. Paul, Minn.: West Publishing Company, 1978.

Hoffenberg, Marvin. "Comments on 'Measuring Progress Towards Social Goals: Some Possibilities at National and Local Levels'." Management Science 16 (August 1970): B979-B983.

Hofshi, Raini and Korsh, James F. "A Measure of an Individual's Power in a Group." Management Science 19 (September 1972): 52-61.

Hofstadter, Douglas. Gödel, Escher, Bach: An Eternal Golden Braid. New York: Vintage Books, 1979.

Holling, C. S. "Resilience and Stability in Ecological Systems." In Evolution and Consciousness: Human Systems in Transition. Ed. Eric Jantsch and Conrad Waddington. Reading, Mass.: Addison-Wesley, 1976, pp. 73-92.

Howard, John A. and Morgenroth, William M. "Information Processing Model of Executive Decision." Management Science 14 (March 1968): 416-428.

Howe, Richard Herbert and Von Foerster, Heinz. "Introductory Comments to Francisco Varela's Calculus for Self-Reference." International Journal of General Systems 2 (1975): 1-3.

Huysmans, Jan H. B. M. "The Effectiveness of the Cognitive-Style Constraint in Implementing Operations Research Proposals." Management Science 17 (September 1970): 92-104.

Inada, K. "On the Simple Majority Decision Rule." Econometrica 37 (1969): 490-506.

Jacob, Jean-Paul. "Potential of Graphics to Enhance Decision Analysis." IBM Research Report. RJ2437. IBM Research Laboratory, San Jose, Calif., 1979.

Jaques, Elliott. A General Theory of Bureaucracy. London: Heinemann Educational Books, 1976.

Jenkins, David. Job Power. Baltimore, Md.: Penguin Books, 1974.

Johnson, Norman and Ward, Edward. "Citizen Information Systems: Using Technology to Extend the Dialogue Between Citizens and their Government." Management Science 19 (December, Part 2, 1972): 21-34.

Kaplan, Abraham. The New World of Philosophy. New York: Vintage Books, 1961.

_____. The Conduct of Inquiry: Methodology for Behavioral Science. New York: Chandler Publishing Company, 1964.

Kaufman, A. Introduction to the Theory of Fuzzy Subsets. Vol. 1: Fundamental Theoretical Elements. With a Foreword by L. A. Zadeh. Trans. D. L. Swanson. New York: Academic Press, 1975.

Keen, Peter G. W. "The Evolving Concept of Optimality." In Starr and Zeleny, eds., 1977, pp. 31-57.

Keen, Peter G. W. and Morton, Michael S. Scott. Decision Support Systems: An Organizational Perspective. Reading, Mass.: Addison-Wesley,

1978.

Keeney, Ralph L. "A Group Preference Axiomatization with Cardinal Utility." Management Science 23 (October 1976): 140-145.

Keeney, Ralph L. and Kirkwood, Craig W. "Group Decision Making Using Cardinal Social Welfare Functions." Management Science 22 (December 1975): 430-437.

Keeney, Ralph L. and Raiffa, Howard. Decisions with Multiple Objectives: Preferences and Value Tradeoffs. New York: John Wiley & Sons, 1976.

Kemeny, J. G. and Snell, J. L. Mathematical Models in the Social Sciences. New York: Blaisdell Publishing Co., 1962.

King, William R. and Cleland, David I. "The Design of Management Information Systems: An Information Analysis Approach." Management Science 22 (November 1975): 286-297.

Klir, G. J. "Identification of Generative Structures in Empirical Data." International Journal of General Systems 3 (1976): 89-104.

Kochen, Manfred and Deutsch, Karl W. "Decentralization by Function and Location." Management Science 19 (April 1973): 841-856.

Kochen, Manfred and Deutsch, Karl W. "A Note on Hierarchy and Coordination: An Aspect of Decentralization." Management Science 21 (September 1974): 106-114.

Kohler, Wolfgang. Gestalt Psychology. New York: The New American Library, 1947.

Koopman, Bernard O. "Intuition in Mathematical Operations Research." Operations Research 25 (March/April 1977): 189-206.

Krippendorff, Klaus. "Communication and the Genesis of Structure." General Systems XVI (1971): 171-185.

_____. "Information Theory." In Communication and Behavior. Ed. Gerald J. Hanneman and William J. McEwen. Reading, Mass.: Addison-Wesley, 1975, pp. 351-389.

_____. "Reliability, The Case of Binary Attributes." Unpublished manuscript, The Annenberg School of Communications, University of Pennsylvania, June 1, 1978.

_____. "On the Identification of Structures in Multi-variate Data by the Spectral Analysis of Relations." Proceedings of the 23rd Annual North American Meeting of the Society for General Systems Research, 1979, pp. 82-91.

Kuhn, Thomas A. The Structure of Scientific Revolutions. 2nd ed. Chicago: University of Chicago Press, 1970.

Lawrence, Paul and Lorsch, Jay. Organization and Environment. Homewood, Ill.: Richard D. Irwin, 1969.

Lee, Sang M. Goal Programming for Decision Analysis. Philadelphia: Auerbach Publishers, 1972.

Levine, Henry D. "Some Things to All Men: The Politics of Cruise Missile Development." Public Policy 25 (Winter 1977): 117-168.

Lewin, Kurt. Principles of Topological Psychology. Trans. Fritz Heider and Grace M. Heider. New York: McGraw-Hill, 1936.

_____. Field Theory in Social Science. Ed. Dorwin Cartwright. Chicago: University of Chicago Press, 1951.

Likert, Rensis. New Patterns of Management. New York: McGraw-Hill, 1961.

_____. The Human Organization: Its Management and Value. New York: McGraw-Hill, 1967.

Lindblom, Charles E. "The Science of 'Muddling Through'." Public Administration Review XIX (Spring 1959): 79-88.

_____. "Contexts for Change and Strategy: A Reply." In Readings on Modern Organizations. Ed. Amitai Etzioni. Englewood Cliffs, N. J.: Prentice-Hall, 1969.

_____. Politics and Markets: The World's Political-Economic Systems. New York: Basic Books, 1977.

Lindley, D. V. Making Decisions. London: John Wiley & Sons, 1971.

Linstone, Harold A. "Eight Basic Pitfalls: A Checklist." In Linstone and Turoff, eds., 1975, pp. 573-586.

Linstone, Harold A. and Turoff, Murray, eds. The Delphi Method: Techniques and Applications. With a Foreword by Olaf Helmer. Reading, Mass.: Addison-Wesley, 1975.

Linstone, Harold A. and Turoff, Murray. "Computers and the Future of Delphi: Introduction." In Linstone and Turoff, eds., 1975, pp. 489-496.

Littauer, S. B.; Yegulap, T. M.; and Zaharlev, G. K. "A Framework for Optimizing Managerial Decision." OMEGA 4 (1976): 35-48.

Lombard, George F. F. "Relativism in Organizations." Harvard Business Review, March/April 1971, pp. 55-65.

Lorange, Peter. "Divisional Planning: Setting Effective Direction." Sloan Management Review, Fall 1975, pp. 77-91.

Lorange, Peter and Vancil, Richard F. Strategic Planning Systems. Englewood Cliffs, N. J.: Prentice-Hall, 1977.

Lucas, Henry C., Jr. "Performance and the Use of an Information System." Management Science 21 (April 1975): 908-919.

MacCrimmon, K. R. Decisionmaking Among Multiple-Attribute Alternatives: A Survey and Consolidated Approach. RM-4823-ARPA. Santa Monica, Calif.: The RAND Corporation, 1968.

_____. "An Overview of Multiple Objective Decision Making." In Multiple Criteria Decision Making. Ed. J. L. Cochrane and M. Zeleny. Columbia, S. C.: University of South Carolina Press, 1973, pp. 18-44.

McCurdy, Howard E. "Fiction, Phenomenology, and Public Administration." Public Administration Review (January/February 1973), pp. 52-60.

McGill, W. J. "Multivariate Information Transmission." Psychometrika 19 (1954): 97-116.

McGregor, Douglas. The Human Side of Enterprise. New York: McGraw-Hill, 1960.

MacKay, Donald M. "The Informational Analysis of Questions and Commands." In Modern Systems Research for the Behavioral Scientist. Ed. Walter Buckley. Chicago: Aldine Publishing Company, 1968, pp. 204-209.

_____. Information, Mechanism and Meaning. Cambridge, Mass.: The M.I.T. Press, 1969.

McKenney, James L. Simulation Gaming for Management Development. Boston: Division of Research, Graduate School of Business Administration, Harvard University, 1967.

McKenney, James L. and Keen, Peter G. W. "How Managers' Minds Work." Harvard Business Review, May/June 1974, pp. 79-90.

MacMillan, Ian C. Strategy Formulation: Political Concepts. St. Paul, Minn.: West Publishing Company, 1978.

March, James G. and Simon, Herbert A. Organizations. New York: John Wiley & Sons, 1958.

Maruyama, Magoroh. "The Second Cybernetics: Deviation-Amplifying Mutual Causal Processes." American Scientist 51 (1963): 164-179.

_____. "Heterogenistics: An Epistemological Restructuring of Biological and Social Sciences." Cybernetica 20 (1977): 69-86.

Maschler, Michael. "The Power of a Coalition." Management Science 10 (October 1963): 8-29.

Maslow, Abraham. Motivation and Personality. 2nd ed. New York: Harper & Row, 1954.

Mason, Richard O. "A Dialectical Approach to Strategic Planning." Management Science 15 (April 1969): B403-B414.

Mason, Richard O. and Mitroff, Ian I. "A Program for Research on Management Information Systems." Management Science 19 (January 1973): 475-487.

Maturana, Humberto R. "Cognitive Strategies." Unpublished Manuscript. Cambridge, Mass.: Massachusetts Institute of Technology, undated.

Merchant, Deepak K. and Rao, M. R. "Majority Decisions and Transitivity: Some Special Cases." Management Science 23 (October 1976): 125-130.

Merton, Robert K. "The Unanticipated Consequences of Purposive Social Action." American Sociological Review 1 (1936): 894-904.

Miller, Danny and Friesen, Peter H. "Archetypes of Strategy Formulation." Management Science 24 (May 1978): 921-933.

Miller, George A. "The Magical Number Seven Plus or Minus Two." Psychological Review 63 (1956): 81-97.

Miller, G. A.; Gallanter, E.; and Pribram, K. Plans and the Structure of Behavior. New York: Holt, Rinehart, & Whinston, 1960.

Mintzberg, Henry. "Patterns in Strategy Formation." Management Science 24 (May 1978): 934-948.

Mintzberg, H.; Raisinghani, D.; and Théorêt, A. "The Structure of 'Unstructured' Decision Processes." Administrative Science Quarterly 21 (June 1976): 246-275.

Mitroff, Ian I. "Fundamental Issues in the Simulation of Human Behavior: A Case in the Strategy of Behavioral Science." Management Science 15 (August 1969): B635-B649.

_____. "A Communication Model of Dialectical Inquiring Systems--A Strategy for Strategic Planning." Management Science 17 (June 1971): B634-B648.

Mitroff, Ian I.; Barabba, Vincent P.; and Kilmann, Ralph H. "The Application of Behavioral and Philosophical Technologies to Strategic Planning: A Case Study of a Large Federal Agency." Management Science 24 (September 1977): 44-58.

Mitroff, Ian I. and Betz, Frederick. "Dialectical Decision Theory: A Meta-Theory of Decision-Making." Management Science 19 (September 1972): 11-24.

Mitroff, Ian I.; Emshoff, James R.; and Kilmannn, Ralph H. "Assumptional Analysis: A Methodology for Strategic Problem Solving." Management Science 25 (June 1979): 583-593.

Mitroff, I. I. and Kilmann, R. H. "On Organizational Stories: An Approach to the Design and Analysis of Organizations Through Myths and Stories." In The Management of Organization Design. Ed. R. H. Kilmann, L. Pondy, and D. Slevin. Amsterdam: North-Holland Publishing Co., 1976, pp. 189-207.

Mitroff, Ian I.; Nelson, John; and Mason, Richard O. "On Management Myth-Information Systems." Management Science 21 (December 1974): 371-382.

Murray, Edwin A., Jr. "Strategic Choice as a Negotiated Outcome." Management Science 24 (May 1978): 960-972.

Myers, Kent C. "Rationale for a Corporate Resilience Strategy." Proceedings of the Twenty-Fourth Annual North American Meeting of the Society for General Systems Research, 1980, pp. 540-547.

Myrdal, Gunnar. Objectivity in Social Research. New York: Pantheon Books, 1969.

Nadler, David A. Feedback and Organizational Development: Using Data-Based Methods. Reading, Mass.: Addison-Wesley, 1977.

Nagel, Ernest and Newman, James R. Gödel's Proof. New York: New York University Press, 1958.

Naylor, Thomas H. and Finger, J. M. "Verification of Computer Simulation Models." Management Science 14 (October 1967): B92-B101.

Naylor, Thomas H. and Schauland, Horst. "A Survey of Users of Corporate Planning Models." Management Science 22 (May 1976): 927-937.

Niemi, Richard G. and Weisberg, Herbert F. "A Mathematical Solution for the Probability of the Paradox of Voting." Behavioral Science 13 (1968): 317-323.

Nutt, Paul C. "An Experimental Comparison of the Effectiveness of Three Planning Methods." Management Science 23 (January 1977): 491-511.

Orchard, Robert A. "On the Laws of Form." International Journal of General Systems 2 (1975): 99-106.

Ouchi, William G. "A Conceptual Framework for the Design of Organizational Control Mechanisms." Management Science 25 (September 1979): 833-848.

Parsons, Talcott. Structure and Process in Modern Societies. New York: The Free Press of Glencoe, 1960.

"Piercing Future Fog in the Executive Suite." Business Week, April 28, 1975, pp. 46-50, 52, 54.

Porter, David O. and Olsen, Eugene A. "Some Critical Issues in Government Centralization and Decentralization." Public Administration Review, January/February 1976, pp. 72-84.

Porter, John C.; Sasieni, Maurice W.; Marks, Eli S.; and Ackoff, Russell L. "The Use of Simulation as a Pedagogical Device." Management Science 12 (February 1966): B170-B179.

Pye, Roger. "A Formal, Decision-Theoretic Approach to Flexibility and Robustness." Journal of the Operational Research Society 29 (1978): 215-227.

Quine, W. V. "Paradox." Scientific American, April 1962, pp. 84-95.

_____. "The Foundations of Mathematics." Scientific American, September 1964, pp. 113-127.

Rainey, Hal G.; Backoff, Robert W.; and Levine, Charles

H. "Comparing Public and Private Organizations." Public Administration Review, March/April 1976, pp. 233-244.

Rapaport, Anatol. Fights, Games, and Debates. Ann Arbor, Mich.: The University of Michigan Press, 1960.

Rein, Martin and White, Sheldon H. "Can Policy Research Help Policy?." The Public Interest, Fall 1977, pp. 119-136.

Rice, Donald B. "New Challenges--and Some Old Ones." OR/MS Today 3 (November/December 1976): 18.

Richards, Laurence D. "Beyond Planning: Controllability vs. Predictability." The Proceedings of the XXIst Annual North American Meeting of the Society for General Systems Research, 1977, pp. 314-323.

_____. "Constraint Theory: A Framework for Social Modeling." Proceedings of the 22nd Annual North American Meeting of the Society for General Systems Research, 1978, pp. 379-388.

_____. "Cybernetics and the Management Science Process." OMEGA 8 (1980): 71-80.

Richards, Laurence D.; Eirich, Peter L.; and Geisler, Murray A. A Concept for the Management of Readiness. Washington, D. C.: Logistics Management Institute, January 1980.

Richards, Laurence D. and Graham, Robert J. "Identifying Problems Through Gaming." Interfaces 7 (May 1977): 76-79.

Riker, William. The Theory of Political Coalitions. New Haven, Conn.: Yale University Press, 1962.

_____. "Arrow's Theorem and Some Examples of the Paradox of Voting." Arnold Foundation Monograph. Dallas, Texas: Southern Methodist University Press, 1965.

Roberts, Fred S. Signed Digraphs and the Growing Demand for Energy. R-756-NSF. Santa Monica, Calif.: The RAND Corporation, May 1971.

386

_____. Weighted Digraph Models for Energy Use and Air
Pollution in Transportation Systems. R-1578-NSF.
Santa Monica, Calif.: The RAND Corporation,
December 1974.

_____. Discrete Mathematical Models. Englewood
Cliffs, N. J.: Prentice-Hall, 1976.

Rockart, John F. "Chief Executives Define Their Own
Data Needs." Harvard Business Review, March/April
1979, pp. 81-93.

Rosenhead, Jonathan; Elton, Martin; and Gupta, Shiv K.
"Robustness and Optimality as Criteria for
Strategic Decisions." Operational Research
Quarterly 23 (1972): 413-431.

Ruefli, Timothy W. "A Generalized Goal Decomposition
Model." Management Science 17 (April 1971):
B505-B518.

Saaty, Thomas L. "A Scaling Method for Priorities in
Hierarchical Structures." Journal of Mathematical
Psychology 15 (1977): 234-281.

Sachs, Wladimir M. "Toward Formal Foundations of
Teleological Systems Science." General Systems
XXI (1976): 145-153.

Sackman, H. Delphi Assessment: Expert Opinion,
Forecasting, and Group Process. R-1283-PR.
Santa Monica, Calif.: The RAND Corporation,
April 1974.

Schein, Edgar H. Process Consultation: Its Role in
Organization Development. Reading, Mass.:
Addison-Wesley, 1969.

Schelling, Thomas C. The Strategy of Conflict.
Cambridge, Mass.: Harvard University Press, 1960.

Schendel, Dan and Patton, G. Richard. "A Simultaneous
Equation Model of Corporate Strategy." Management
Science 24 (November 1978): 1611-1621.

Schick, Allen. "A Death in the Bureaucracy: The
Demise of Federal PPB." Public Administration
Review, March/April 1973, pp. 146-156.

Selznick, Philip. TVA and the Grass Roots. Berkeley,

Calif.: University of California Press, 1949.

_____. Leadership in Administration. New York:
Harper & Row, 1957.

Sen, A. K. "A Possibility Theorem on Majority
Decision." Econometrica 34 (1966): 491-499.

_____. Collective Choice and Social Welfare. San
Francisco: Holden-Day, 1970.

Sen, Amartya and Pattanaik, Prasanta K. "Necessary and
Sufficient Conditions for Rational Choice Under
Majority Decision." Journal of Economic Theory 1
(1969): 178-202.

Shakun, Melvin F. "Management Science and Management:
Implementing Management Science via Situational
Normativism." Management Science 18 (April
1972): B367-B377.

_____. "Policy Making Under Discontinuous Change:
The Situational Normativism Approach." Management
Science 22 (October 1975): 226-235.

Shannon, Claude E. and Weaver, Warren. The Mathematical Theory of Communication. Urbana, Ill.:
University of Illinois Press, 1949.

Sherrard, Willaim R. and Steade, Richard D. "Power
Comparability--Its Contribution to a Theory of
Firm Behavior." Management Science 13 (December
1966): B186-B193.

Siedman, Eileen. "Why Not Qualitative Analysis?."
Public Administration Review, July/August 1977,
pp. 415-417.

Simon, Herbert A. Administrative Behavior. New York:
The Free Press, 1957.

_____. Models of Man. New York: John Wiley & Sons,
1957.

_____. The New Science of Management Decision. New
York: Harper & Row, 1960.

_____. "On the Concept of Organizational Goal."
Administrative Science Quarterly 9 (1964): 1-22.

_____. "Motivational and Emotional Controls of Cognition." _Psychological Review_ 74 (1967): 29-39.

_____. _The Sciences of the Artificial_. Cambridge, Mass.: The M.I.T. Press, 1969.

Smith, Robert D. and Greenlaw, Paul S. "Simulation of a Psychological Decision Process in Personnel Selection." _Management Science_ 13 (April 1967): 409-419.

Snow, C. P. _The Two Cultures and the Scientific Revolution_. New York: Cambridge University Press, 1960.

Somerhoff, G. _Analytical Biology_. London: Oxford University Press, 1950.

Sorley, Lewis. "Profesiional Evaluation and Combat Readiness." _Military Review_, October 1979, pp. 41-53.

Souder, William E. "Achieving Organizational Consensus with Respect to R&D Project Selection Criteria." _Management Science_ 21 (February 1975): 669-681.

Spencer-Brown, G. _Laws of Form_. New York: The Julian Press, 1972.

Spencer-Brown, George [James Keys]. _Only Two Can Play This Game_. Preface by R. D. Laing. New York: Julian Press, 1972.

Starr, Martin K. "Planning Models." _Management Science_ 13 (December 1966): B115-B141.

Starr, Martin K. and Zeleny, Milan. "MCDM--State and Future of the Arts." In Starr and Zeleny, eds., 1977, pp. 5-29.

Starr, Martin K. and Zeleny, Milan, eds. _Multiple Criteria Decision Making_. Amsterdam: North-Holland Publishing Company, 1977.

Statland, Norman. "Computer Systems: Centralized or Dispersed." _Administrative Management_, March 1978, pp. 57-60, 62, 98.

Steinbruner, John D. _The Cybernetic Theory of_

Decision. Princeton, N.J.: Princeton University Press, 1974.

Steiner, George A. and Minor, John B. Management Policy and Strategy. New York: Macmillan Publishing Co., 1977.

Stockfish, J. A. Analysis of Bureaucratic Behavior: The Ill-Defined Production Process. P-5591. Santa Monica, Calif.: The RAND Corporation, January 1976.

Swanson, E. Burton. "Management Information Systems: Appreciation and Involvement." Management Science 21 (October 1974): 178-188.

Sweeney, Dennis J.; Winkofsky, E. P.; Roy, Probir; and Baker, Norman R. "Composition vs. Decomposition: Two Approaches to Modeling Organizational Decision Processes." Management Science 24 (October 1978): 1491-1499.

Swinth, Robert L. "Organizational Joint Problem-Solving." Management Science 18 (October 1971): B68-B79.

Taylor, F. W. Scientific Management. New York: Harper & Brothers, 1911.

Taylor, Ronald N. "Perception of Problem Constraints." Management Science 22 (September 1975): 22-29.

Terleckyj, Nestor E. "Measuring Progress Towards Social Goals: Some Possibilities at National and Local Levels." Management Science 16 (August 1970): B765-B778.

Thompson, James D. Organizations in Action: Social Science Bases of Administrative Theory. New York: McGraw-Hill, 1967.

Toffler, Alvin. Future Shock. New York: Bantam Books, 1970.

Turoff, Murray. "The Policy Delphi." In Linstone and Turoff, eds., 1975, pp. 84-101.

_____. "An Alternative Approach to Cross Impact Analysis." In Linstone and Turoff, eds. 1975, pp. 338-368.

Umpleby, Stuart A. "Second Order Cybernetics and The Design of Large Scale Social Experiments." The Proceedings of the XXth Annual North American Meeting of the Society for General Systems Reseach, 1976, pp. 69-75.

Vail, Hollis. "The Automated Office." The Futurist, April 1978, pp. 73-78.

Vancil, Richard F. "Strategy Formulation in Complex Organizations." Sloan Management Review, Winter 1976, pp. 1-18.

Van Horn, Richard L. "Validation of Simulation Results." Management Science 17 (January 1971): 247-258.

Varela, Francisco J. "A Calculus for Self-Reference." International Journal of General Systems 2 (1975): 5-24.

_____. Principles of Biological Autonomy. New York: Elsevier North-Holland, 1979.

Vickers, Geoffrey. Value Systems and Social Process. Middlesex, England: Penguin Books Ltd., 1968.

_____. Freedom in a Rocking Boat: Changing Values in an Unstable Society. Middlesex, England: Penguin Books Ltd., 1970.

Von Foerster, Heinz. Cybernetics of Cybernetics. Urbana, Ill.: Biological Computer Laboratory, University of Illinois at Urbana-Champaign, 1974.

Wagner, Harvey M. "The Next Decade of Logistics Research." In Science, Technology, and the Modern Navy. Ed. Edward I. Salkovitz. ONR-37. Arlington, Virginia: Office of Naval Research, 1976, pp. 97-109.

Warfield, John N. Societal Systems: Planning, Policy, and Complexity. New York: John Wiley & Sons, 1976.

Waterman, D. A.; Anderson, R. H.; Hayes-Roth, Frederick; Klahir, Philip; Martins, Gary; and Rosenschein, Stanley J. "Design of a Rule-Oriented System for Implementing Expertise." RAND

Note N-1158-1-ARPA. Santa Monica, Calif.: The
RAND Corporation, May 1979.

Watzlawick, Paul; Beavin, Janet Helmick; and Jackson,
Don D. Pragmatics of Human Communncation. New
York: W. W. Norton & Company, 1967.

Watzlawick, Paul; Weakland, John; and Fisch, Richard.
Change: Principles of Problem Formation and
Problem Resolution. New York: W. W. Norton &
Company, 1974.

Weber, Max. The Theory of Social and Economic
Organizations. Trans. A. M. Henderson. Ed.
Talcott Parsons. New York: The Free Press of
Glencoe, 1947.

Weick, Karl E. The Social Psychology of Organizing.
Reading, Mass.: Addison-Wesley, 1969.

Weinberg, Gerald M. An Introduction to General Systems
Thinking. New York: John Wiley & Sons, 1975.

Weiss, Herman L. "Why Business and Government Exchange
Executives." Harvard Business Review, July/August
1974, pp. 129-140.

Whinston, Andrew. "Price Guides in Decentralized
Organizations." In New Perspectives in
Organization Research. Ed. William W. Cooper,
Harold J. Leavitt, and Maynard W. Shelly, II.
New York: John Wiley & Sons, 1964, pp. 405-448.

Whitehead, Alfred North and Russell, Bertrand.
Principia Mathematica. 2nd ed. London: Cambridge
University Press, 1925.

Wiener, Norbert, "A Simplification of the Logic of
Relations." Proceedings of the Cambridge
Philosophical Society 17 (1914): 387-390.

_____. Cybernetics. 2nd ed. Cambridge, Mass.: The
M.I.T. Press, 1961.

Wittgenstein, Ludwig. Tractatus Logico-Philosophicus.
With an Introduction by Bertrand Russell. Trans.
D. F. Pears and B. F. McGuiness. London and
Henley: Routledge & Kegan Paul, 1922.

Wolfe, Joseph. "Effective Performance Behavior in a

Simulated Policy and Decision Making Environment."
Management Science 21 (April 1975): 872-882.

Yu, P. L. "A Class of Solutions for Group Decision
Problems." *Management Science* 19 (April 1973):
936-946.

Zadeh, L. A. "Fuzzy Sets." *Information and Control*
8 (1965): 338-353.

_____. "Outline of a New Approach to the Analysis
of Complex Systems and Decision Processes."
In *Multiple Criteria Decision Making*. Ed. J. L.
Cochrane and M. Zeleny. Columbia, S. C.:
University of South Carolina Press, 1973,
pp. 686-725.

Zeleny, Milan. "Compromise Programming." In *Multiple
Criteria Decision Making*. Ed. J. L. Cochrane and
M. Zeleny. Columbia, S. C.: University of South
Carolina Press, 1973, pp. 262-301.

_____. "The Attribute-Dynamic Attitude Model (ADAM)."
Management Science 23 (September 1976): 12-26.

_____. "Adaptive Displacement of Preferences in
Decision Making." In Starr and Zeleny, eds.,
1977, pp. 147-157.

_____. *Multiple Criteria Decision Making*. New York:
McGraw-Hill, 1982.

deterministic,8,56-57,66
econometric,7
generalized,56-57,64,120
normative,1,55-58,120
optimization,26,27,30-31,63,119,200,221
predictive,30-31,56,67,119,149,200,221
probabilistic,56-57
process-oriented,12,30,56-57,76-77,122
qualitative,9,55-56,70,76,160
quantitative,2,9,55-56,160
role of,xix,1,11,12,47,56-57,120,137
structure of,xix,1,2,5,10,12,55-57,76,137
validation of,55,57,66-68,74
Monte Carlo methods,66
Morphogenetic system,27
Multidimensional scaling,62,68
Multiple criteria decisionmaking,58,62-66,75,79

Negative reasoning,xx,12,24,29,36,46,96,97,100,105,107,
124,221,305,308
Negotiating zone,136
Nested analysis,128
Newtonian mechanics,42,96

Objectives. See Goals; Functions, objective
Objectivity,9,16,42,43,45,55,57,66,96,202,225,303
Office of the Secretary of Defense (OSD),xix,4,14,181,
198-203,219,222,230,233,237
Operation, definition of,104
Optimality,27,64,77,79,107,122,123,168-179. See also
Models, optimization
Organization, definition of,88,109,123
Organizational development (OD),45,70,74-75,188,305
Organizations:
bureaurcratic,21,26-27,42,113,221,244. See also
Bureaucracy
centralized,24,71
charts of,22,24,190,199,240-241
decentralized,24,71
hierarchical,21,22,24
informal,21,38,71
levels of,3,22,239
matrix of,22,24
pluralistic,22

Paradigms,2,10,29,33,76,96,100,125,200,308-309. See
also Negative reasoning; Rational decisionmaking
Paradox,11,47,48,96,98
Paradox of administration,24,140
Paradox of voting,58

Parameter estimation,57,79
Pareto optimality,63,64
Participant-observer,12,55-56,70,76,78,125,171,306
Participation,xx,2,70,130,134,169,185,193,225,243,
   266-270,299,302,307
Pattern recognition,45,128,156,193,308,310
Perception, selective,43,128,150
Performance standards,23,35,74,111,204,260-262,266-269
Personnel:
   policies,3,229,244,247,256-270,299
   selection,63,299
   turnover,5,32,184,243,255,257,264-269,270,296,301.
      See also Turnover rate
PERT,72
Phenomenology,41,45-47
Planning:
   capacity,25
   contingency,107,120
   dialectical,72-74,76
   long-range,23,171
   product,25
   project,25
   strategic,13,22,70,72-74,171
   transportation,25
Planning, Programming, and Budgeting System (PPBS),4,
   14,200,205,221,222,230
Plant location,25
Policy. See also Logistics policy; Personnel policies:
   criteria for,12,34-35,140-142,204,208,210-214,306
   definition of,13,23,137
   public,8,14,130,208-209
   robust,xx,170,185,203,311
   value-rich,xx,2,33,130,134,170,185,306
Policy actor, definition of,126
Policy domain, discussion of,147,188
Policy support system,1,4,68,69,71,100,104,181,183,190,
   197,231-233,240,302,309,311
Politics,9,29-30,70,200. See also Structure, political
Portfolio selection,63
Positivism,41-42
Pragmatism,41,43-45,55,305
Pricing,63,71
Probability. See Models, probabilistic; Uncertainty,
   probabilistic
Problem:
   definition of,30-31
   ill-structured,xix,13,22,56,77,121,126,154,308
Problem solving,24,30-36,63,70,73,80,120,126
Process, definition of,104
Production scheduling,23,25

State transition graph,160-161
Statistical inference,44
Statistical techniques,8,58,69,154,156,159,181,236
Straight-through analysis,128
Strategic posture,32,272
Strategy, See also Planning, strategic:
    definition of,13
    growth,23,184,242-243,247,252-254,269,300
    long-term,5,252
    market,23,184,243,247,252-254,269,288
    organizational,23,184,247,252,255-256,272,299
Structural decomposition,128,149,156-164
Structural uncertainty. See Uncertainty, structural
Structure. See also Models, structure of:
    definition of,109-111
    digraph,68-69,156,160-162
    flow graph,68,160-161,190,193,210,214-221,231,244
    hierarchical,22,156,157-160,165,190,193,210-214
    mathematical,10,11,41,67,75,156,219
    political,134
    power,133-134,200
    strategy and,24
Structured group process,2,74,172,185,192,230,274,
    275,310
Subjectivity,xx,2,9,42-43,45,49,55,96
Survival,23,141,244
System, definition of,104-105
System Dynamics (SD),66-68,183,190

Task structure,184,269,271-297,299-301,307-308
Technology and organization,24,42,100
Technology assessment,161
T-groups,74
Theory of Logical Types,47,97
Theory of relativity,47
Time:
    concepts of,79,96,171
    modelling of,98-100,101,124,170
    perception of,170,311
Topological concepts,123-124,162,311
Trend analysis,181-182,189,193,231-232
Turbulent environments,8,106,113,170,244,269,311. See
    also Richly-joined environments
Turnover rate,4,5,32,73,244-245,247,255-258,273,279,
    288,296-300. See also Personnel turnover

Ultrastability,112
Uncertainty:
    primary,138
    probabilistic,7,120-121,137-138,167